IMAGES
of America

OAK RIDGE

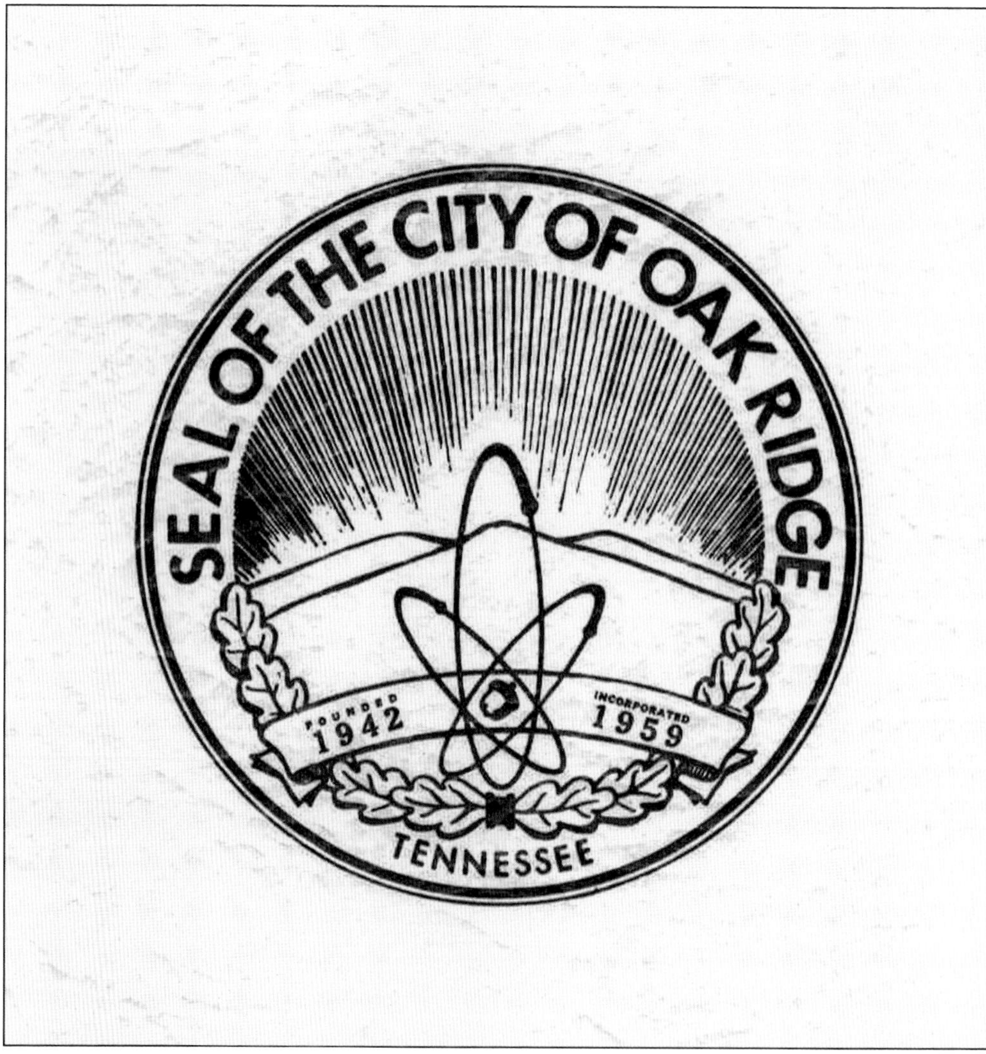

SEAL OF THE CITY OF OAK RIDGE. Created originally as the Kingston Demolition Range, the city transitioned through several project names such as the Clinton Engineer Works and the Manhattan Engineering District before finally selecting the city name Oak Ridge. The city was officially founded in 1942 and incorporated in 1959.

On the Cover: The cover photograph was made on August 6, 1945, by photographer and Images of America: *Oak Ridge* author Ed Westcott at around 10:00 p.m., as crowds began to gather in the Townsite shopping area after news had spread of Japan's surrender. Ed, as the only authorized photographer inside the Oak Ridge reservation, climbed up on the back of a flatbed truck and captured his "War Ends" photograph as the crowd reacted to the happy occasion.

IMAGES
of America

OAK RIDGE

Ed Westcott

ARCADIA
PUBLISHING

ISBN 978-0-7385-4170-9

Published by Arcadia Publishing
Charleston, South Carolina

Printed in the United States of America

Library of Congress Catalog Card Number: 2005926592

For all general information contact Arcadia Publishing at:
Telephone 843-853-2070
Fax 843-853-0044
E-mail sales@arcadiapublishing.com
For customer service and orders:
Toll-Free 1-888-313-2665

Visit us on the Internet at www.arcadiapublishing.com

This book is dedicated to my mother and father, Lucille and Jamie Westcott, and to my wife and partner of 56 years, Esther Westcott, who supported and encouraged my passion for photography throughout my career. This book is also dedicated to all of the wonderful people of Oak Ridge who made such great subjects for my photographs for over 60 years.

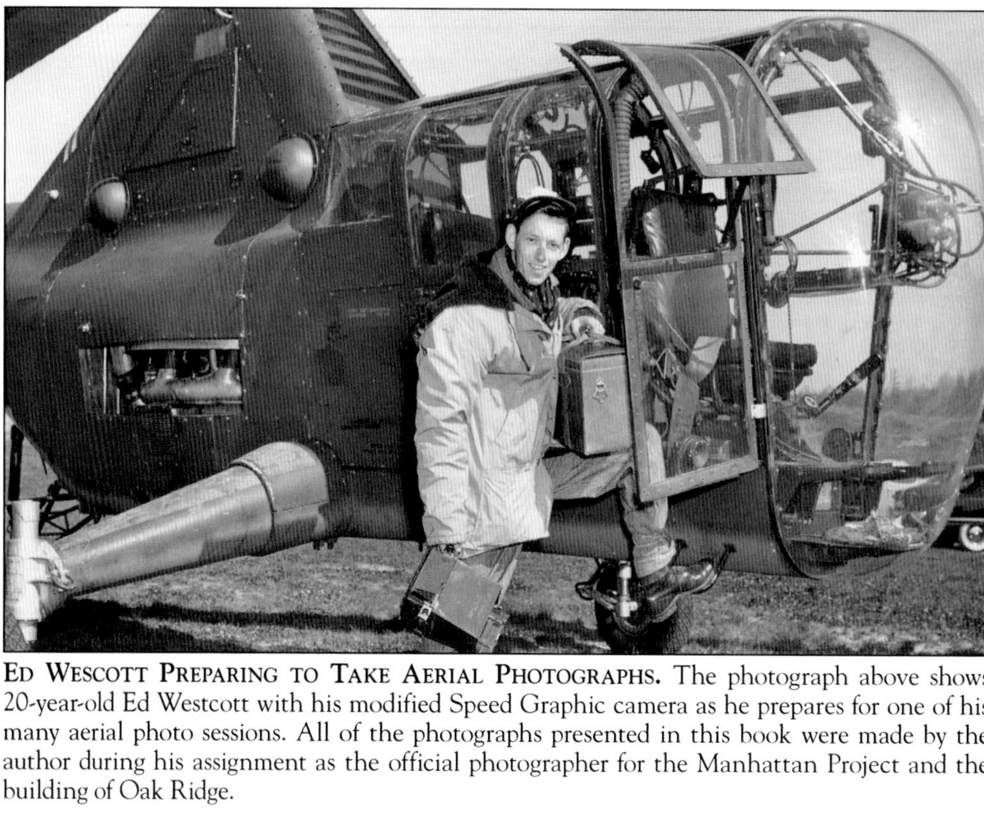

ED WESCOTT PREPARING TO TAKE AERIAL PHOTOGRAPHS. The photograph above shows 20-year-old Ed Westcott with his modified Speed Graphic camera as he prepares for one of his many aerial photo sessions. All of the photographs presented in this book were made by the author during his assignment as the official photographer for the Manhattan Project and the building of Oak Ridge.

Contents

ACKNOWLEDGMENTS

A special debt of gratitude is reserved for all of my family for their support and hard work to help bring my photographs of Oak Ridge to print. Thanks to my daughter, Emily Hunnicutt, to my sons, Jim, David, William, and John Westcott, to my son-in-law, Don Hunnicutt, and to my daughter-in-law, Danielle Westcott.

SOURCES CONSULTED:

Manhattan District History. Volume 12: *Clinton Engineer Works, Central Facilities*, Book I: General. September 13, 1946.

Celebrate Oak Ridge. A Celebrate 2000 Publication, *The Oak Ridger*, 2000.

Overholt, James. *These Are Our Voices: The Story of Oak Ridge, 1942–1970*. Oak Ridge, TN: Children's Museum of Oak Ridge, 1987.

Robinson, George O. *The Oak Ridge Story*. Kingsport, TN: Southern Publishers, Inc., 1950.

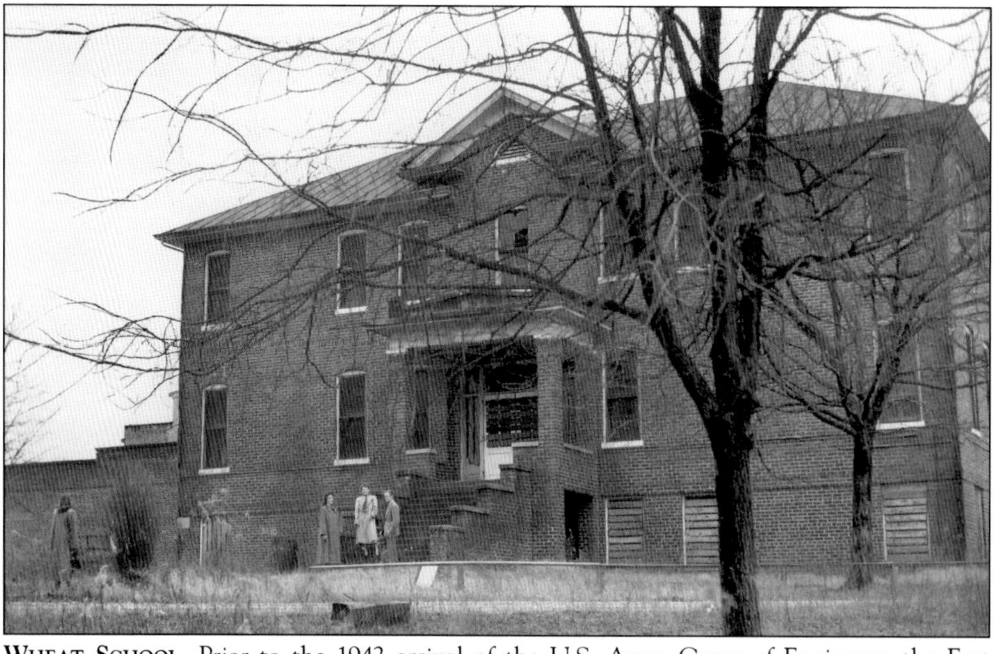

WHEAT SCHOOL. Prior to the 1942 arrival of the U.S. Army Corps of Engineers, the East Tennessee Valley area 25 miles west of Knoxville contained numerous small communities. An area known as the Wheat community existed in the space that would eventually become the Manhattan Project's K-25 Gaseous Diffusion Plant. The photograph above shows Wheat High School, which was originally part of Roane College until 1908.

INTRODUCTION

Oak Ridge, Tennessee, is located in the Anderson County portion of the valley of East Tennessee and covers approximately 92 of the county's 450 square miles. Settlement did not begin in earnest until the county was established in 1801.

Significant change first came to the region in 1838 with the dislocation of the Cherokees, but Native Americans were not the only people to be dislocated; 100 years later, the Tennessee Valley Authority (TVA) was born, and 2,900 families from the county were displaced in order to build the first TVA hydroelectric dam at Norris. Many relocated to the valley, which was bordered on three sides by the Clinch River. Homes, farms, and businesses were re-established and eventually became part of communities such as Wheat, Robertsville, Elza, and Scarboro.

The dislocation to the southern portion of Anderson County provided a comfortable distance for the relocated families for a while, but in 1942, government land appraisers once again appeared and began the hasty removal of close to 1,000 families in order to begin a secret war effort for the federal government.

The area selected was considered "marginal farmland," consisting of many large Victorian homes, barns, frame houses, and log cabins. By November 1, 1942, all of the landowners had received notices of condemnation ordering them to vacate no later than January 1, 1943. It was an extreme hardship for the families to be given just two months to find another home, especially with the scarcity of building materials due to war rationing, but move they did, as their homes, farms, and businesses were erased and the area was transformed into an industrial community with 75,000 people within two years' time.

"I've seen it. . . . It's coming," said Tennessee backwoods mystic John Hendrix in the early 20th century. Hendrix was describing the monumental changes that he had predicted would eventually descend upon the quiet valleys and ridges of Anderson County. John made no predictions about the dates that these "visions" would occur, but, true to his prophecies, monumental changes did occur in 1942, as the land began to transform from rolling hills and valleys into factories and a "secret city."

Hendrix's visions and prophecies included the prediction that "there would be a city built on the Black Oak Ridge" and that the valley "would contain factory buildings that would help towards winning the greatest war that ever was or ever will be." Most of the folks living in the small communities considered the predictions made by Hendrix as just stories from his own imagination—certainly not prophecies or visions that would change life as they knew it. But true to Hendrix's visions, life did change for the families in the area, just as change also came to the nation and world as the result of the Manhattan Project's contributions to the building of the atomic bomb and the ending of World War II.

Oak Ridge represents a photographic history of the building of a city from the groundbreaking in 1942 up through the completion of the city. Most of the photographs provided for this book were made in the 1943–1945 period in order to chronicle one of the world's most significant engineering feats, the equivalent of building a Panama Canal once each year for three straight years.

The author's first introduction to Oak Ridge came in 1942, when he was selected to create the Photographic Unit for the U.S. Army Corps of Engineers in an area first referred to as the Kingston Demolition Range, which became the Corps of Engineer's Manhattan District/ Clinton Engineer Works and eventually the city of Oak Ridge. Ed Westcott was 20 when he accepted the transfer from Nashville to Knoxville and was the 29th employee to arrive. No one had any suspicion that the sole purpose of the Manhattan Project was to produce the atomic bomb, but as the official photographer, Westcott was directed to create a photographic history of everything significant within the project from the town and factory construction to public-relations events and everyday life in the community.

In January 1943, the northeast corner of the Manhattan Project reservation was set aside for the town of Oak Ridge. The town was to be located entirely within Anderson County in a valley between two parallel ridges. The area consisted of a slender strip of wooded land approximately one-and-a-half miles wide and seven miles long. The town occupied 9,000 of the 59,000 total reservation acres.

Over the span of those few short years, Westcott photographed the birth of a city that included massive engineering factories and plants, one of which (K-25) covered 44 acres under one roof, for the purpose of producing enriched uranium to be used for the explosive core of the atomic bomb. Westcott's photographs included the construction of 3,050 homes, thousands of dormitories, hutments, apartments, barracks, and other residential buildings, schools, medical facilities, shopping and recreation centers, libraries, 300 miles of roads and streets, and 163 miles of wooden sidewalks.

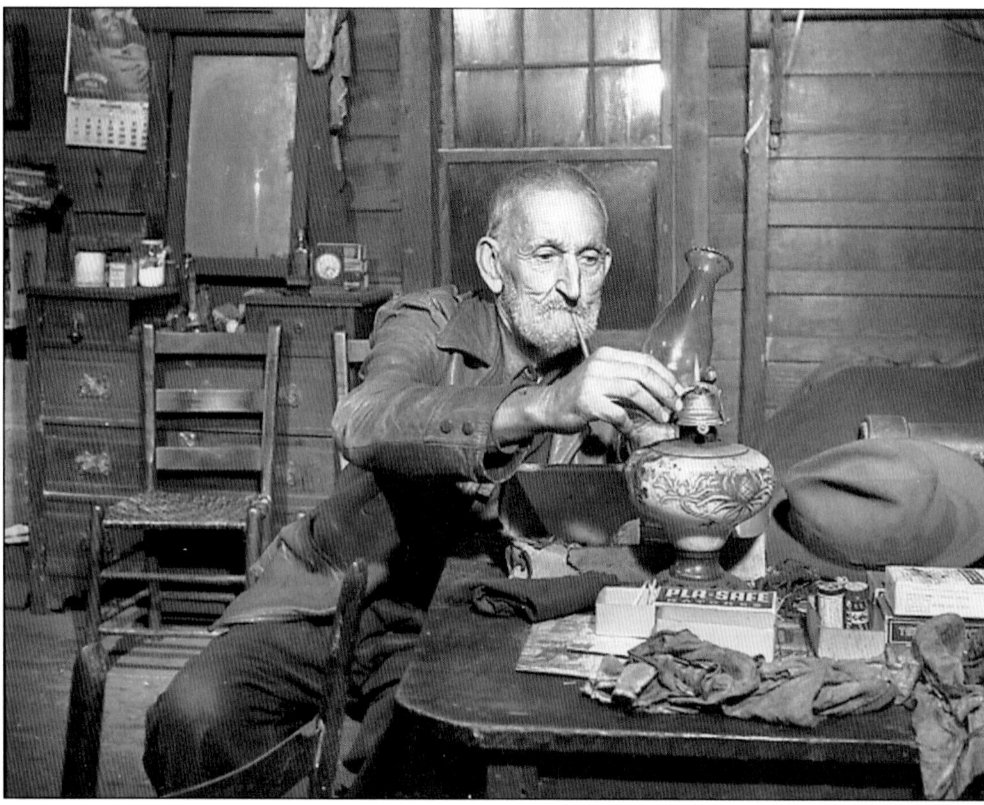

AN OLD-TIMER. Over 1,000 residents of Roane and Anderson Counties had to be relocated to make way for Oak Ridge. One of the lucky ones, William Henry Alonzo, lived just outside Blair gate and was able to remain in his home place. In the evening, when traffic through the gate was slow, the guards visited Mr. Alonzo to listen to him spin a yarn about the good old days.

One

Building and Operating Plants for the Manhattan Project

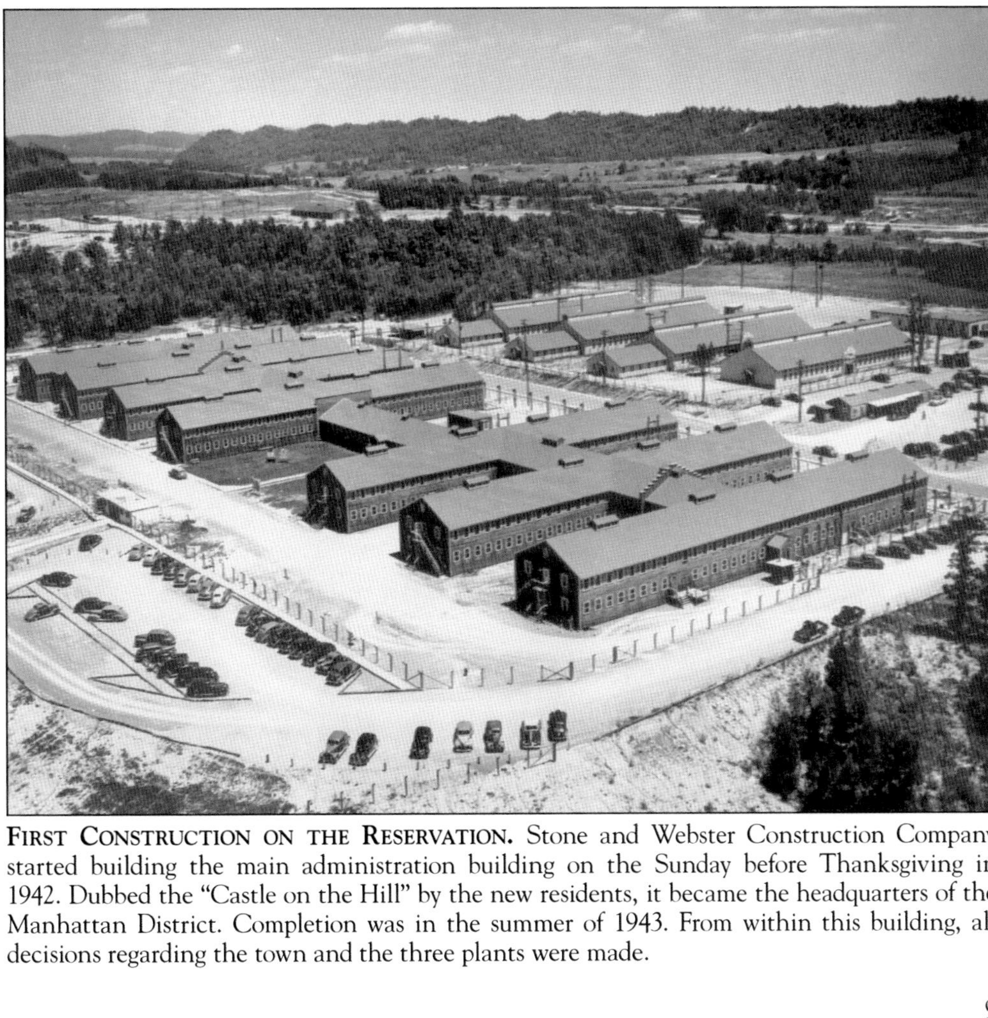

First Construction on the Reservation. Stone and Webster Construction Company started building the main administration building on the Sunday before Thanksgiving in 1942. Dubbed the "Castle on the Hill" by the new residents, it became the headquarters of the Manhattan District. Completion was in the summer of 1943. From within this building, all decisions regarding the town and the three plants were made.

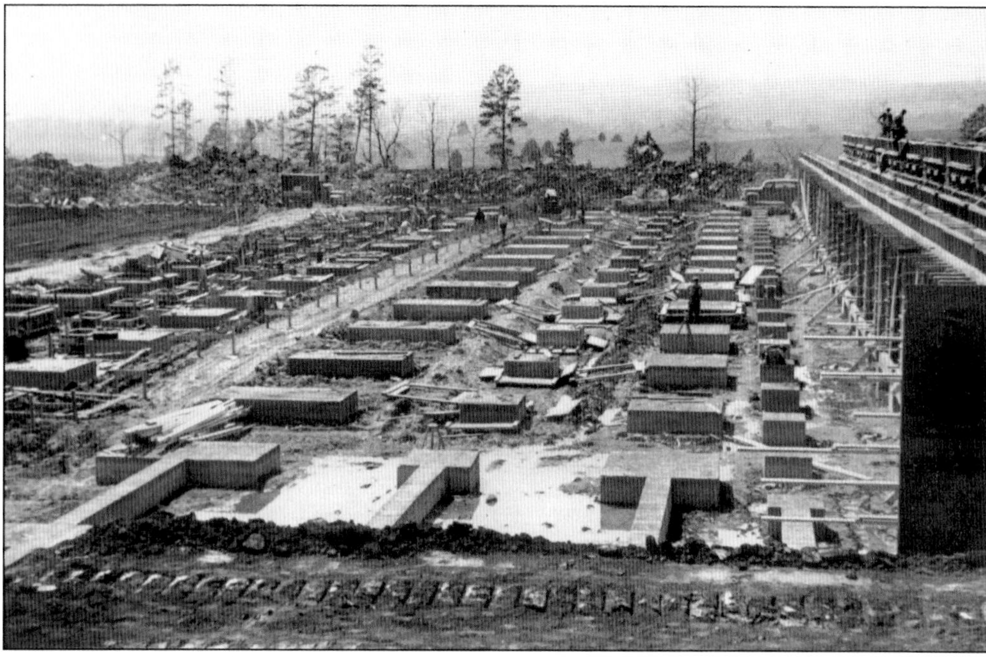

FOUNDATION FOR K-25. On September 10, 1943, the construction on the world's largest building under one roof began. Rain, snow, cold, and mud created a challenge for the construction workers. The chief construction contractor was the J. A. Jones Construction Company of Charlotte, North Carolina.

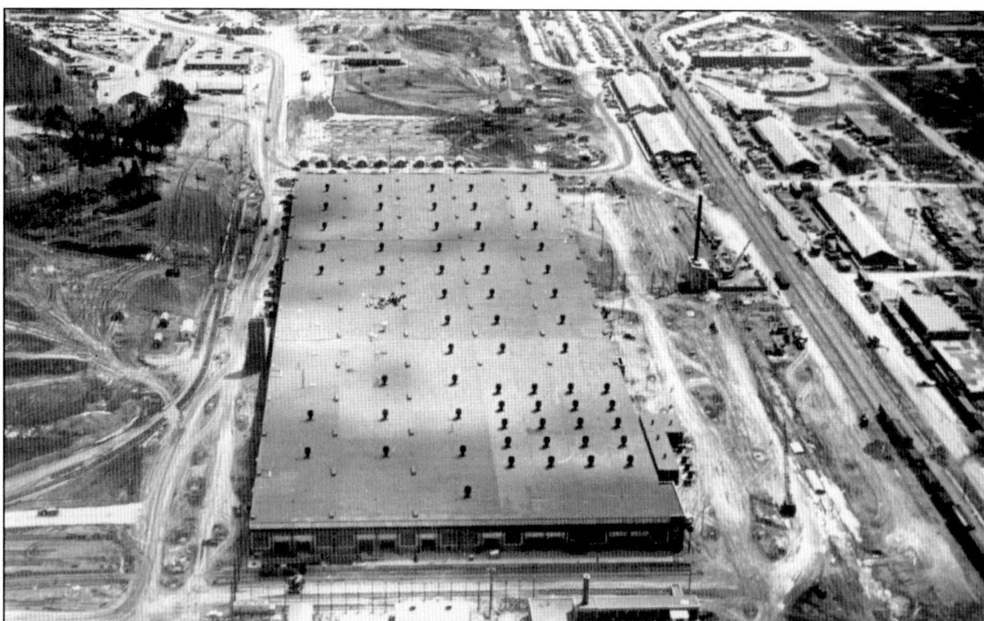

K-25 MAINTENANCE SHOP. This is an aerial view of Building 1401, which housed the weld shop, motor shop, pipe shop, general maintenance, and machine shop. To the right are shipping and receiving warehouses. Off-site construction material was transported in by rail cars and staged at these warehouse terminals.

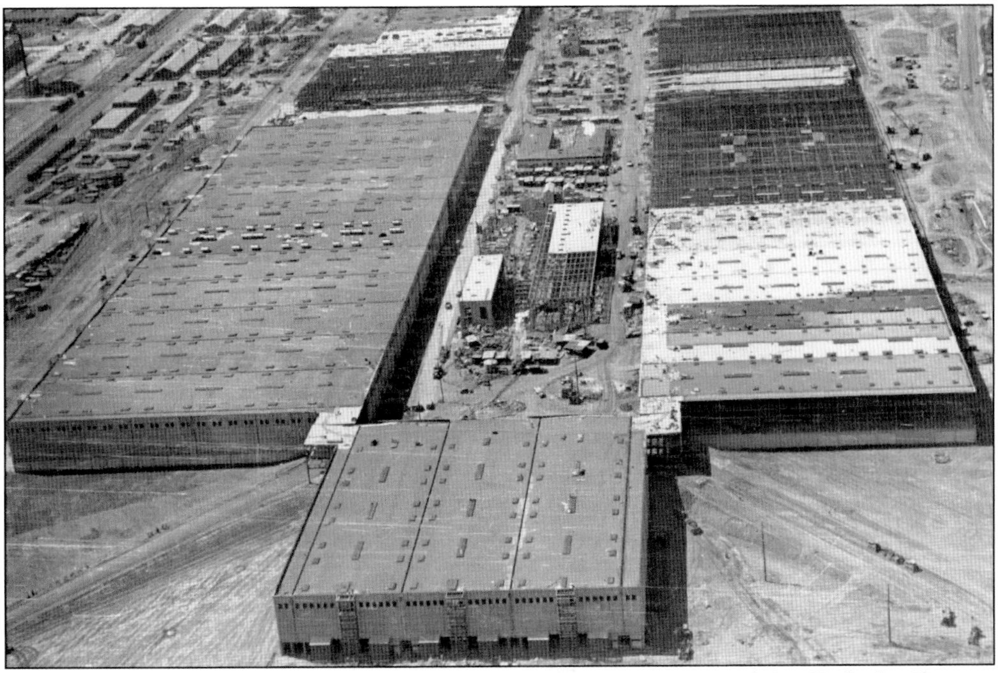

K-25 BUILDING CONSTRUCTION. Designed by the Kellex Corporation of New York, the Gaseous Diffusion Process Building has two wings. Each is 2,450 feet long, averages 400 feet in width, and is 60 feet in height. The total area of the building covers 44 acres.

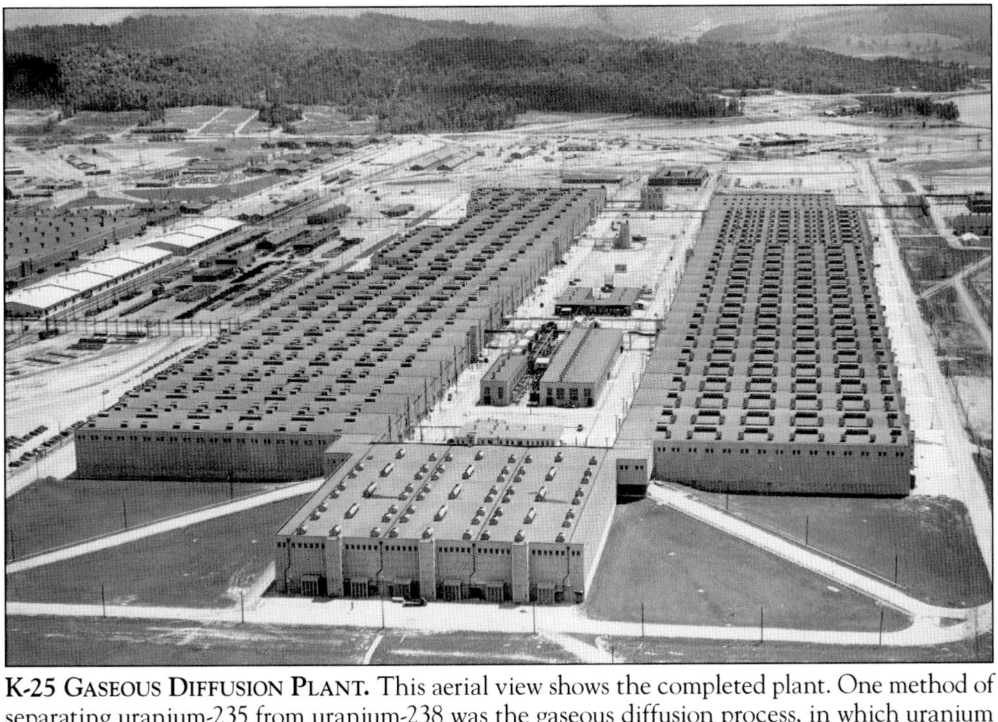

K-25 GASEOUS DIFFUSION PLANT. This aerial view shows the completed plant. One method of separating uranium-235 from uranium-238 was the gaseous diffusion process, in which uranium gas was pumped against a porous barrier, capturing the lighter molecules of gas containing uranium-235. The K-25 Plant was one of the largest industrial plants built.

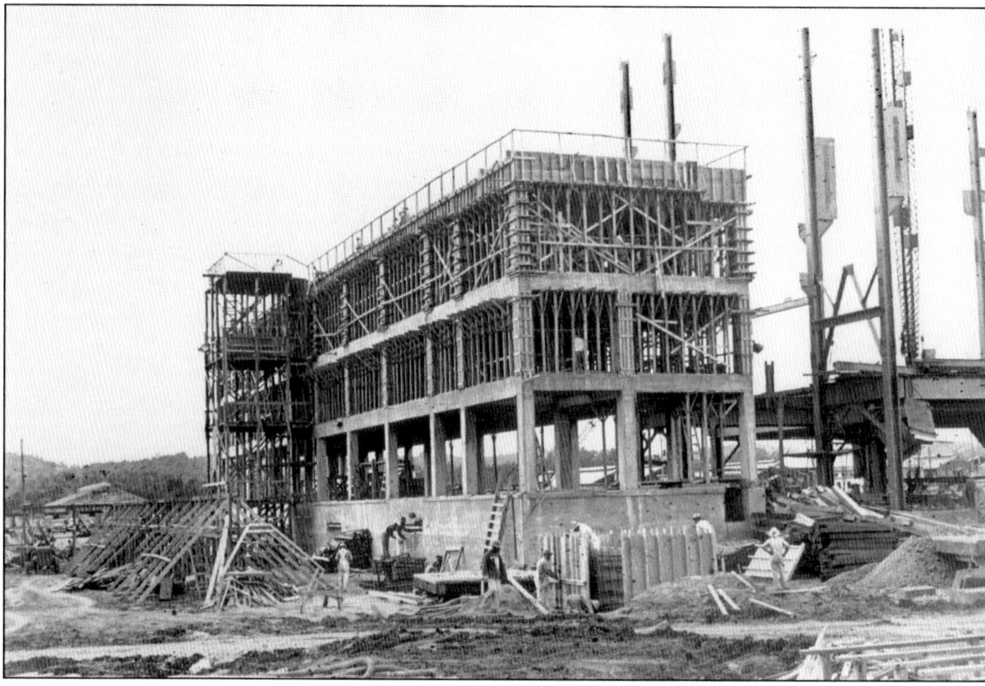

K-25 POWER PLANT. A. S. Schulman Electrical Company started construction in July 1943 on the world's largest steam power plant at an estimated cost of $5,685,761. Coal was brought in by rail car, and water was provided by the Clinch River, which flowed beside the plant. Below, the completed power facilities in the K-25 area consisted of a steam generating station with a total installed capacity of 238,000 kilowatts and a high-voltage substation having a capacity of 120,000 kilovolts. The Tennessee Valley Authority also supplied 154-kilovolt lines.

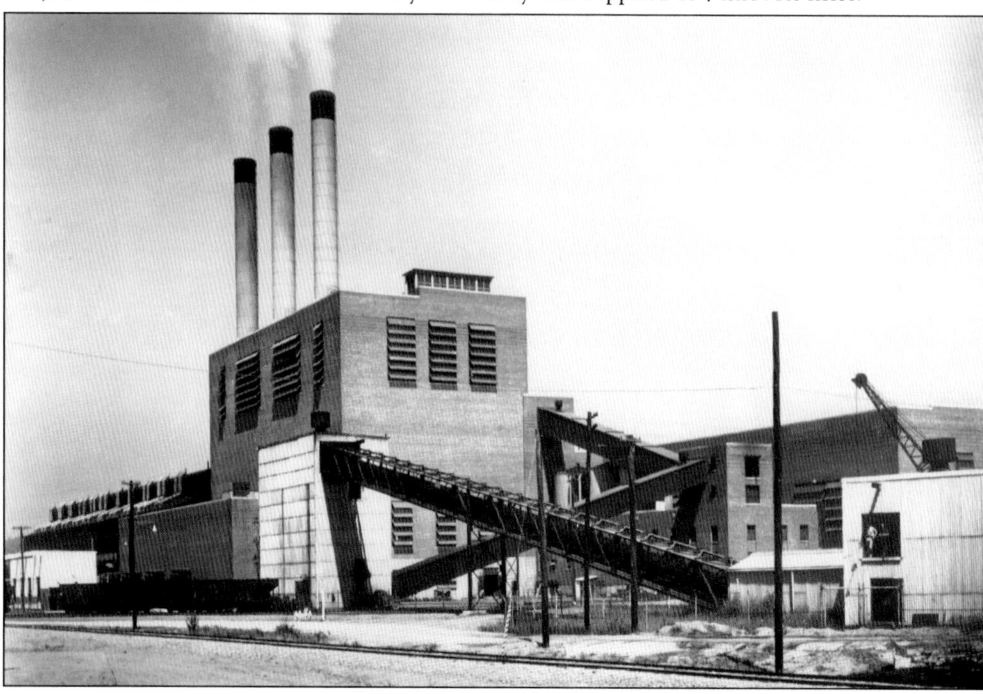

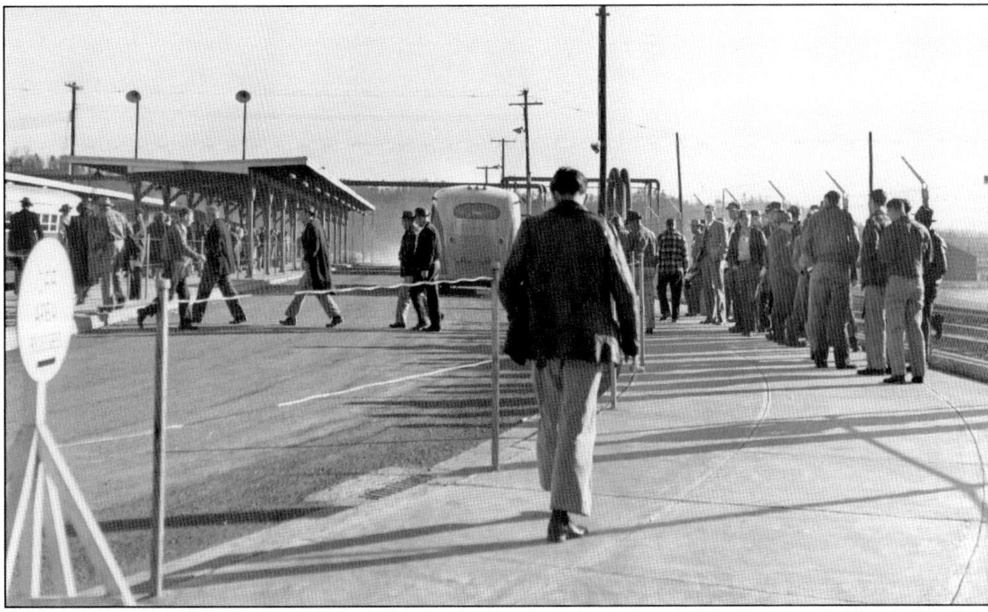

SHIFT CHANGE. Some of the 12,000 workers leaving at end of their shift board buses back to their homes. Bus service was started by the Clinton Engineer Works Bus Authority on March 4, 1944. Buses ran from the main terminal in Oak Ridge to the K-25 Plant area. By the end of March, 29 round-trips were being made each day, with a total of 7,500 passengers a month.

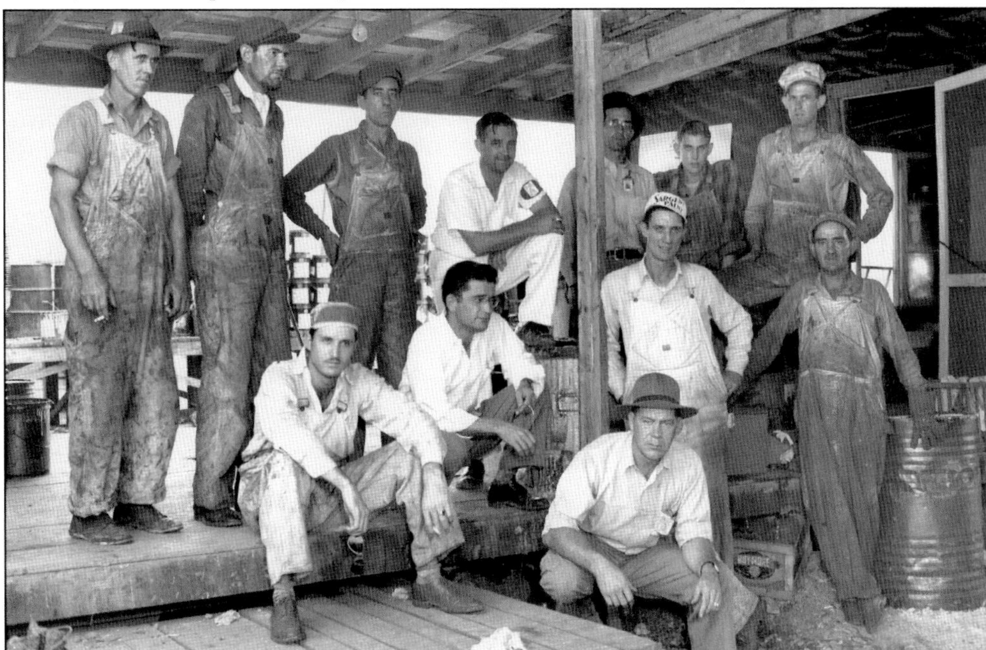

WORKING VETERANS. These ex-service men, veterans of World Wars I and II, are part of the K-25 paint shop and rolling spray crew. They came to Oak Ridge to continue work in support of the war effort, even though 10 of the men narrowly escaped with their lives during their enlistment in the military. The crew was highly praised for their attendance and work ethics by R. V. Ward, superintendent of the paint shop.

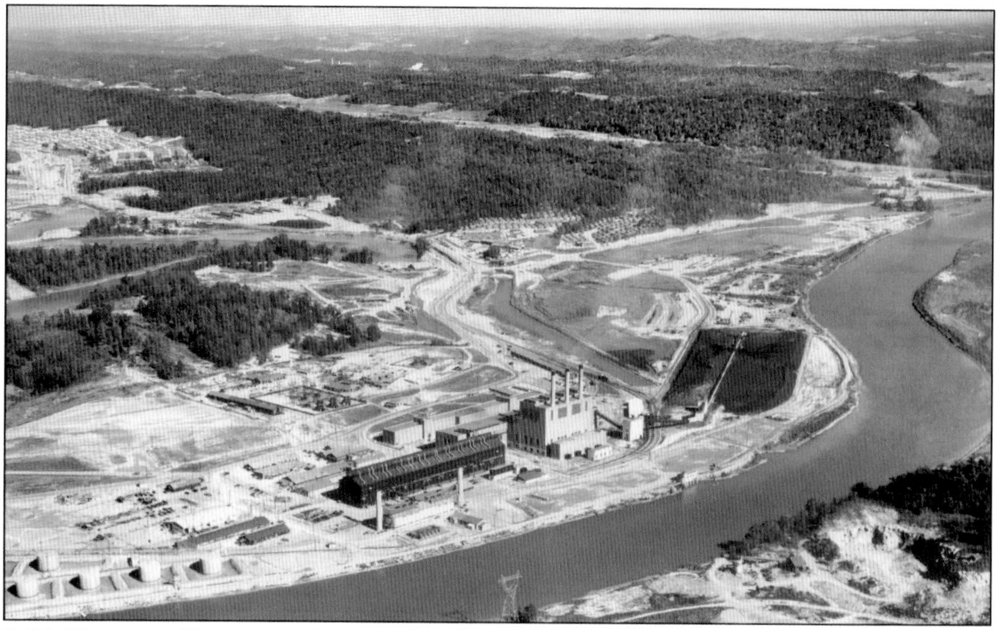

S-50 THERMAL DIFFUSION PLANT. Another system of gaseous diffusion was the thermal diffusion process. On July 9, 1943, construction began on a huge barn-like structure of black coated metal siding more than 500 feet long, 80 feet wide, and 75 feet high. This building was located next to the K-25 Power House, center right, on the Clinch River. This process was impractical on an industrial scale, so in 1944, on the recommendation of J. Robert Oppenheimer, this process was disbanded.

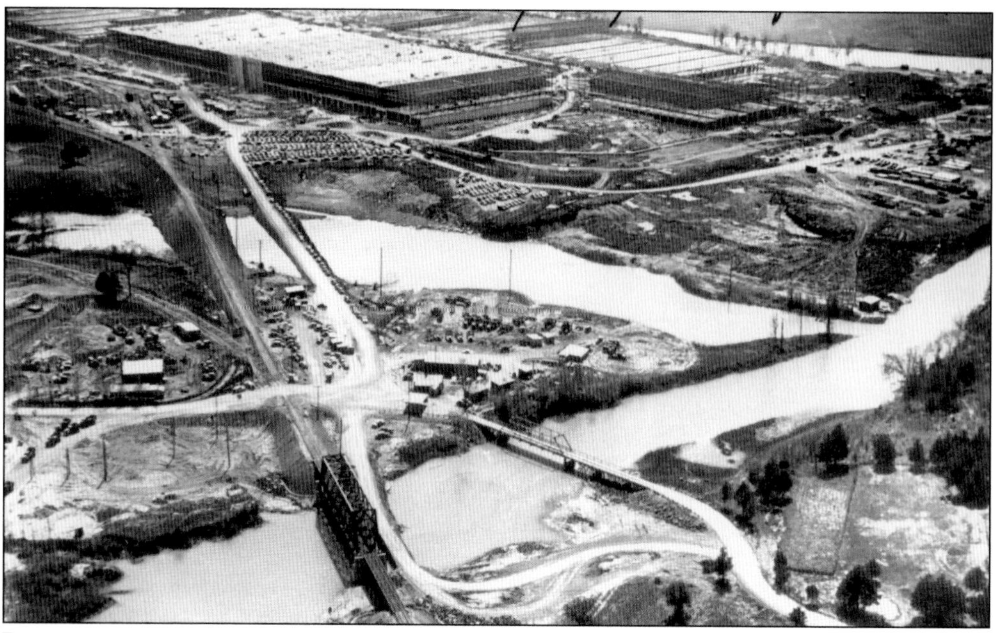

BLAIR AREA. There were two methods for entry into the north side of the K-25 site through the Blair gate, which crossed Popular Creek. The railroad bridge on the left was part of the main line from Blair. Parallel to this bridge was an earth-dam bridge used for vehicle traffic until the steel bridge downstream could be completed.

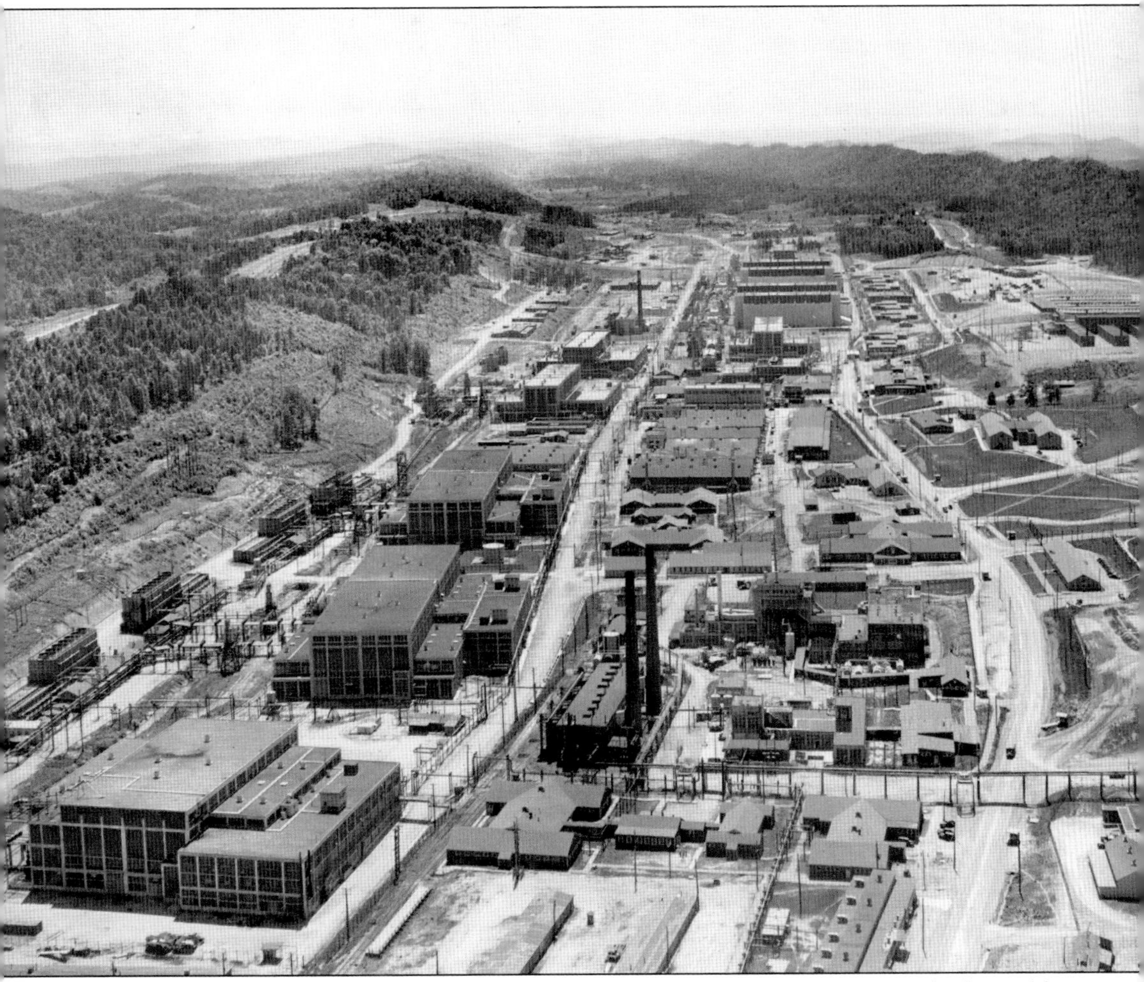

Y-12 Plant. This aerial view shows the electromagnetic plant code-named Y-12, which would separate uranium-235. The plant name had no meaning except to confuse enemy agents. The size and cost was enormous. Over 24,000 people were on the payroll. Construction costs ran over $300 million by 1946.

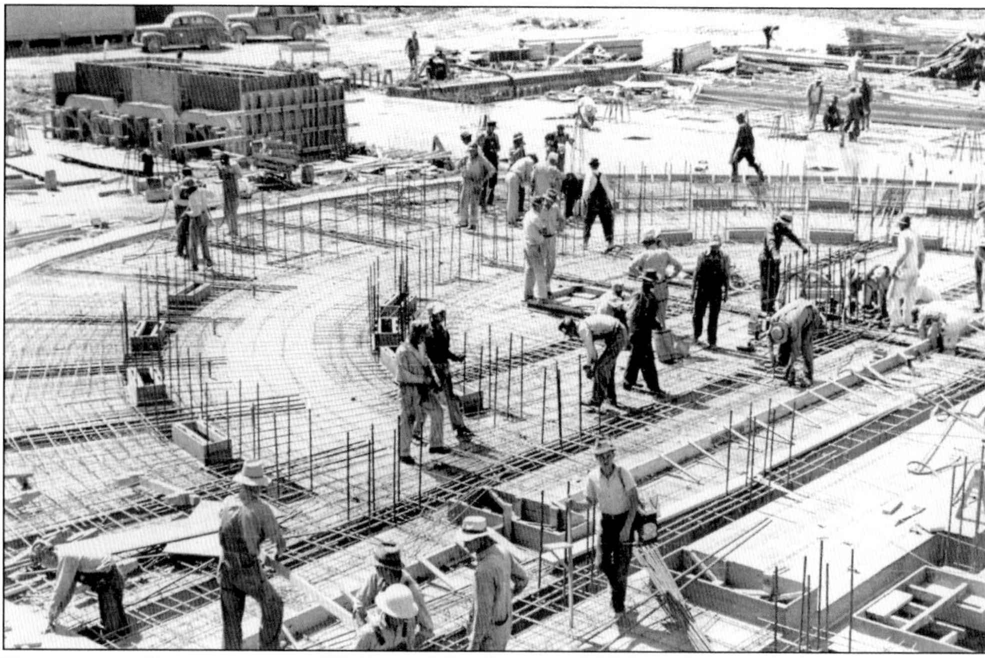

Racetrack Construction. Workers of the Stone and Webster Engineering Company install steel reinforcing rods that will form the base of one of the Alpha electromagnetic racetracks. Construction on the racetracks continued around the clock in order to meet the deadline for the needed enriched uranium.

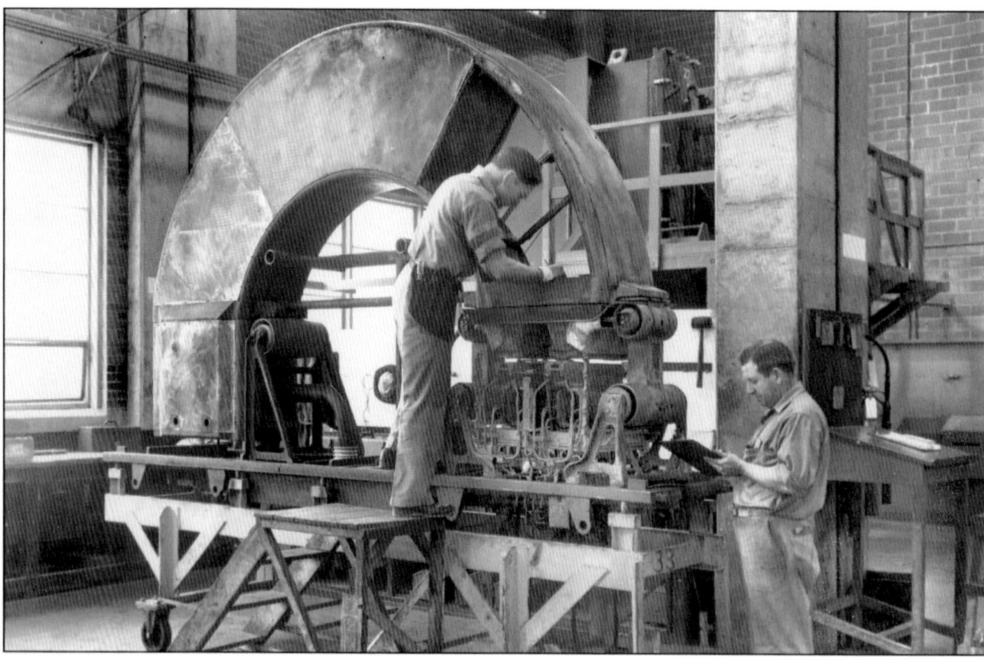

Racetrack Maintenance Area. Maintenance workers prepare a type-1 D-unit, a calutron, to be used in the Alpha racetrack. The unit rests on a storage dolly and the cover on the right has been removed, showing the double source area. On the left end of the D-unit is a cover over the receiver area. This area is where the final separation product was finally retrieved.

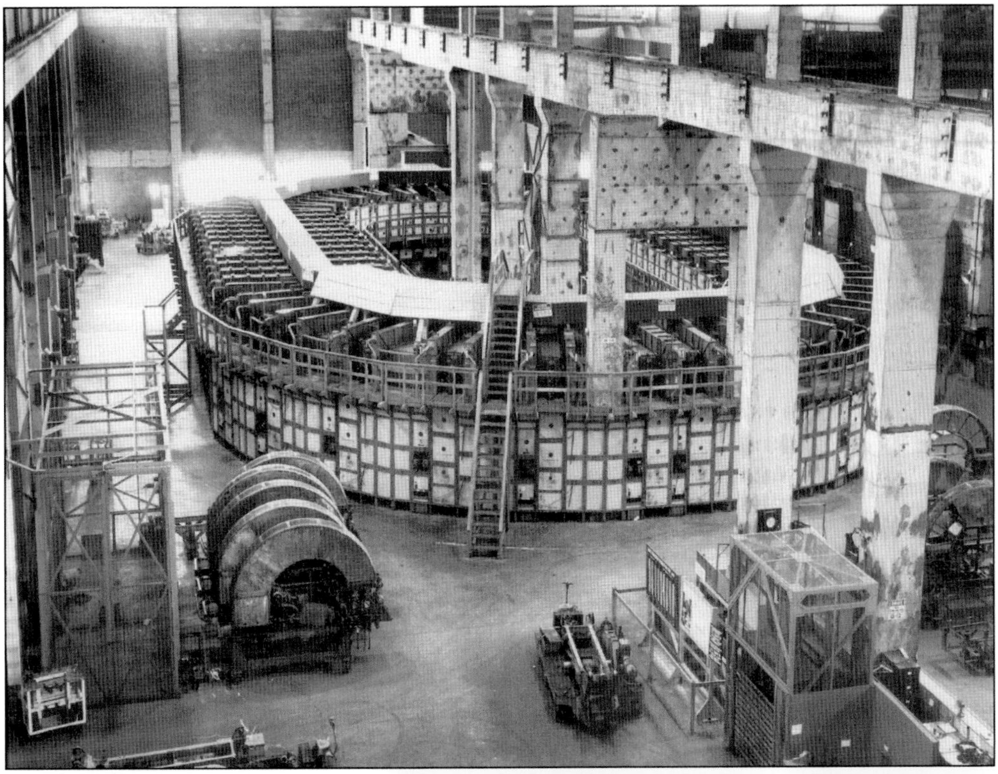

ALPHA RACETRACK. During summer and fall of 1943, the first electromagnetic plant began to operate. Due to electrical and oil related problems, the first racetrack was shut down. In January 1944, the second racetrack began start-up. This process produced 200 grams of 12 percent uranium-235 by the end of February 1944.

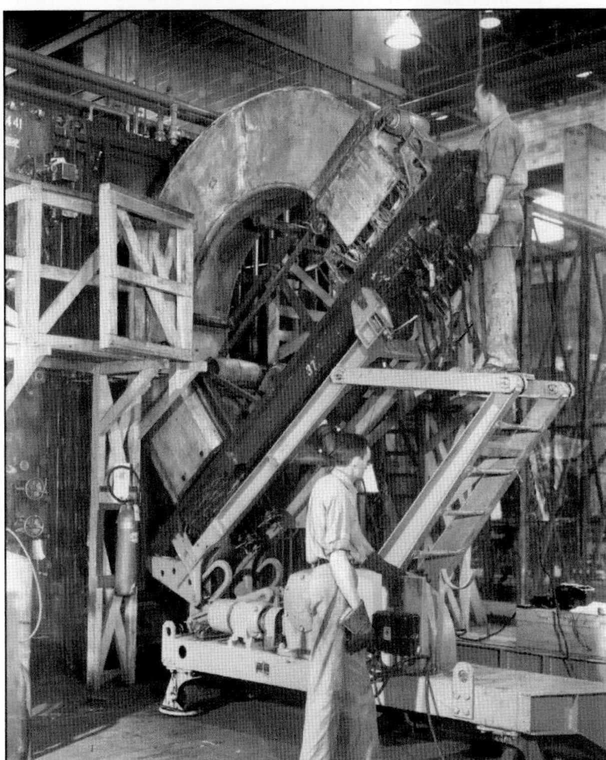

D-UNIT LOADING OPERATION. Loading handlers are using a loading dolly to install a calutron (D-unit) into the Alpha racetrack. Inside the D-unit was the E-unit, where the refined uranium was received. During the war, these machines were never referred to as calutrons but as Ds.

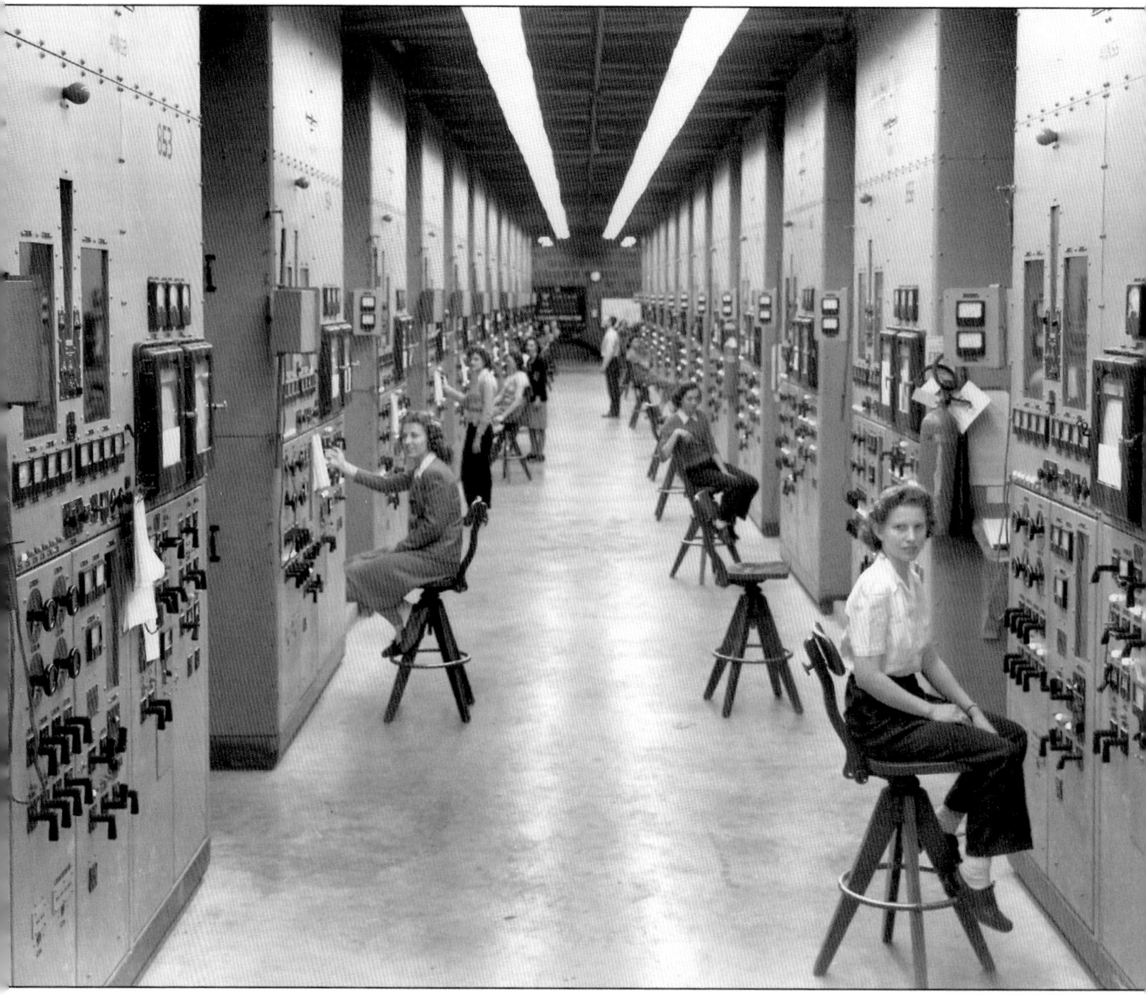

CUBICLE OPERATORS. Due to the shortage of men workers, women workers were used throughout the Y-12 plant. Like Gladys Owens, right front stool, these women monitored the control panels of the calutrons. Seven days a week, usually ten hours a day, they stared intently at the rows of dials that represented the activities within the giant oval "racetrack" for the electromagnetic process. The man standing center at the back is Connie Bolling, the supervisor for the operators.

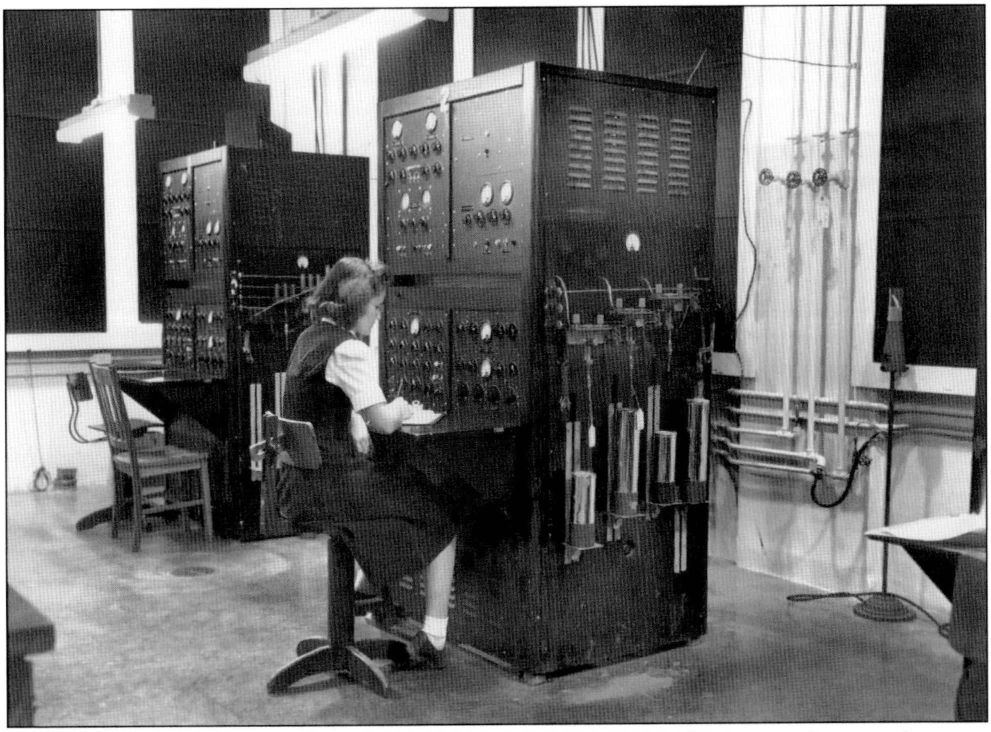

VACUUM CONTROL PANEL. The women workers shown in these two photographs were monitoring the vacuum system of the electromagnetic separation process, taking data and adjusting the dials to provide the proper vacuum during the uranium separation process at the Y-12 plant.

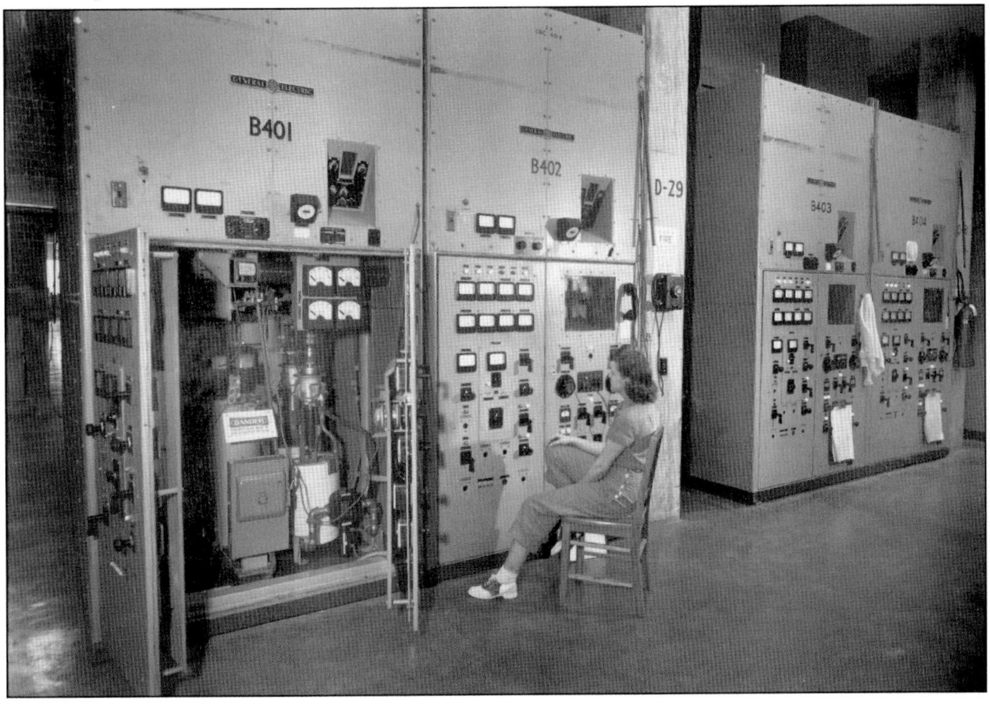

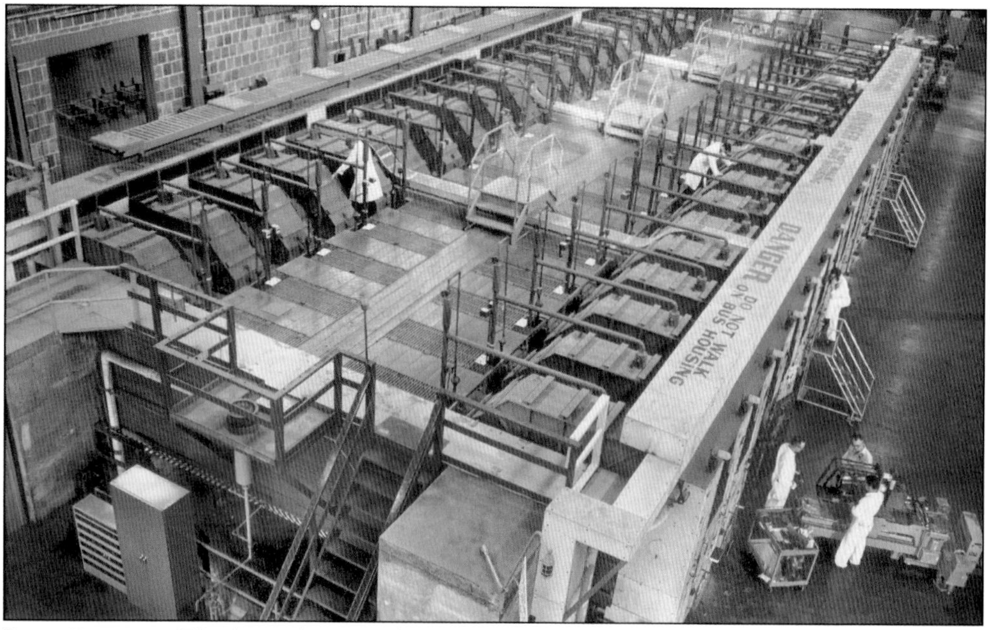

BETA PROCESS. The beta plant was located in three beta buildings in Y-12 and housed two tracks of 36 tanks each. The tracks would be divided into two banks, the tanks in each bank facing the same way to simplify supply lines. This process was the second stage that took the feed material from the alpha process and enriched it to over 90 percent bomb-grade material. On the floor level, workers are preparing an M-unit to be installed into one of the 36 tanks of the beta process.

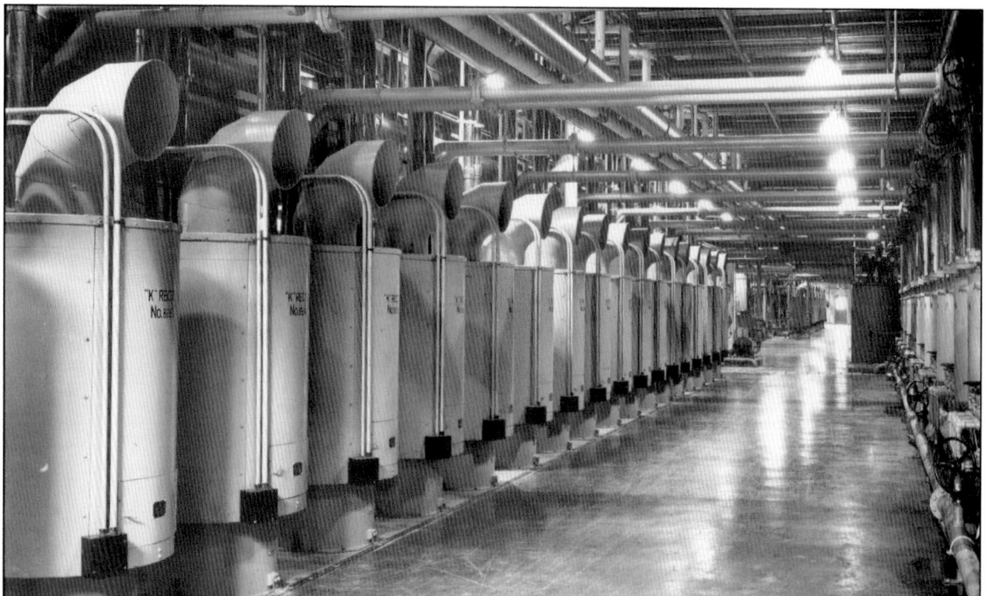

RECTIFIERS. Some of the many electrical rectifiers used in the beta (second-stage) racetracks are shown here. Voltage was needed for the separation process, so each stage had its own rectifier. Cubicle operators sat in front of their control panels, monitored meters, and adjusted the voltage as necessary for proper operation of the beta process.

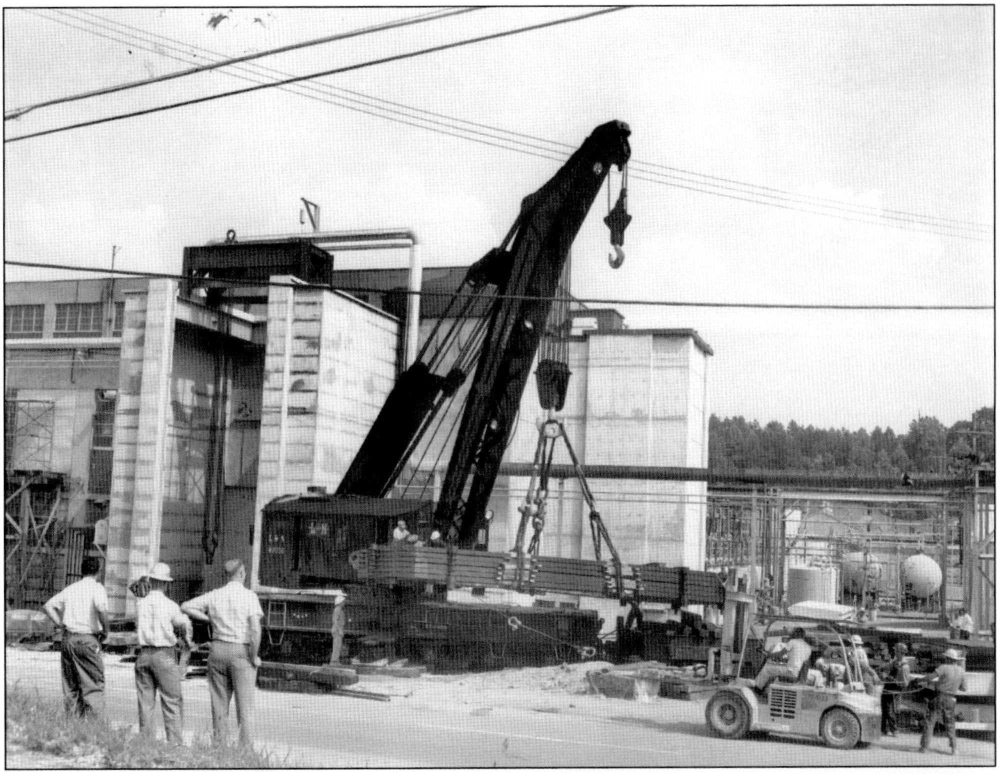

REMOVING SILVER. Huge bus bars of silver, a square foot in cross section, ran around the top of the racetrack. These bus bars were fabricated at the Y-12 plant. Shown is a stack of bus bars awaiting transporting to the cutting and weighing area for return to the U.S. Treasury Department. Silver, a great conductor of electricity, was used because of the wartime shortage of copper.

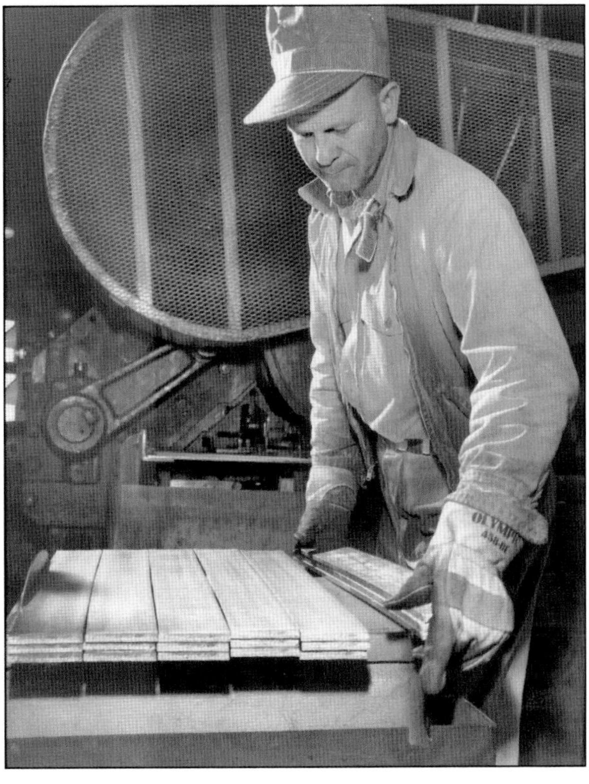

STAGING SILVER. A Y-12 worker is shown stacking silver strips after they have been cut from 40-foot bars into 3-foot lengths for weighing and packaging. After each bar was weighed, it was packed into wooden crates for return to the U.S. Treasury Department.

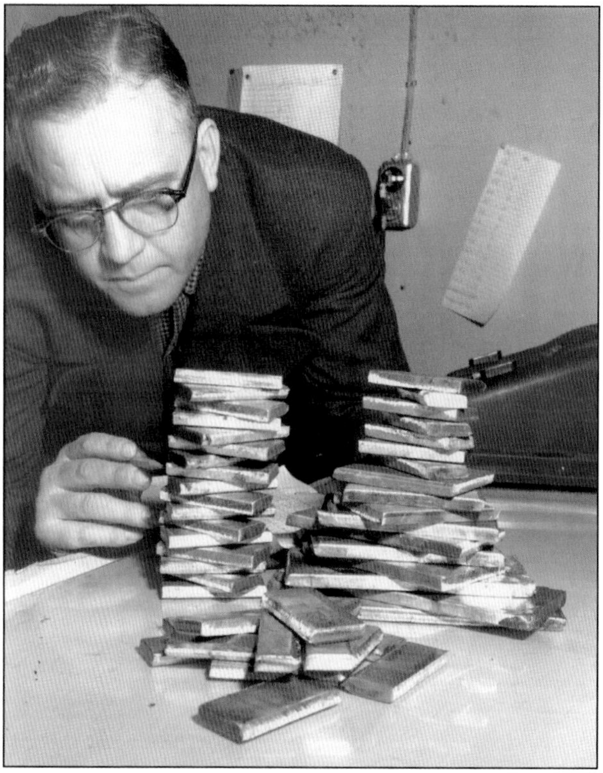

ACCOUNTABILITY. After the separation process was no longer needed, the silver on loan from the U.S. Treasury Department was removed from the process buildings. Each fragment of silver had to be accounted for. In the picture at left, Otis Sharpe is counting odd-sized silver pieces. The photograph below shows the small trimmings from the bar-cutting process. In the final accounting of the 14,700 tons of silver borrowed, only a minuscule one percent was missing.

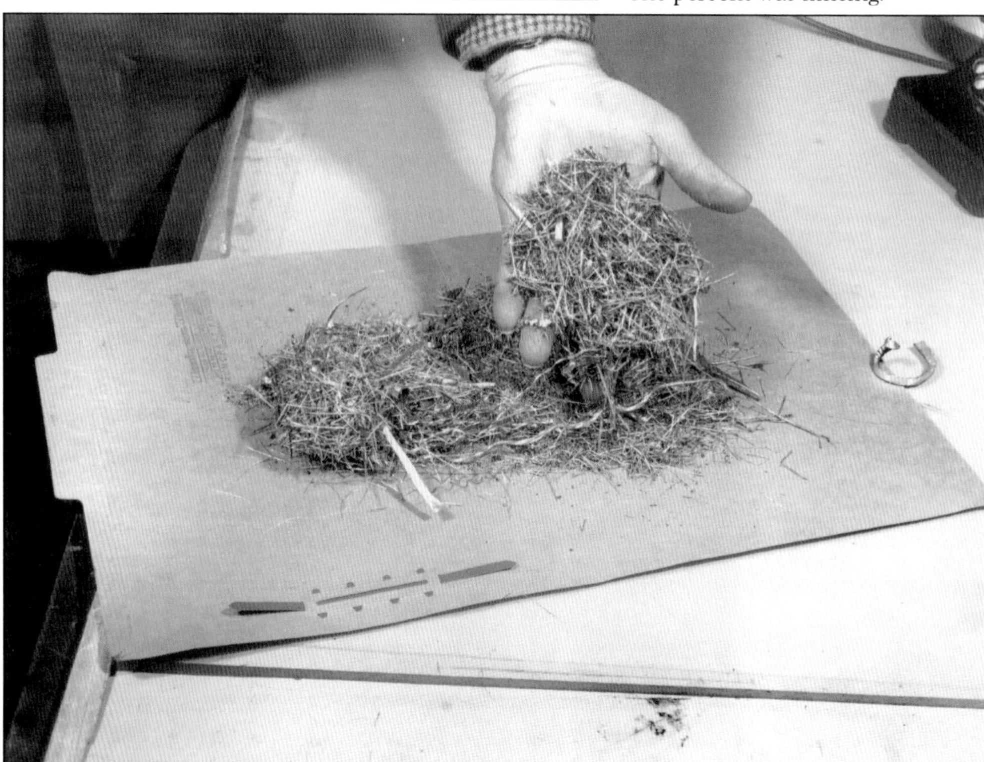

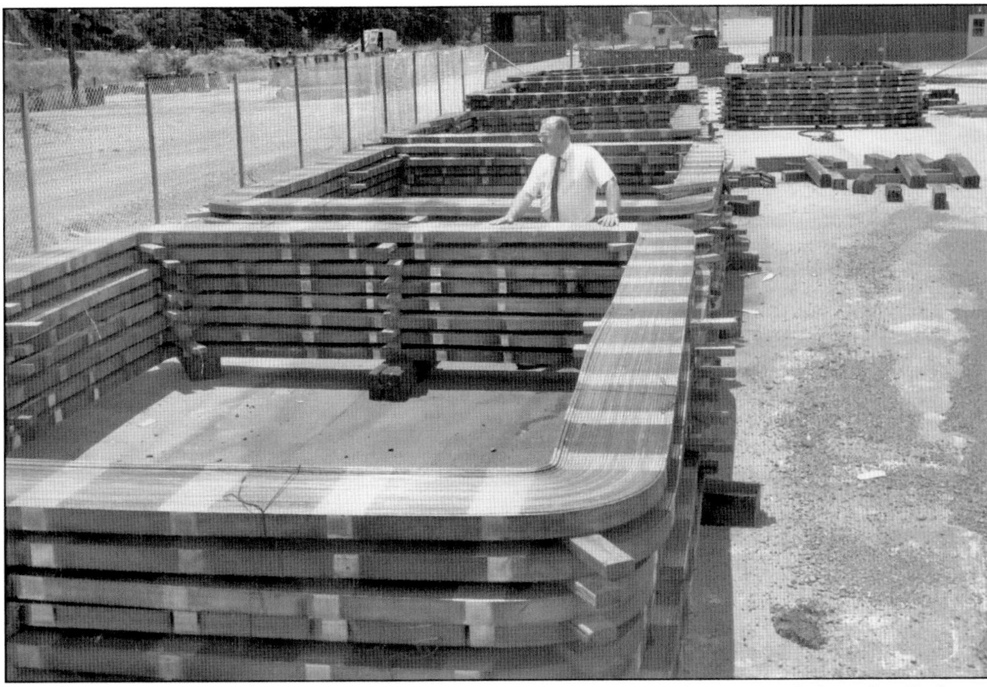

Return of Silver. The 14,700 tons of silver was cast into billets, extruded, and rolled into strips. The strips, 5/8 of an inch thick, 3 inches wide, and about 40 feet long, were wound on the magnetic coils by Alice Chalmers for the separation process. The above photo shows some of the 940 magnetic coils fabricated between 1943 and 1944 being prepared for return to the U.S. Treasury Department. Below, crates of cut silver bars are awaiting shipment. The total value of the silver was more than $400 million.

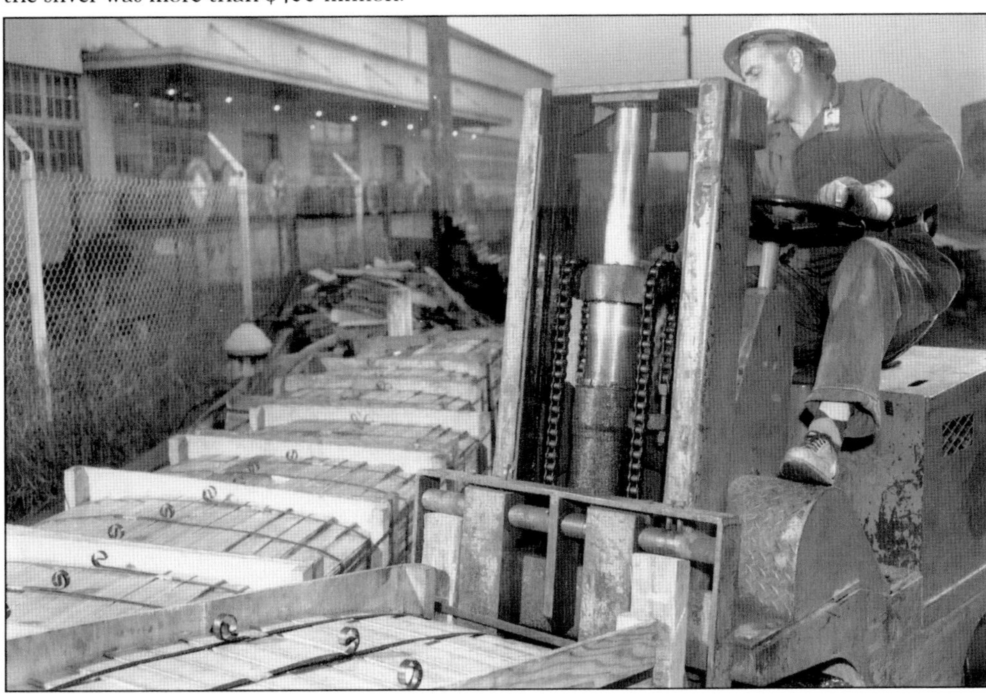

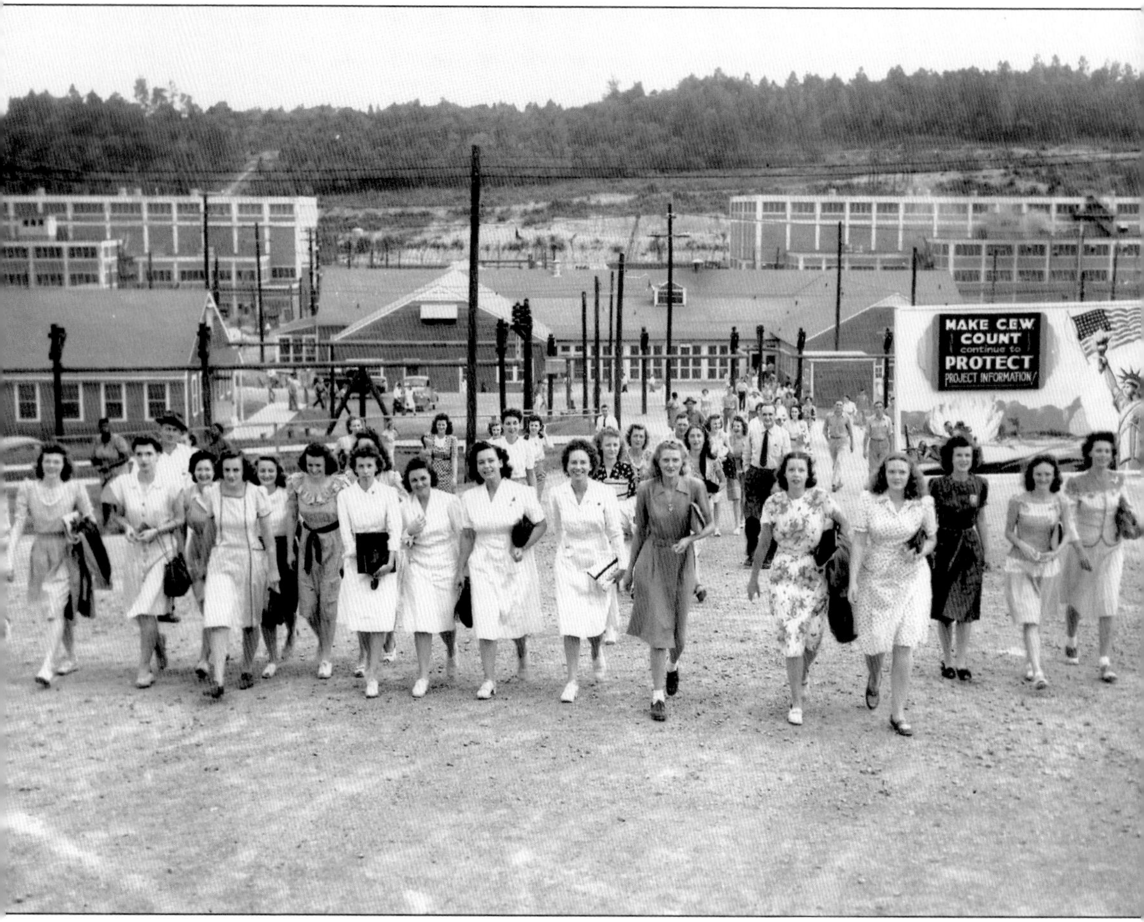

Y-12 Workers. Some of the 24,000 workers are seen here leaving at shift change. The female work force vividly demonstrates the role women played in Oak Ridge during the war. Operators worked three shifts over a 24-hour period, rotating every seven days.

Two

BRIDGES, ROADS, AND HOUSING

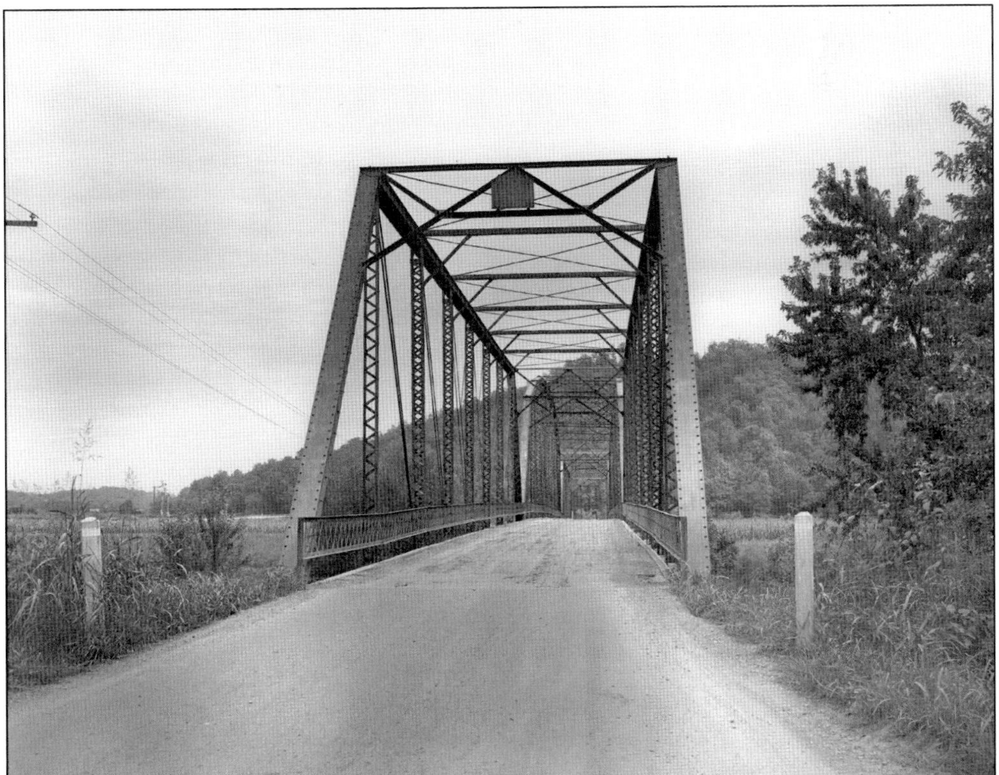

EDGEMOOR BRIDGE. As the reservation was bordered on three sides by the Clinch River, bridges became an important feature of the access to the area. Edgemoor Bridge, originally a steel and wooden structure, existed before the reservation was established and was one of the main river-crossing points for workers coming from Knoxville and the surrounding areas.

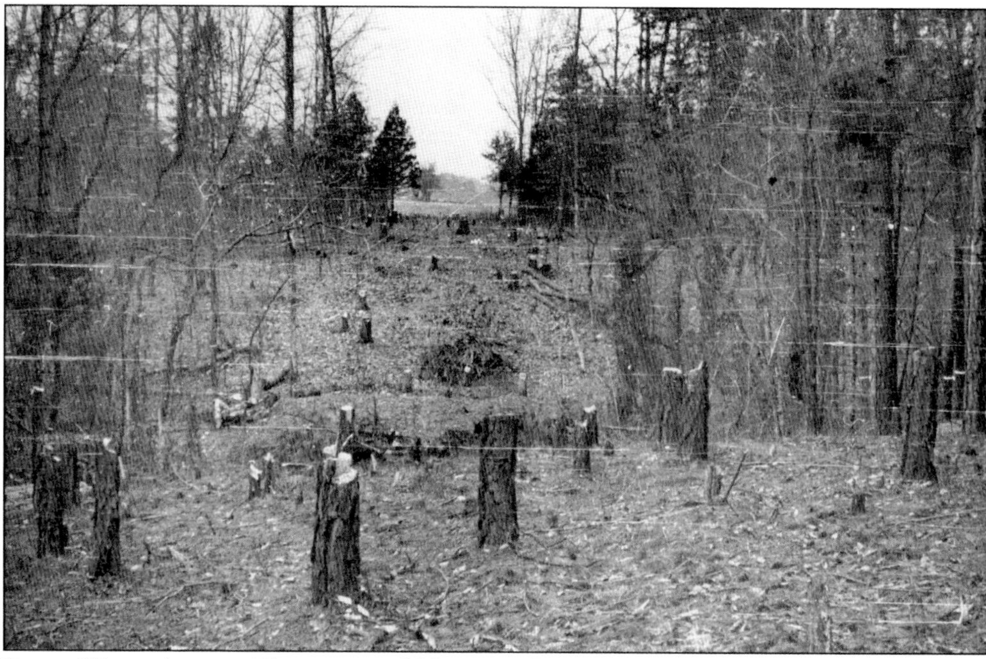

ROAD WORK AHEAD. This site would become Tennessee Avenue, one of the main roads running east to west through the city. One of the primary factors in site selection for the Clinton Engineer Works was the necessity of isolation. Road and highway entrance to the area was limited, although many dirt trails existed.

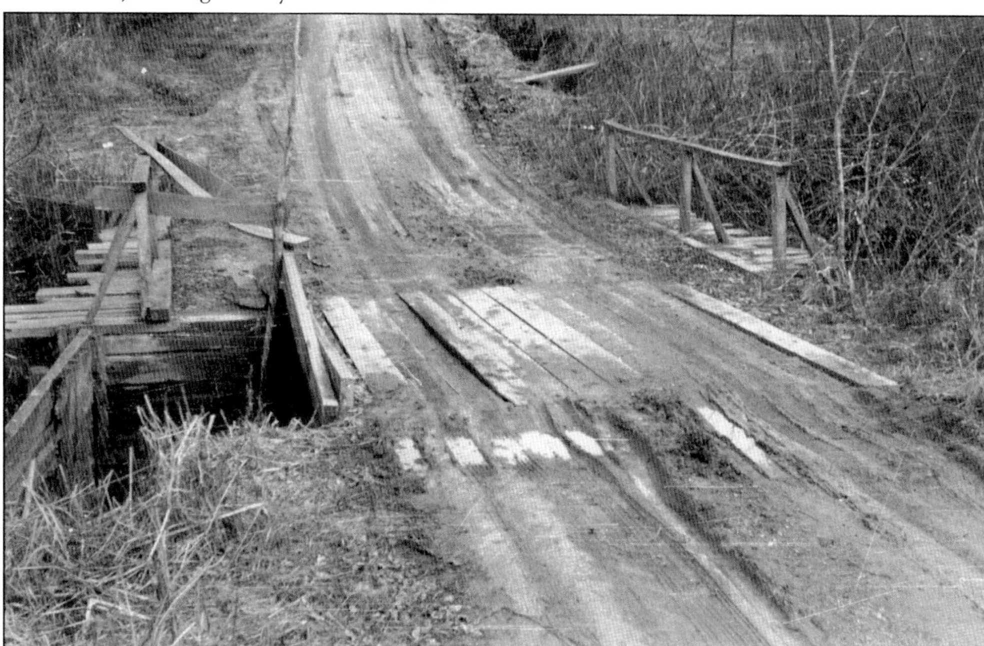

HAZARDOUS CONDITIONS. When the planners of the Clinton Engineer Works arrived in the area, they were faced with narrow country dirt roads, wooden bridges in need of repair, and a terrain of clay and rolling hills. As construction traffic increased, the many dirt roads on the site became a hazard. Each rain would cause the roads to rut and make travel difficult.

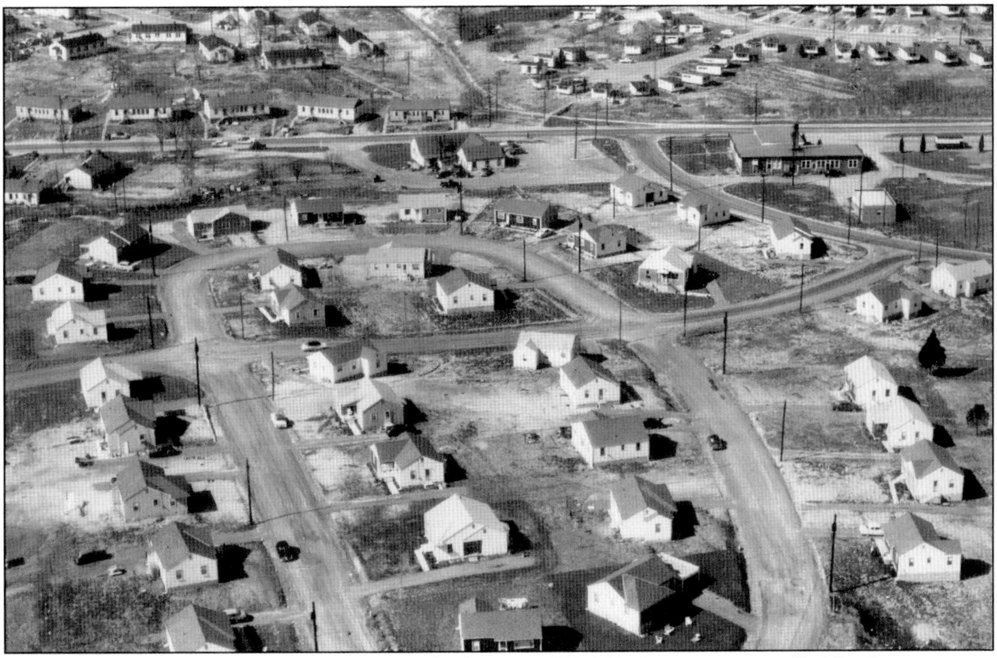

THE DESIGN OF STREETS AND ROADS. The layout of Oak Ridge was controlled by the contours and grades of the area. Several main roadways run east and west. "Avenues" run north and south, or up and down hills. The avenues, which are named for states, start in the east, progressing to the west alphabetically—California, Delaware, Florida, Georgia, and so on.

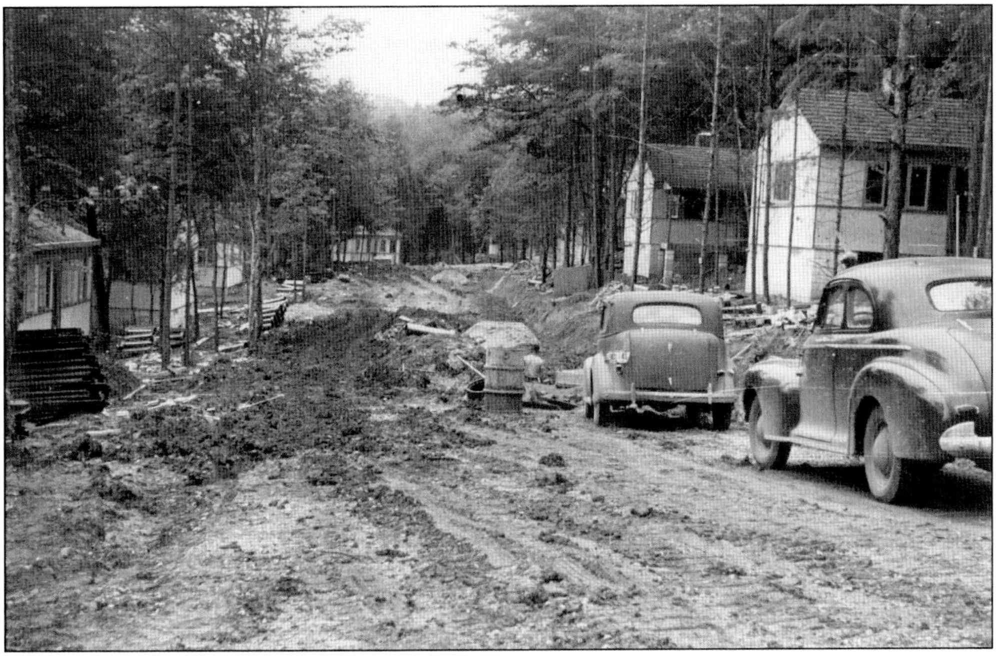

MUD, MUD, EVERYWHERE. Looking east down Tucker Road shows a typical challenge residents had to face in the early days of Oak Ridge. Construction was going 24 hours a day with heavy trucks delivering building materials up and down the roads and streets. In 1946, after the bulk of construction was complete, the town undertook a large-scale paving program.

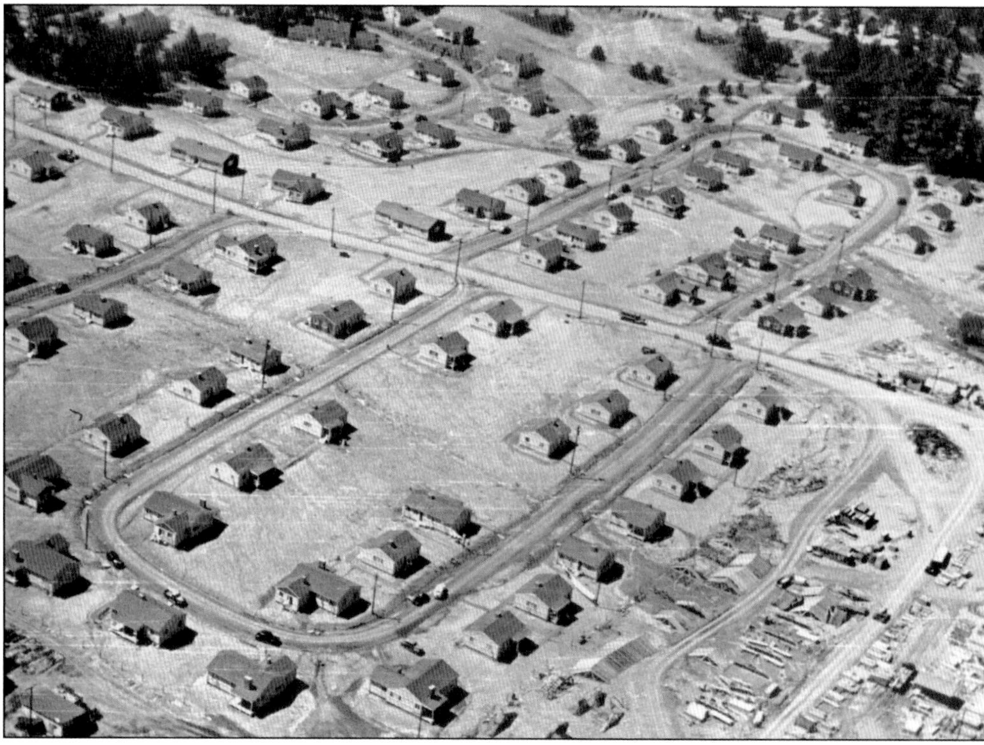

Cemesto Construction. These houses were constructed with exterior walls of horizontal cemesto-board panels supported by horizontal structural wood framing. (Cemesto was thin cement and asbestos sheets.) Floors were conventional, supported by wood joists and girders. Roofs were cello (tar and gravel) roofing supported on trusses. The homes were heated with central warm air (coal furnaces) supplemented by fireplaces.

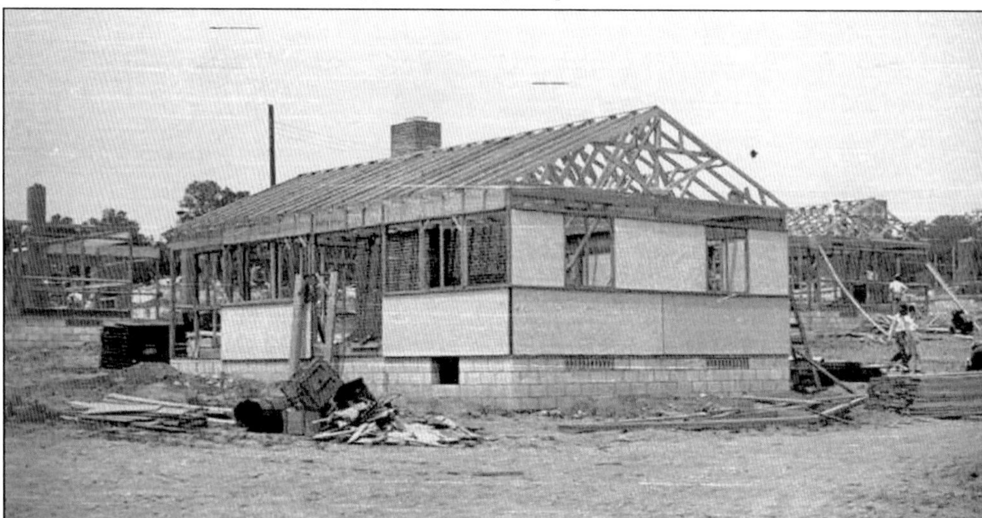

Cemesto Type A. These houses consisted of two bedrooms, a bathroom, a living room, a kitchen, and a utility room that housed the coal furnace. The cemesto houses were the first 3,050 homes built. There were 700 A-type units constructed at a total cost of $2,907,800. Rent on these homes was $38 per month.

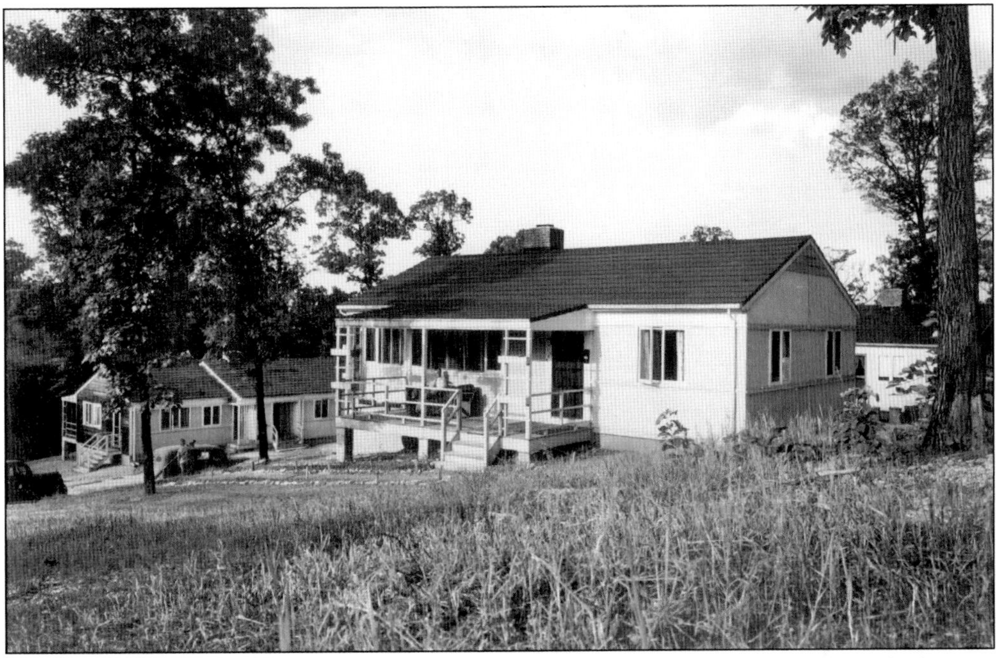

CEMESTO TYPE B. Houses of this type were constructed with two bedrooms, a bathroom, a living/dining room, a kitchen, and a utility room that housed the coal furnace. The total number of B-type homes built was 800 with a total cost of $4,012,000. Monthly rental was $48.50 per unit.

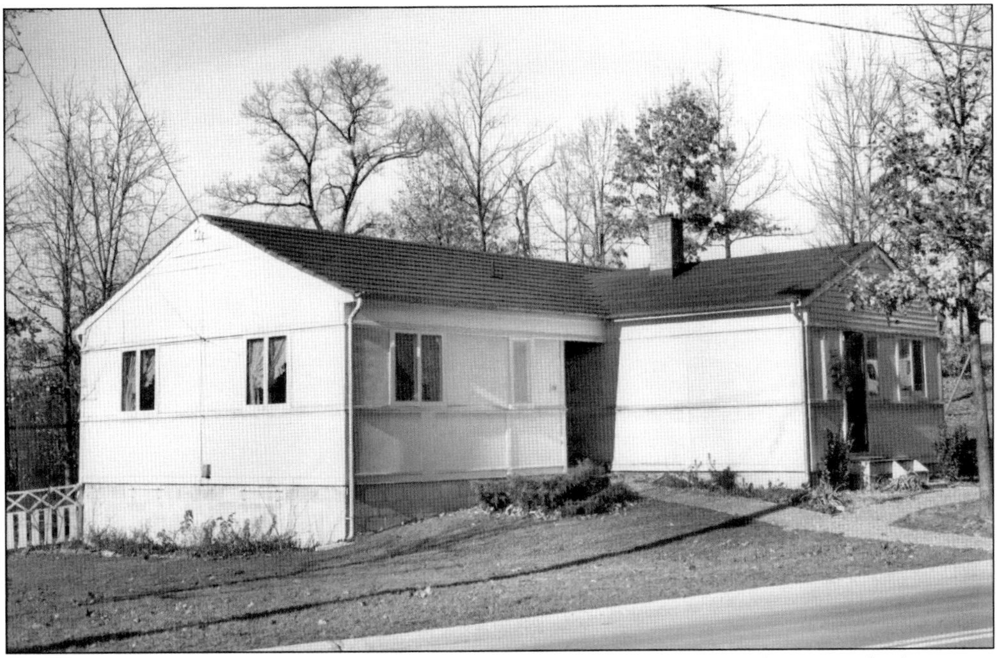

CEMESTO TYPE C. Families living in this type house enjoyed three bedrooms, a bathroom, a living/dining room, a kitchen, and a utility room. This design had three entrance/exit doors—the front, the back, and the utility room. The total number built was 400 at a cost of $2,369,200. Units rented for $56 per month.

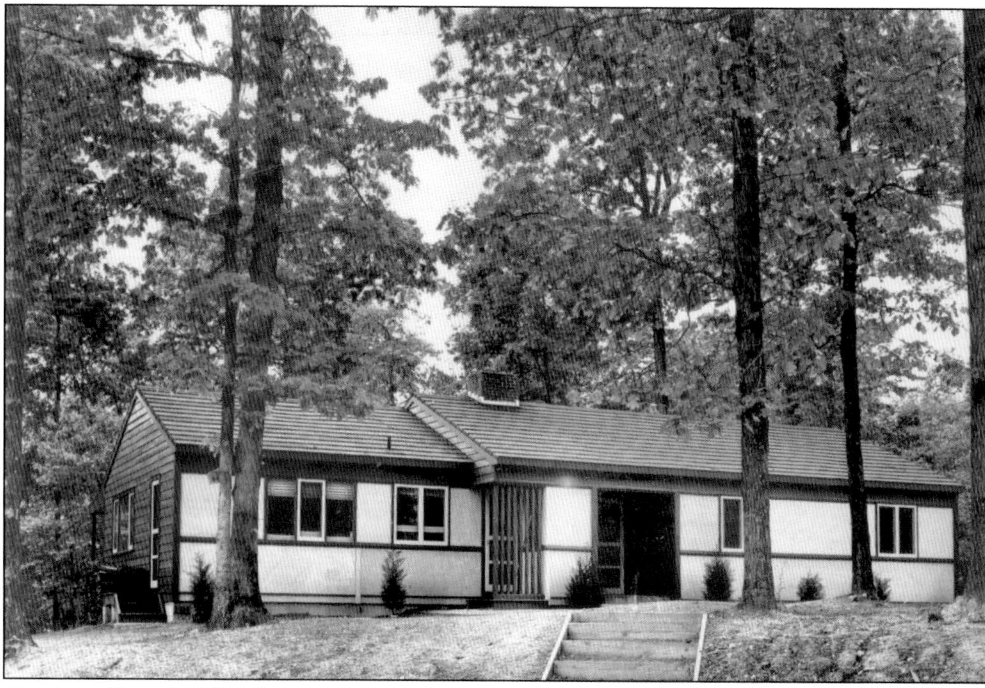

CEMESTO TYPE D. This design was one of two that consisted of a separate dining room. A few of these units housed two bathrooms. The home had three bedrooms, a living room, a kitchen, and a utility room. There were 447 of these units built totaling $3,169,230. Rent per month was $68.50.

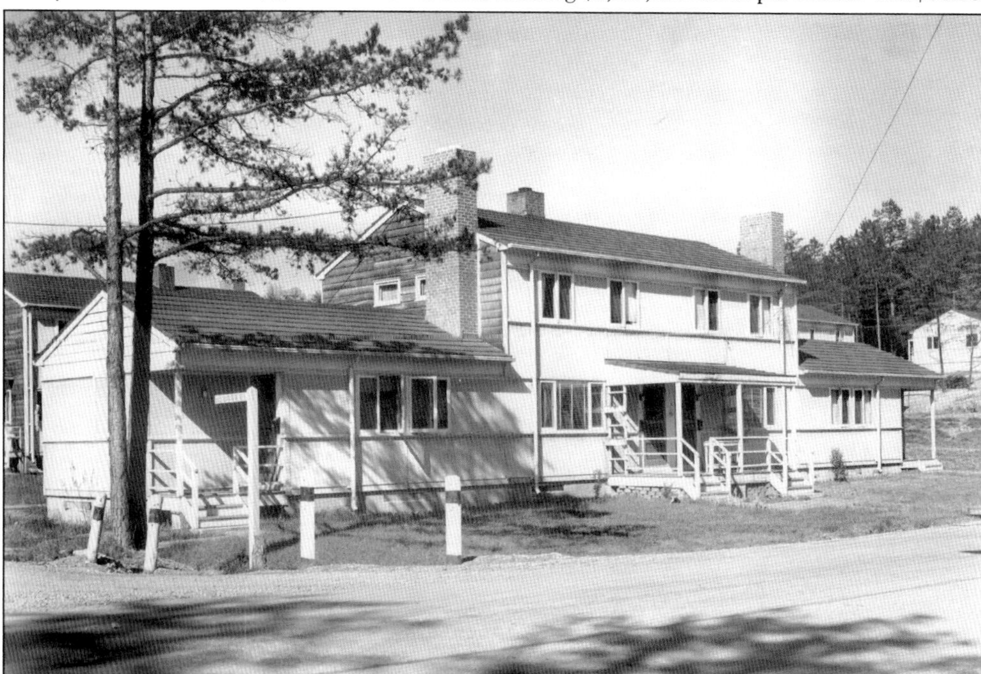

CEMESTO TYPE E. Four families could be housed in this cemesto. It had two one-bedroom units and two two-bedroom units. Each shared a central utility room. The 600 units were built for $2,003,400 with rent for one-bedroom units at $30 per month and two-bedroom units at $40.

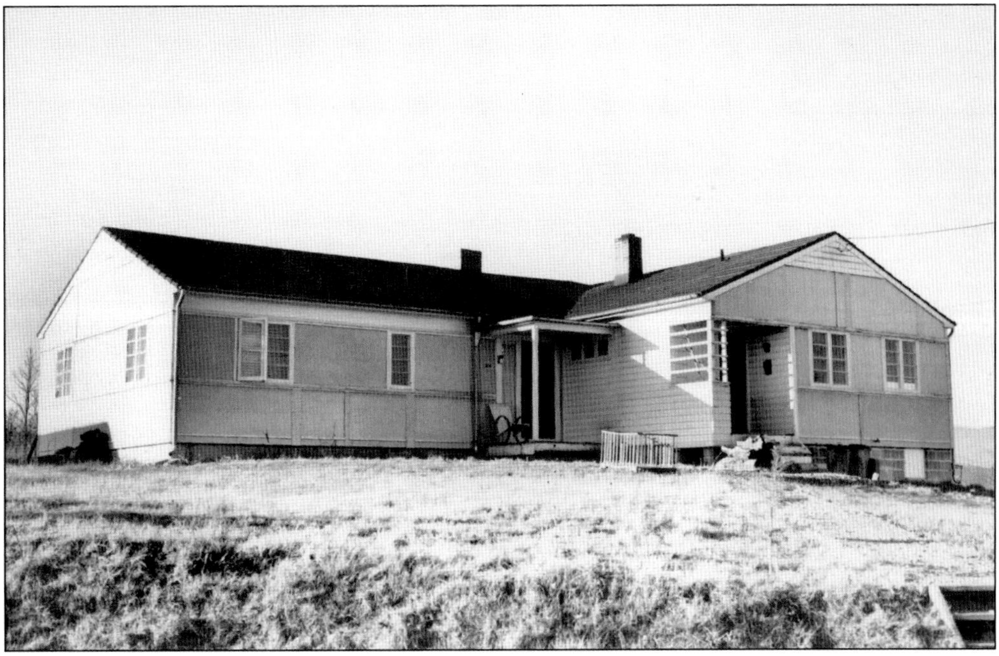

CEMESTO TYPE F. The F-type dwelling had three bedrooms, a living room, a separate dining room, a kitchen, and two baths. The government built 53 of these units and rented them for $73 a month. Housing was allocated by the job you had. Plant managers were likely to be assigned to this type of house.

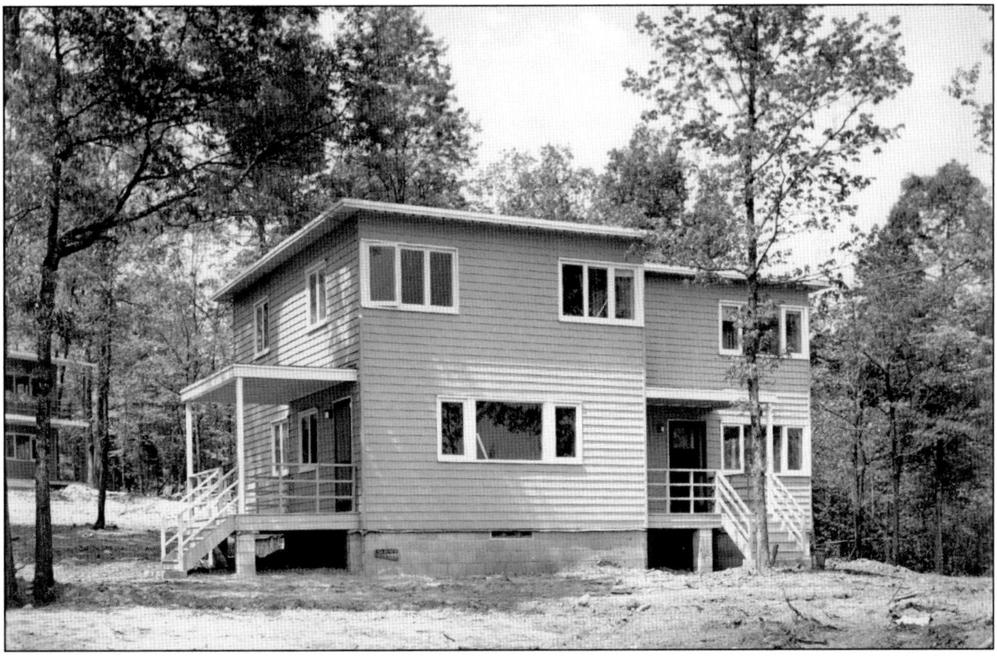

MULTI-FAMILY UNITS. Dwelling type K contained two two-bedroom units or two one-bedroom units and rented from $31.50 to $37 per month. This rate included utilities and fuel; there was an extra rental charge for furniture. Two hundred of this type housing units were built at a total construction cost of $796,000.

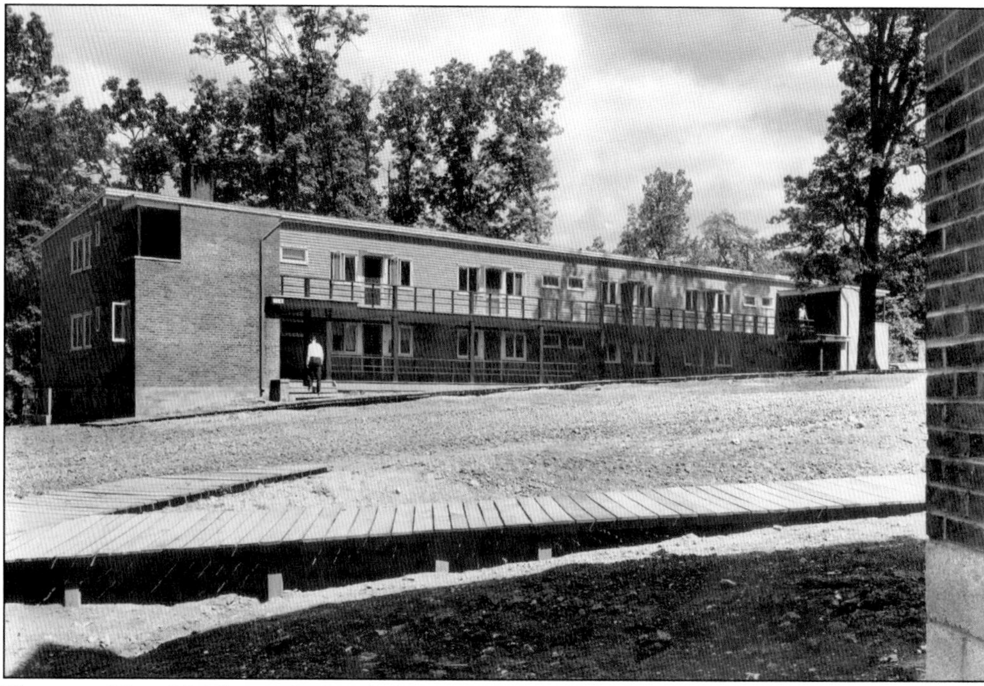

HOUSING TYPE N. This multi-family housing unit consisted of 12 one-bedroom units. A rental cost of $30 per month included utilities and fuel. Total construction cost for 180 units was $632,700. In the foreground is seen the boardwalk that served the city as a sidewalk.

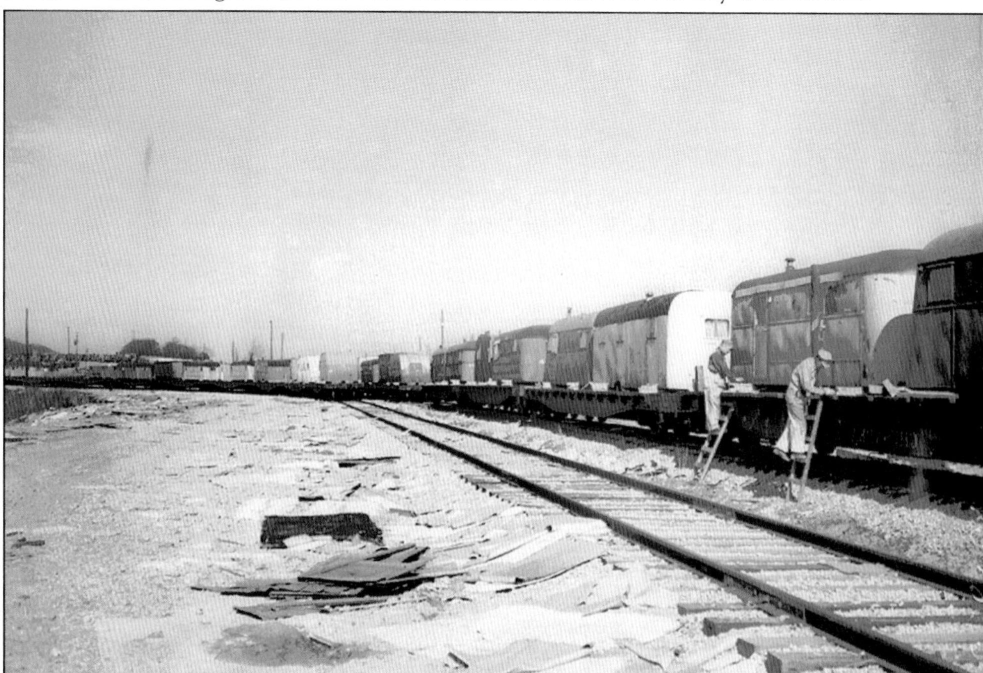

TRAILERS. With the need to house construction men and their families, trailers were purchased from the Federal Public Housing Authority and shipped by railcar from as far away as New York and Florida. Seven trailer camp sites were eventually built with a capacity of 4,173 trailers.

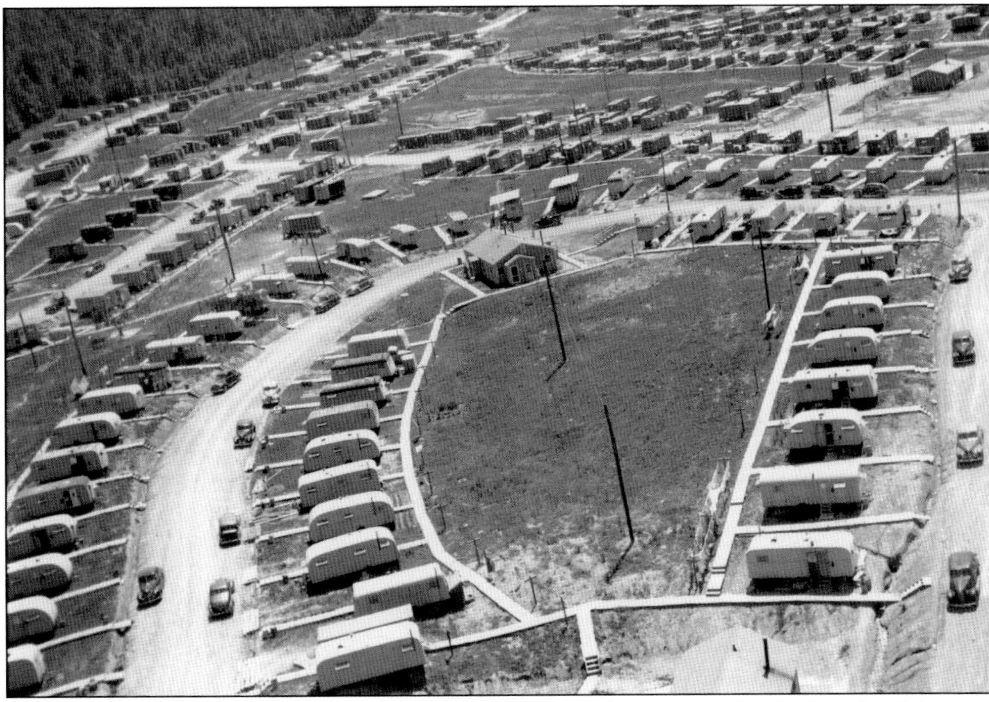

TRAILER HOMES. Housing for construction labor was made necessary by the fact that labor was imported from 500 to 600 miles away. Seven trailer camps with a capacity of 4,173 trailers were constructed to house some of these workers and their families at a total cost of $1,314,118. Below, Mrs. Wilson J. Schreck picks a flower from the vine in front of her trailer in the Middletown Trailer Camp. The Schrecks came to Oak Ridge from Lexington, Kentucky.

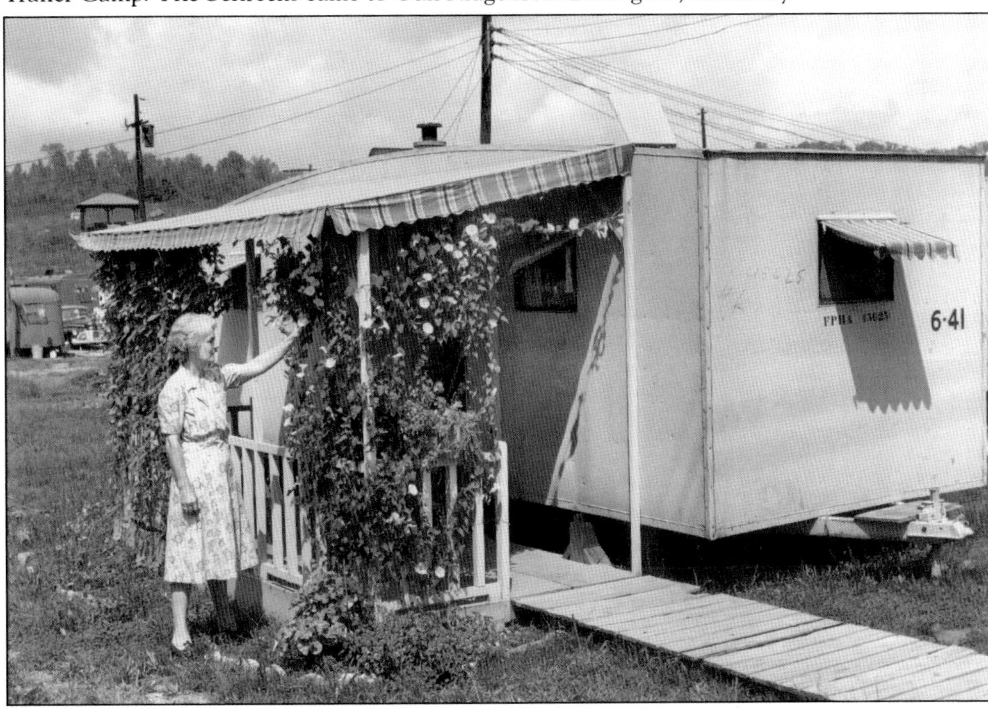

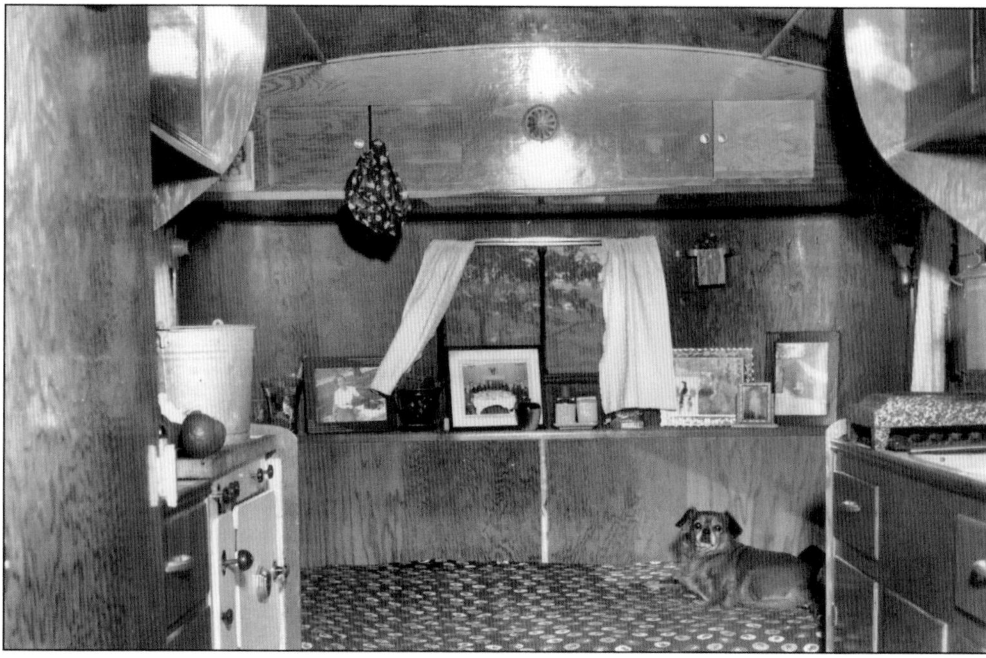

GOVERNMENT TRAILER LIVING QUARTERS. If you had your own trailer, you could rent a space for $3 per week, including water, electricity, and use of a bathroom. Government-owned trailers rented for $3.45 per week for a single and $4.60 per week for an expandable type. Rent included normal utility services.

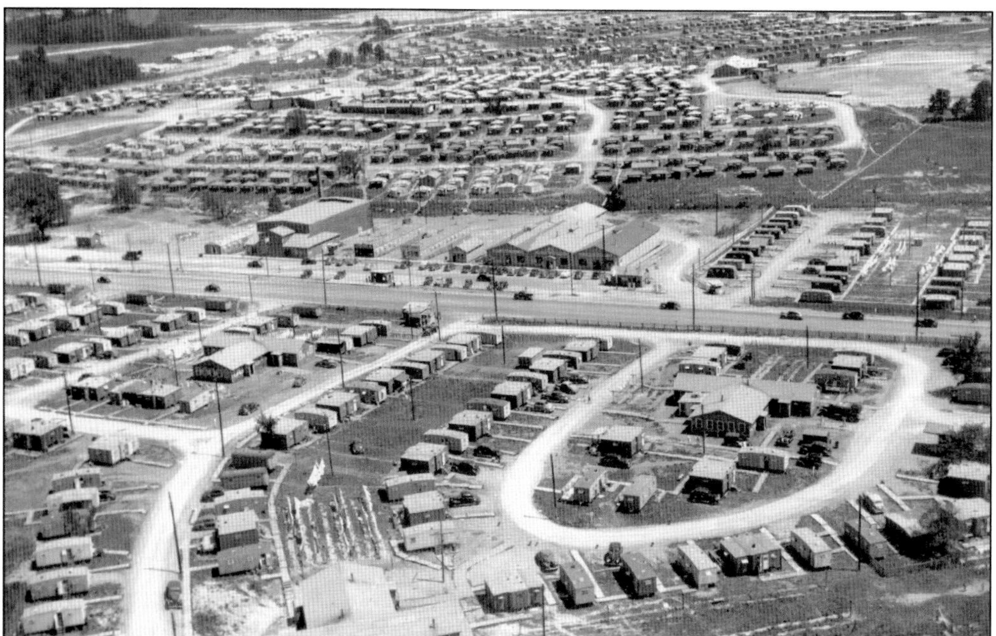

MIDDLETOWN TRAILER CAMP. This typical housing area was one of seven trailer camps built at a cost of $1,314,118, exclusive of trailers but including cost of assembly and construction of utilities. Upon arrival, the trailers were placed on foundations prepared in advance, connected to the electrical distribution system, and otherwise made ready for occupancy.

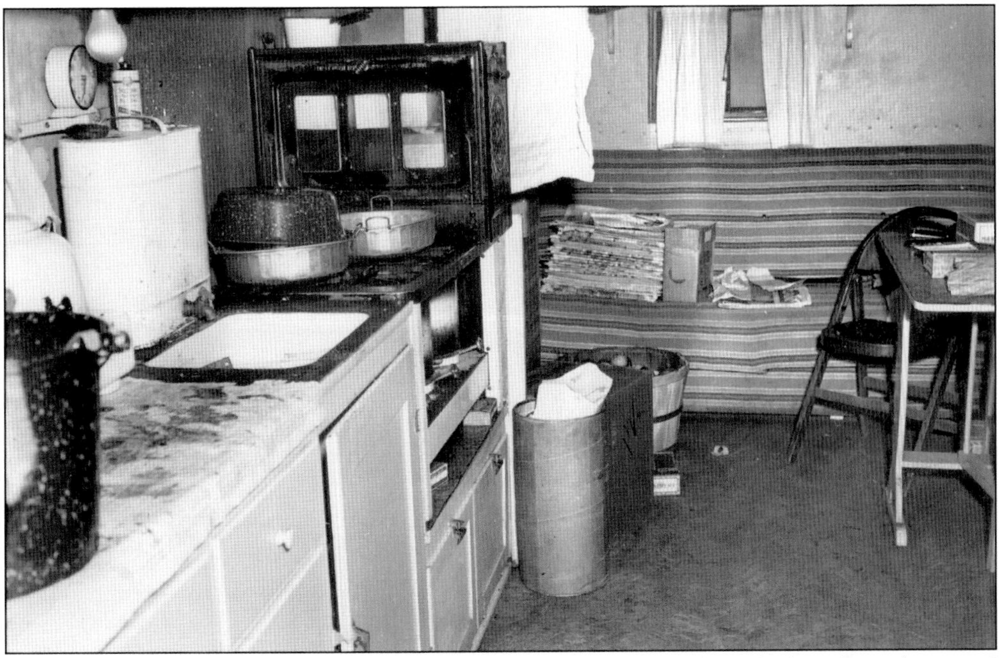

TRAILER LIVING QUARTERS. The units were small but nicely furnished with cooking and sleeping areas. Each trailer was equipped with electricity, but water had to be carried from a water distribution center daily. The water was stored in a holding tank next to the sink. No bathrooms were in the trailers, so residents had to use the bathroom facility within the trailer camp.

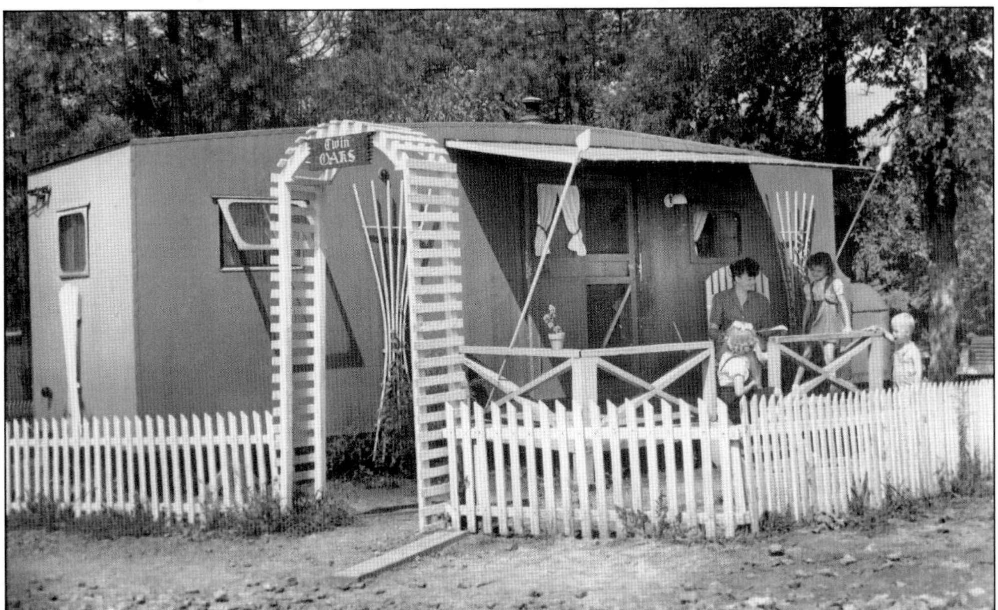

FIRST TRAILER CAMP. Located in the area known as Middletown, this camp was ready for operation in June 1943. The camps were provided with lights and conveniently located utility buildings, bathhouses, toilets, laundries, stores, and recreational areas. Residents were encouraged to fix their areas up, as Mrs. Rebecca Martin did with a white picket fence, to make the small trailers feel more like home and help promote morale.

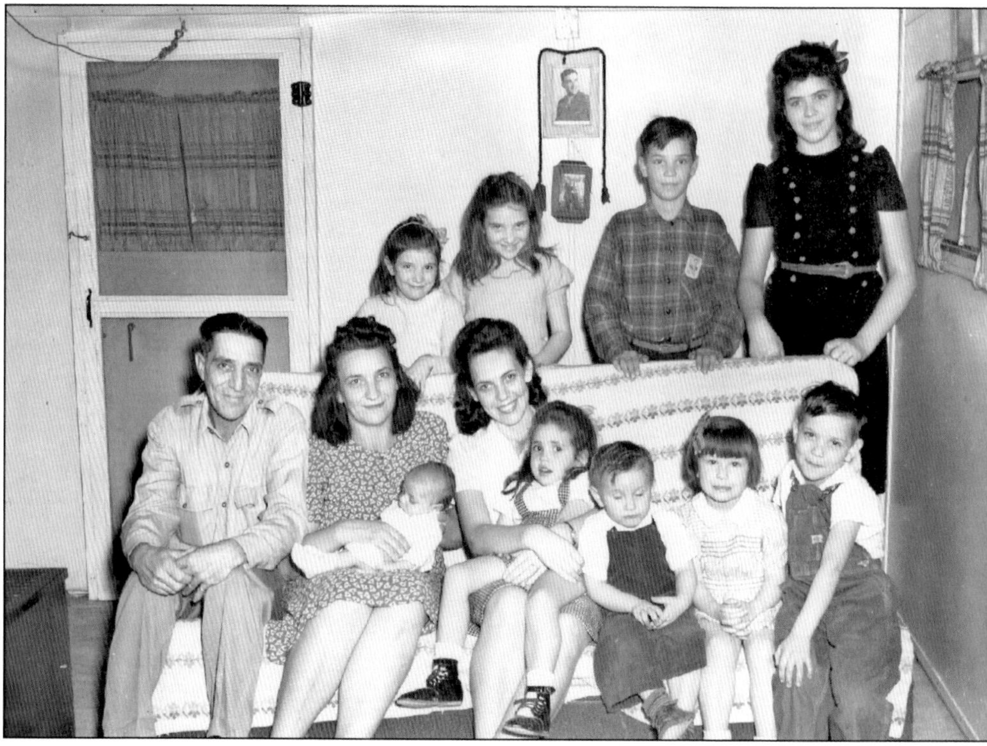

AN EVEN DOZEN. The largest family living in Oak Ridge was that of Mr. and Mrs. Melvin Otto Sportsman from Little Rock, Arkansas. The family of 12 inhabited an expandable trailer located in the Gamble Valley Trailer Camp. Mrs. Sportsman is seated second from left; beside her is her daughter-in-law, wife of the pictured Marine and eldest child, Charles Sportsman (seated left).

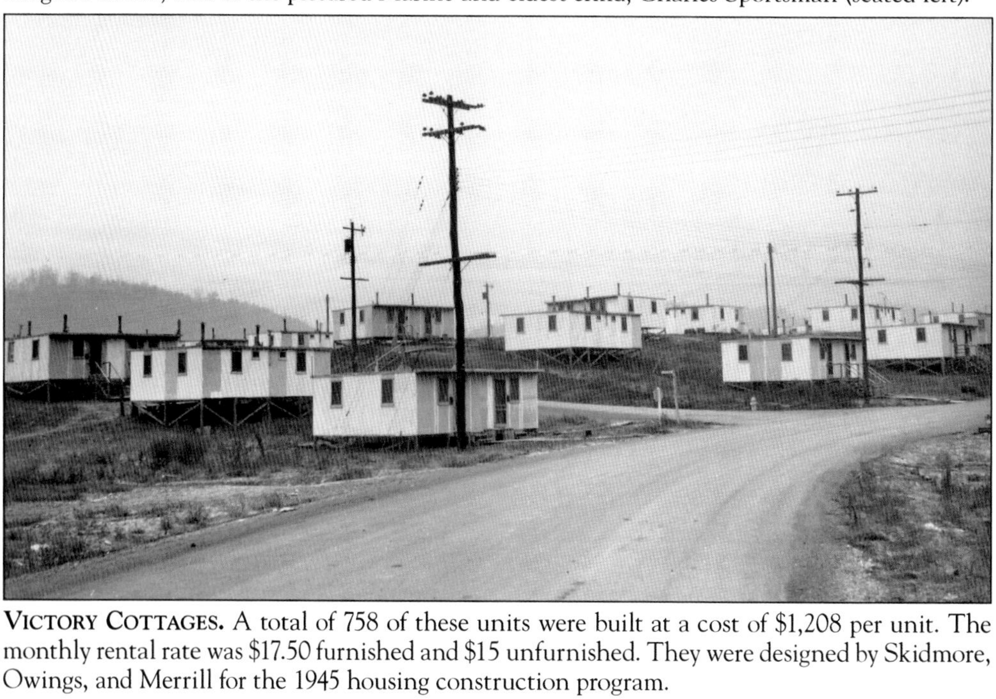

VICTORY COTTAGES. A total of 758 of these units were built at a cost of $1,208 per unit. The monthly rental rate was $17.50 furnished and $15 unfurnished. They were designed by Skidmore, Owings, and Merrill for the 1945 housing construction program.

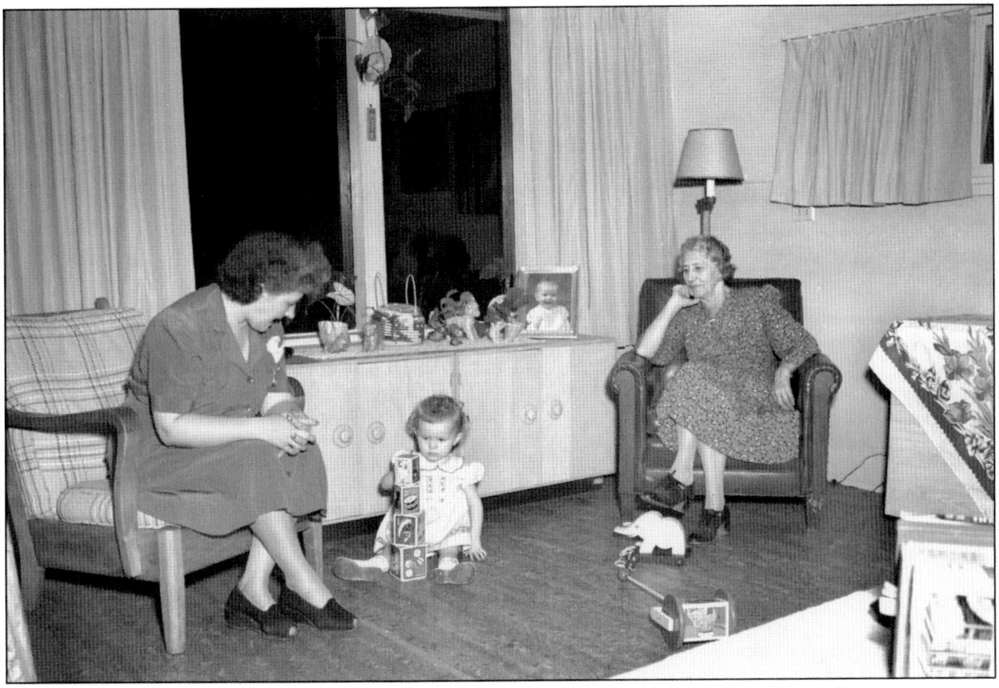

CONSIDER IT A VICTORY TO LIVE HERE. Equipped with running water and a coal-burning stove, this marginal, partly prefabricated–type home was particularly desirable for the government from the standpoint of reducing on-site labor costs. As can be seen with this unidentified family, even the prefabricated housing could be made more comfortable by adding personal touches such as window treatments and upholstered furniture.

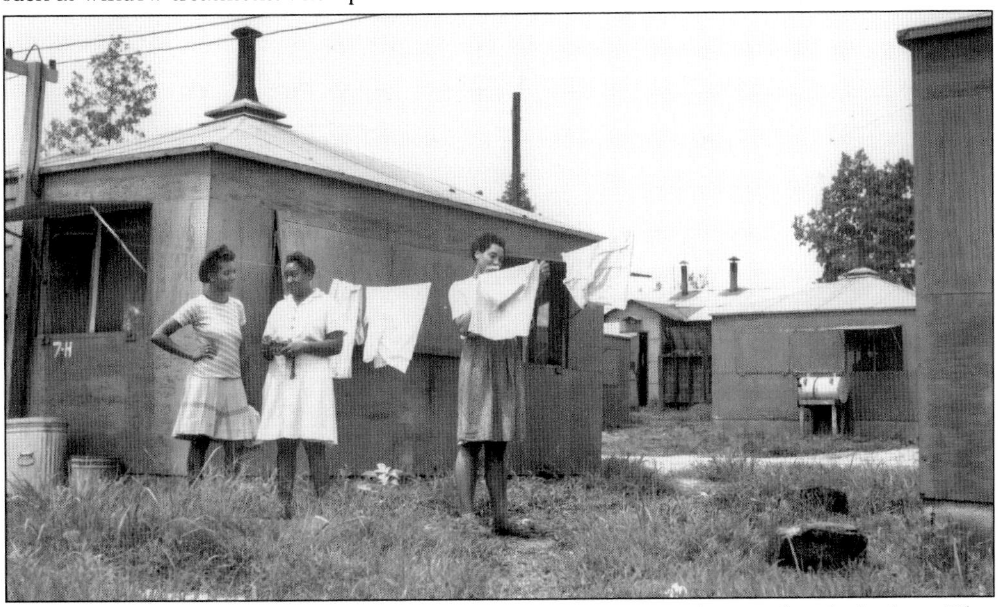

LIFE IN THE BLACK VILLAGE. African American women socialize at the clothesline. This activity was an important part of their daily lives. Segregated living arrangements existed during the war years in Oak Ridge. Black workers were housed in hutments, with men and women separated by a fence.

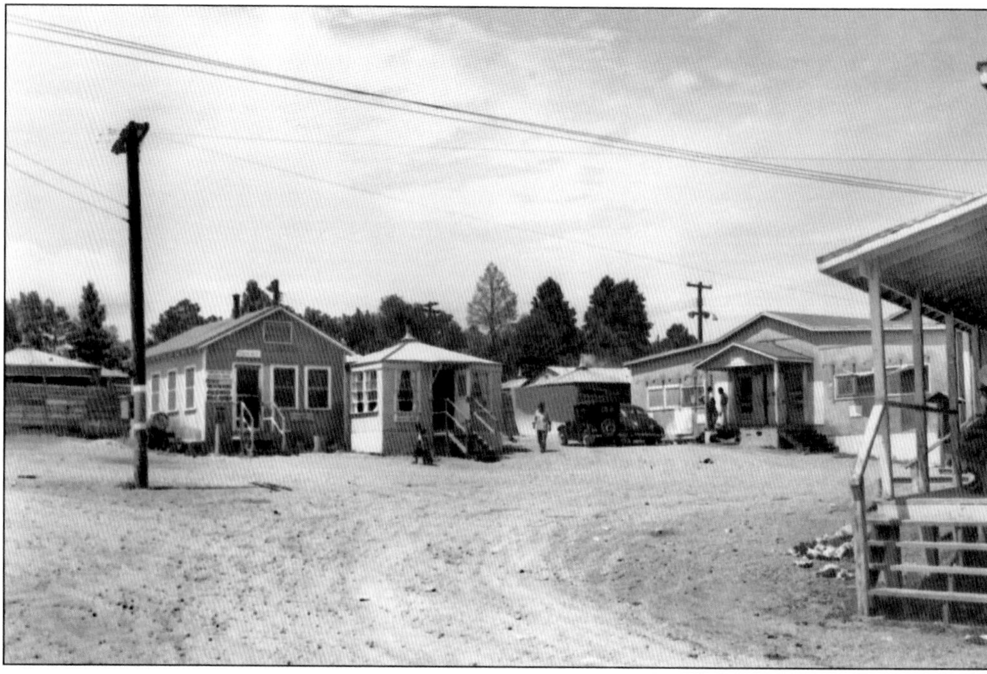

AREA WHERE BLACKS LIVED. Dirt roads were everywhere in early Oak Ridge. Between mud in the winter and dust in the summer, getting from hutments to the barber or beauty shop, the recreation hall, and the cafeteria was a real challenge.

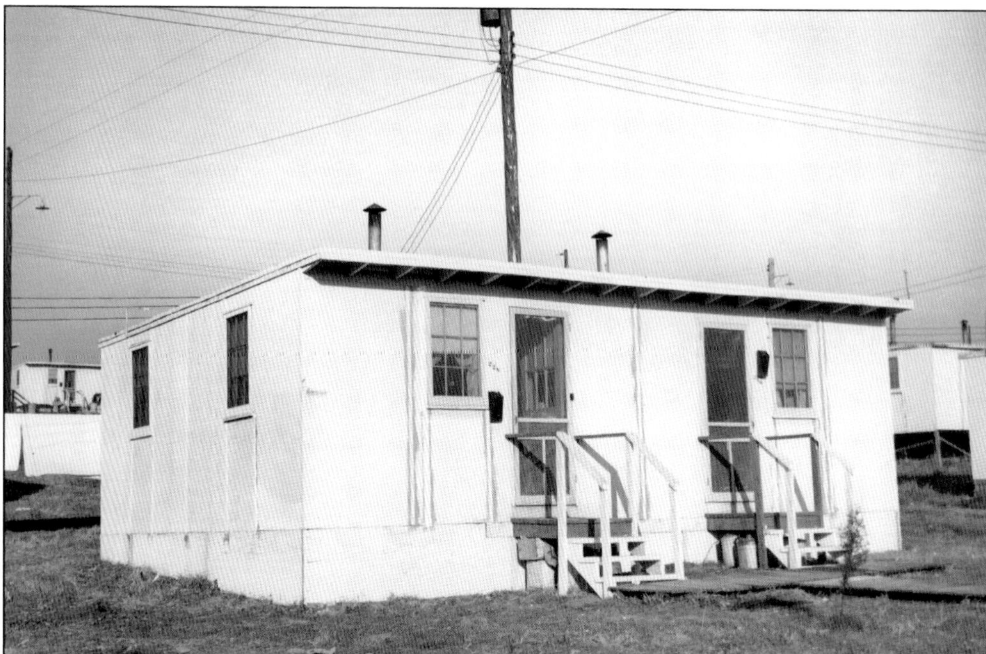

MARGINAL-TYPE HOUSING UNIT. These units were called Victory Cottages and designated VC-1. Shipped in by rail car, they were assembled on-site from prefabricated panels and parts, largely of plywood walls with rolled roofing. It was a one-story structure containing two family units, each with one bedroom.

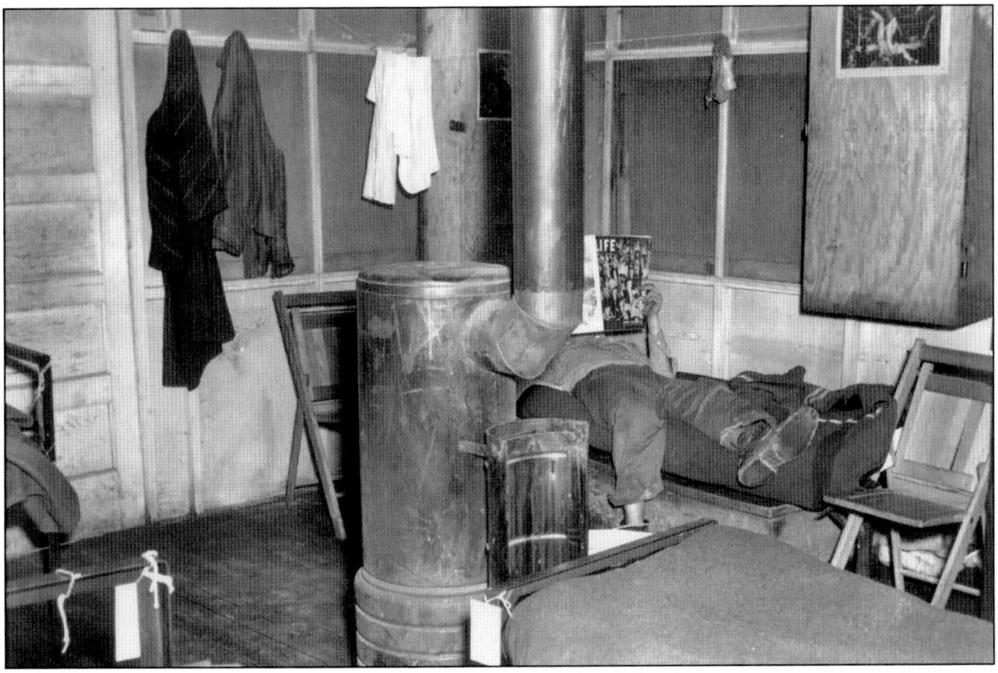

MOST CONSTRUCTION WORKERS' DOMAIN. The inside of the hutments was sparse. Five men shared a hut, slept on cots, shared a heater, and had a nail or two to hang their clothes on. Attached to each cot was a tag bearing the worker's name. Each group of 10 huts had its own utility buildings, a cafeteria, a recreation building, a barbershop, and other facilities.

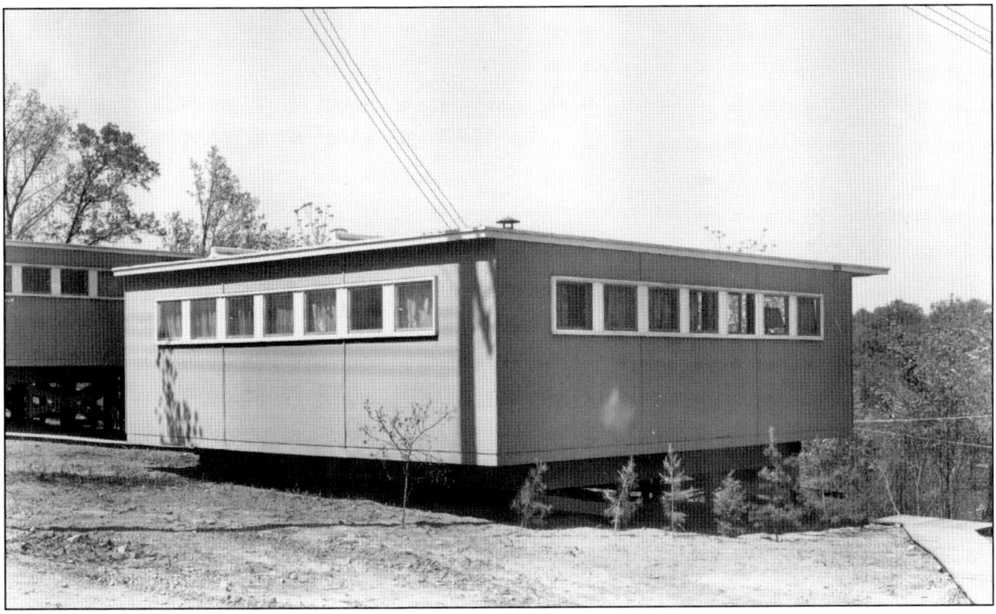

MORE HOUSING NEEDED. In 1943, as work began to progress rapidly on building the plants and the community, it was obvious more housing was needed. The Tennessee Valley Authority made available drawings of prefabricated units they used during construction of Fontana Dam in North Carolina. These units were called "flat tops" and were transported to the city partially assembled.

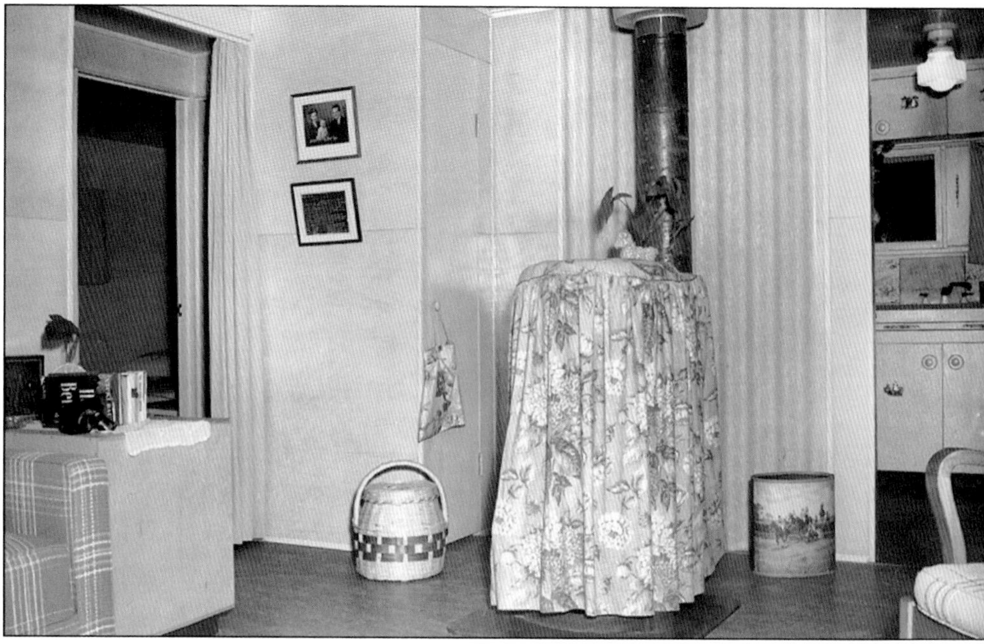

The Challenges Ahead. Coming to work for the Clinton Engineer Works and being part of creating a new city was like settling the West in the frontier days. Each day was a new adventure, and the residents took it in stride. Homemakers had to be creative in their new surrounds, and with little to work with, they tried to make their homes welcome places to come to after a hard day's work. With a little fabric, this flat top–unit resident dressed the heating stove to make it attractive and useful.

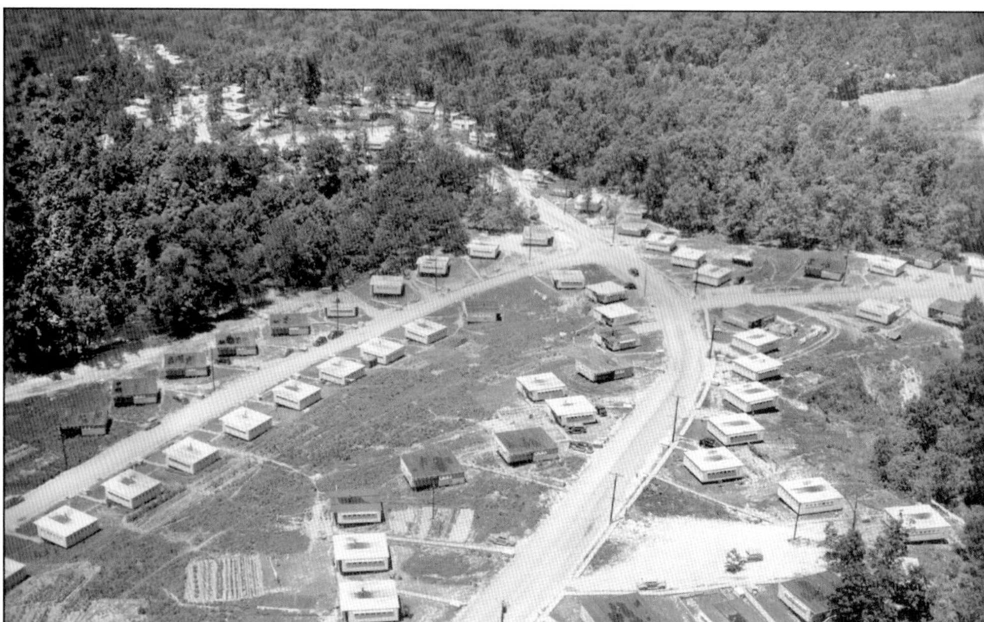

Flat Top Units. With the exploding population, this type of home was easy to assemble and ready for use quickly. The units were transported to the city in sections—two or three depending on the number of bedrooms—rejoined, and placed on lots. They even came furnished!

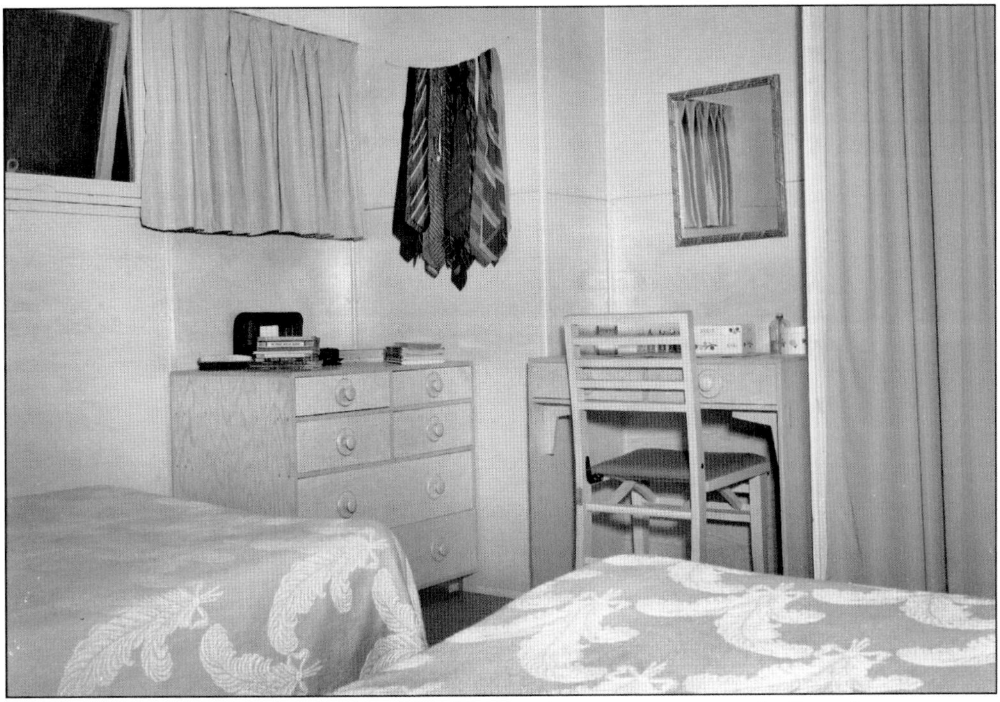

QUALITY IN WORKMANSHIP. Even though many housing units were built to be temporary, quality materials and craftsmanship was used. The furniture for the flat top houses was built on-site. The design was simple but the quality good. Many units are still being used in the city today, and some still have the original hardwood furnishings.

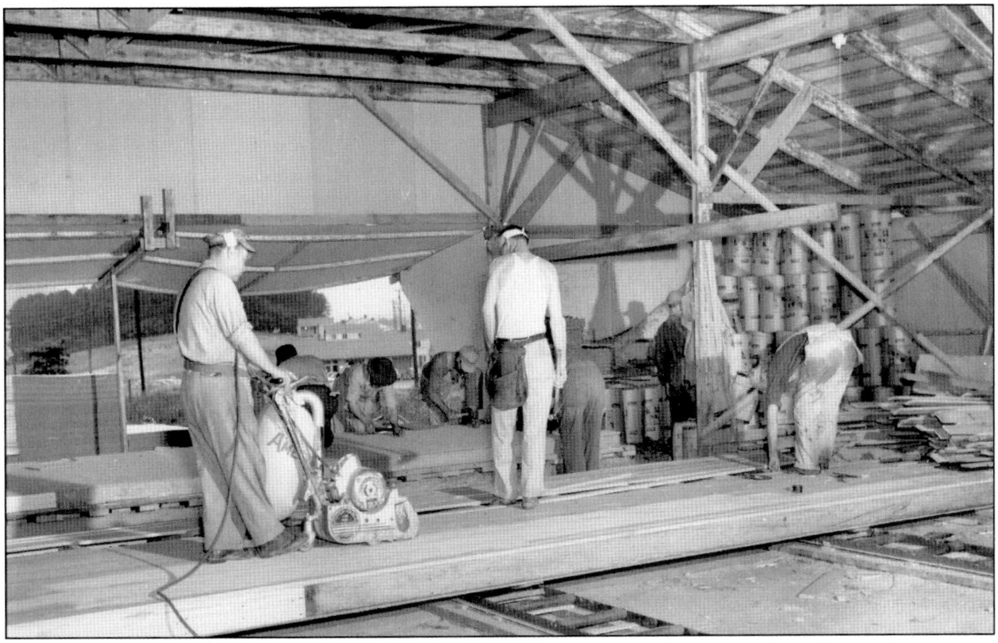

MEN AT WORK. Workers are putting the finishing touches to the wood floor that will connect the prefabricated flat top sections together. On-site labor was used for most of the assembly of the 3,373 homes, which amounted to a total cost of $10,590,866.

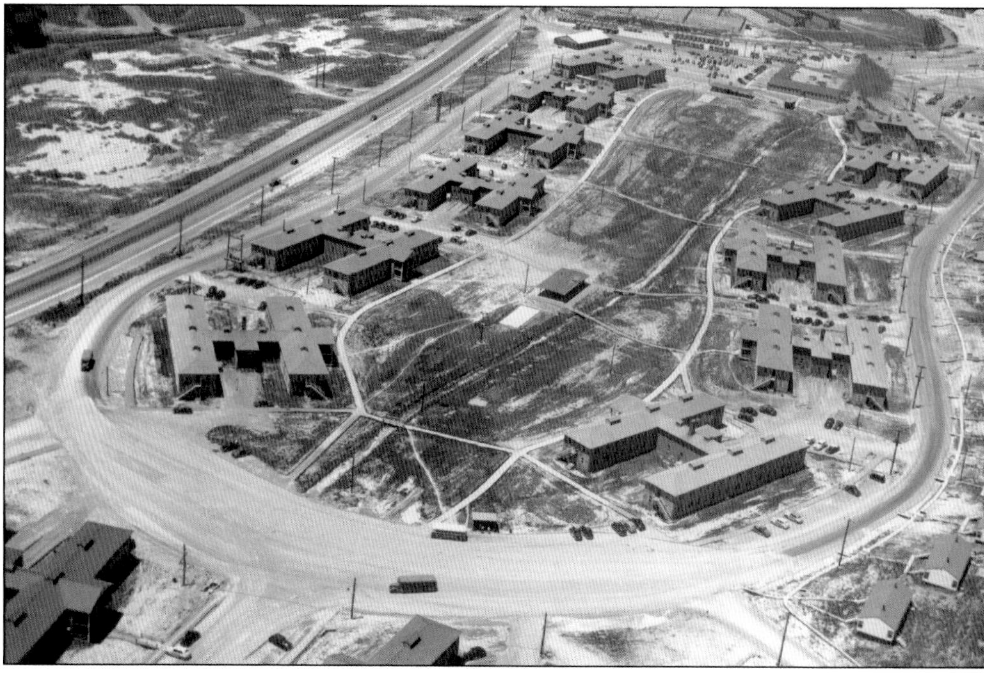

H Dormitories. A total of 89 dormitories were built in Oak Ridge. Under the construction supervision of Stone and Webster, 49 H-type dorms were built at a total price of $6,803,698. Monthly rent for these units was $15 for a double and $10 for a single.

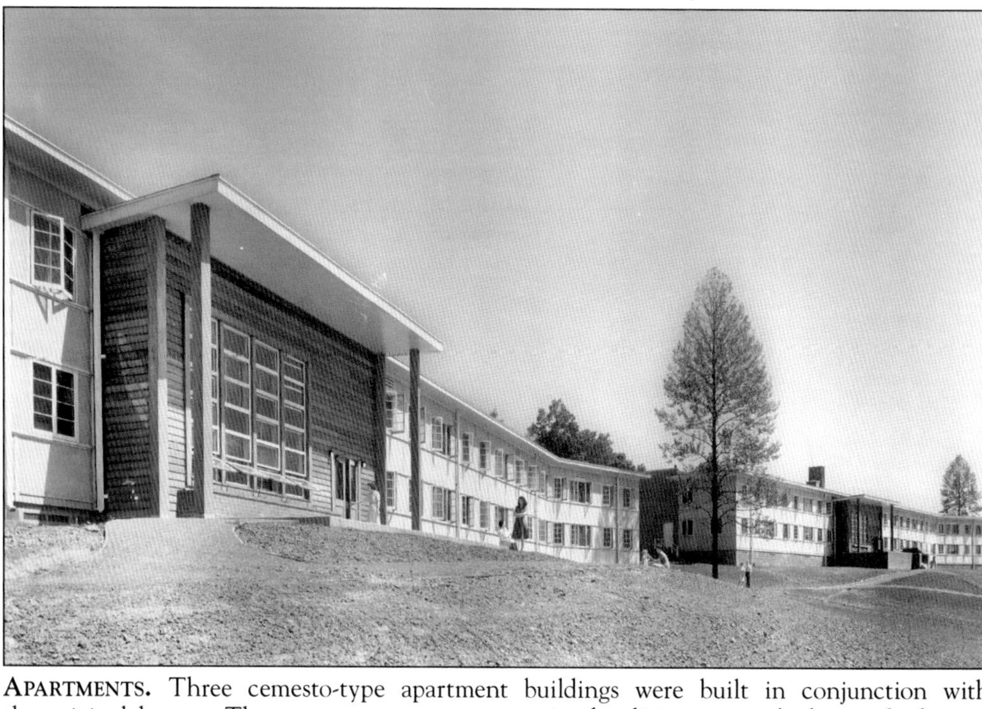

Apartments. Three cemesto-type apartment buildings were built in conjunction with the original houses. The two-story structure contained a living room, bedroom, bath, and kitchenette. Available for use by the residents was a lobby, a lounge, an office, a laundry, and two public toilets.

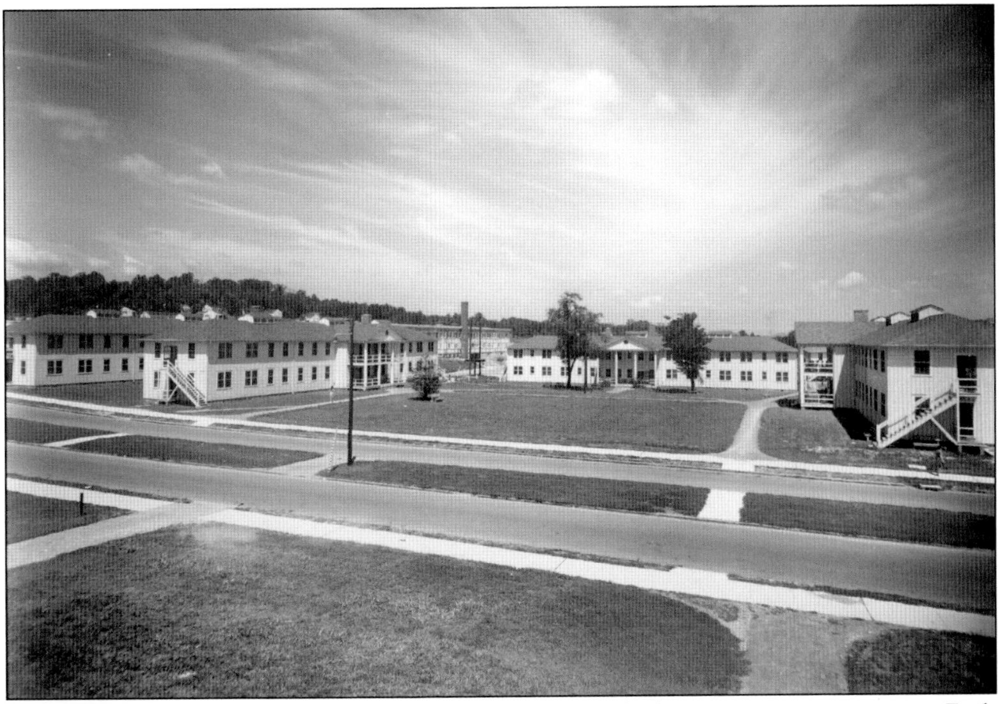

Dormitory Facilities. Residents of this type of housing had access to many amenities. Each dormitory had 2 recreation rooms, 38 double rooms, 65 single women's bedrooms, 73 men's bedrooms, 4 laundry and ironing rooms (women only), and 4 toilet and shower rooms. Separate dorms housed men and women. Below, a young lady has decorated her furnished dorm room with bright accessories.

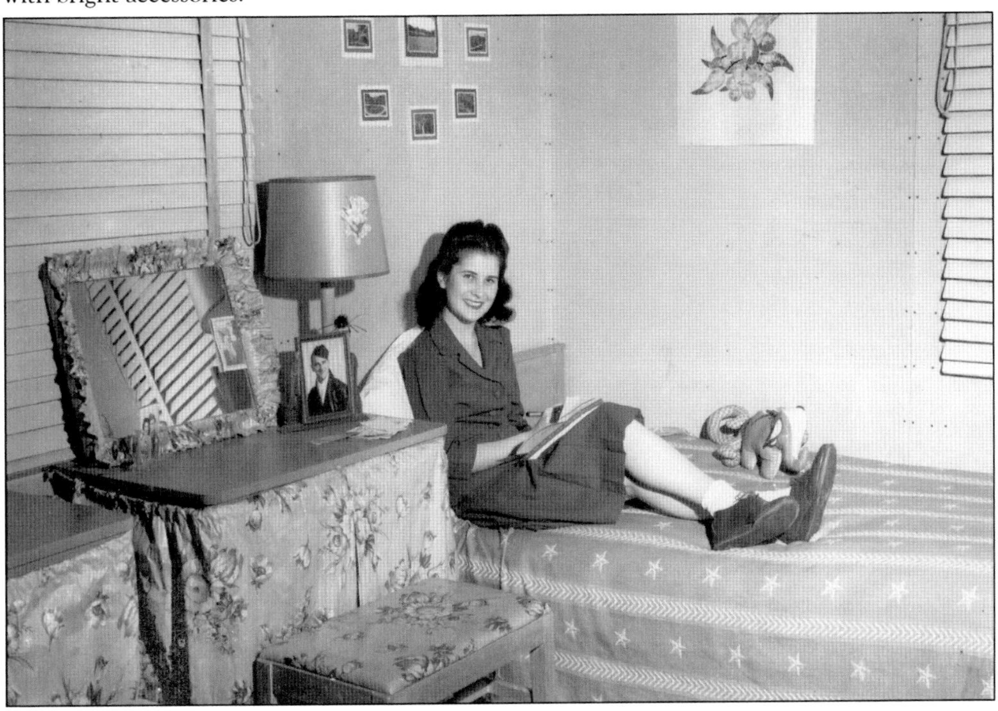

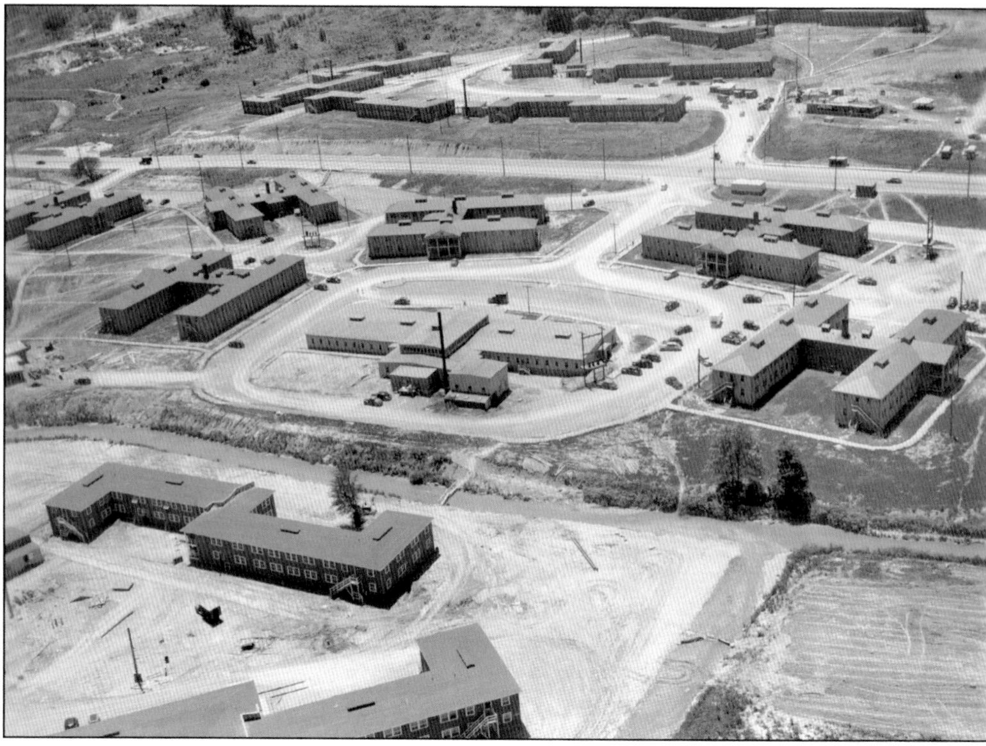

Dormitory Names

Abilene Hall
Adrian Hall
Asheville Hall
Aurora Hall
Batavia Hall
Bayonne Hall
Beacon Hall
Beaumont Hall
Boone Hall
Brockton Hall
Cambridge Hall
Canton Hall
Carlisle Hall
Casper Hall
Charleston Hall
Charlotte Hall
Chester Hall
Cheyenne Hall
Claremont Hall
Clayton Hall
Columbia Hall
Corning Hall
Cortland Hall
Covington Hall
Danville Hall
Darby Hall
Davenport Hall
Dayton Hall
Dearborn Hall
Denison Hall

Donora Hall
Dothan Hall
Duluth Hall
Dunkirk Hall
Dunmore Hall
Durman Hall
Fairfield Hall
Fargo Hall
Farrell Hall
Ferndale Hall
Finlay Hall
Flint Hall
Florence Hall
Fostoria Hall
Frankfort Hall
Frederick Hall
Freeport Hall
Fremont Hall
Gadsden Hall
Galesburg Hall
Gariner Hall
Gary Hall
Gastonia Hall
Glendale Hall
Goldsboro Hall
Goshen Hall
Greely Hall
Greenwood Hall
Griffin Hall
Guthrie Hall

Laconia Hall
Lafayette Hall
Lakewood Hall
Laramie Hall
Laredo Hall
Racine Hall
Rahway Hall
Redlands Hall
Redondo Hall
Richmond Hall
Ridgewood Hall
Riverside Hall
Roanoke Hall
Rochester Hall
Rockford Hall
Rome Hall
Roswell Hall
Rutherford Hall
Rutland Hall
Sacramento Hall
Saginaw Hall
Salina Hall
Sandusky Hall
Saratoga Hall
Saugus Hall
Sedalia Hall
Sharon Hall
Shelby Hall
Springfield Hall
Stanford Hall
Sterling Hall

A TIGHT SITUATION. As the population peaked to 75,000 in 1945, housing space was at a premium. Even though 89 H- and S-type dormitories had been built (90 including the nurses' dorm), an emergency measure was found necessary in October 1944 that all unoccupied dormitory rooms be assigned on the basis of two occupants for single rooms and three for double rooms. All vacated rooms were added to this category, and current occupants were invited to volunteer for doubled-up accommodations to carry over the occupancy peak expected for 1944–1945. The image at left lists the names of the dormitories, which were scattered east to west across the city.

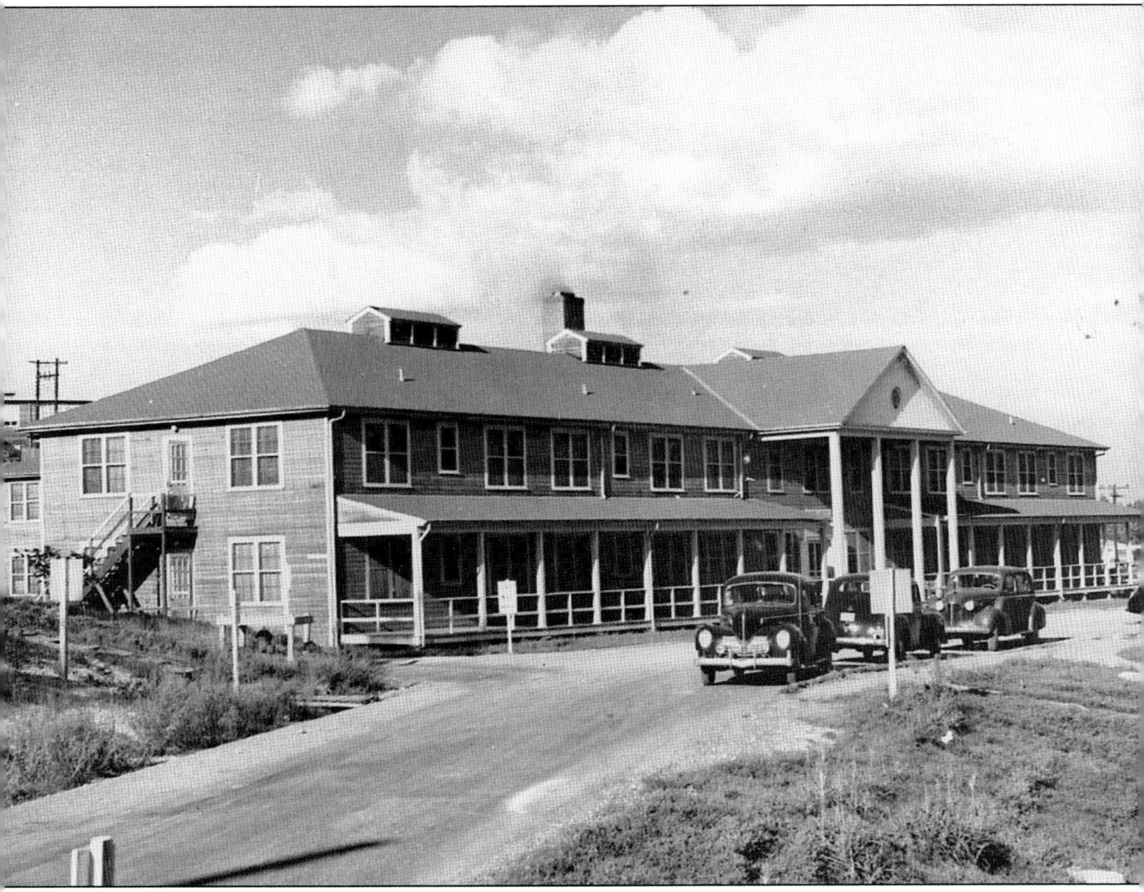

THE GUEST HOUSE. This transient hotel opened August 5, 1943, with 52 rooms. Each room had two beds, and rooms could be assigned to persons not acquainted with each other. This wooden structure served as a stopover for many scientists and dignitaries.

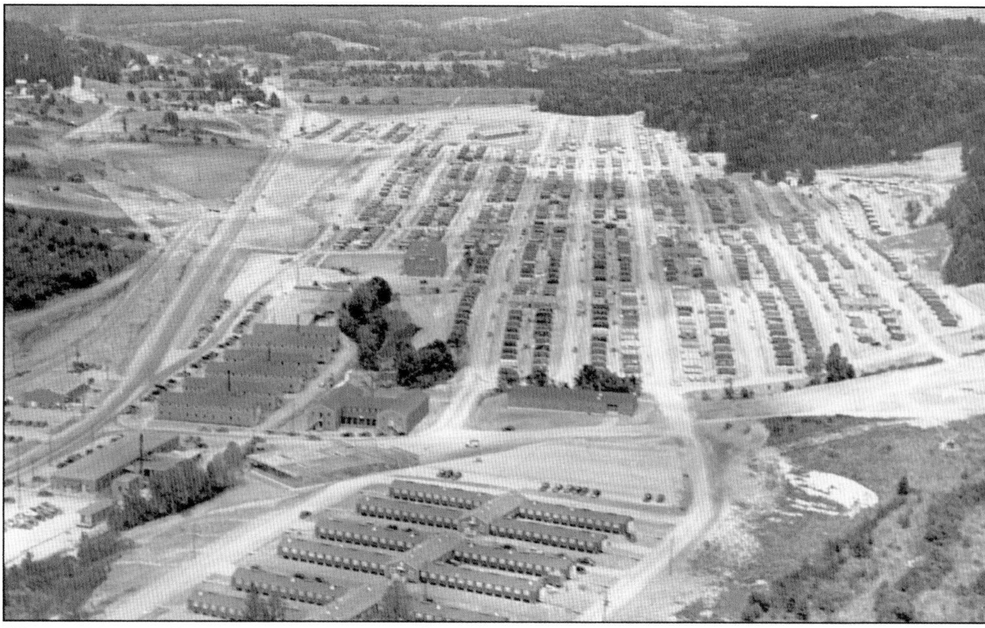

Happy Valley Community. In 1943, when the construction of the K-25 complex began, there was a community created for a population of 15,000 construction workers and their families. These people were housed in trailers, hutments, and barracks. Because headquarters at Oak Ridge was 11 miles away, the K-25 site developed into a satellite town. They had a post office, stores, cafeterias, a bank, recreational facilities, and a nearby school for the children.

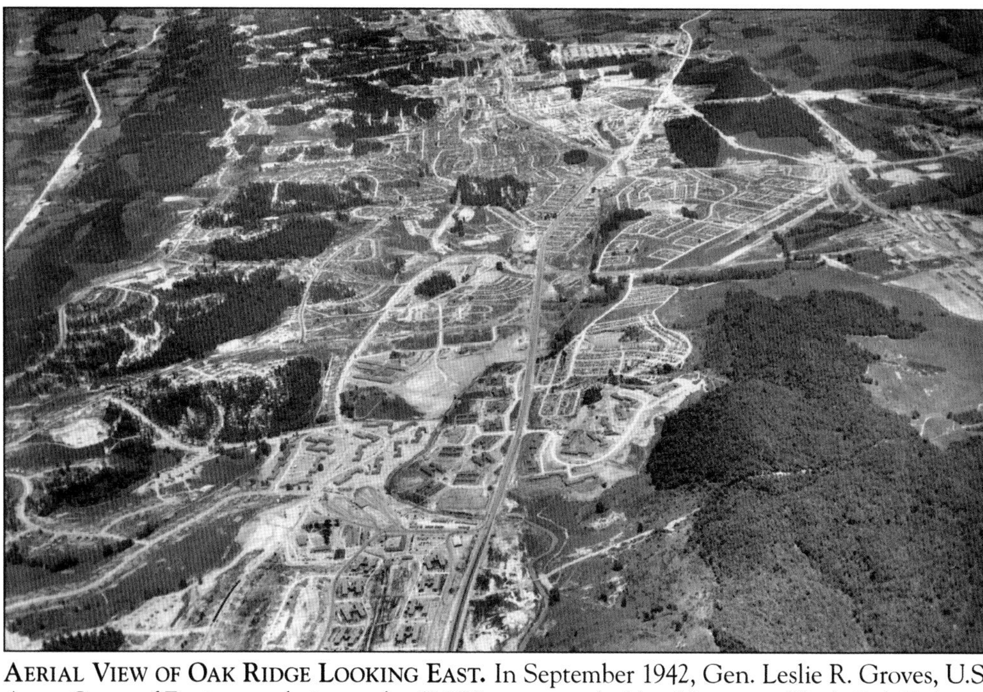

Aerial View of Oak Ridge Looking East. In September 1942, Gen. Leslie R. Groves, U.S. Army Corps of Engineers, designated a 59,000-acre parcel of land between Black Oak Ridge to the north and the Clinch River to the south as the first federal reserve for producing nuclear materials for the atomic bomb.

Three

Recreation, Businesses, Churches, and Services

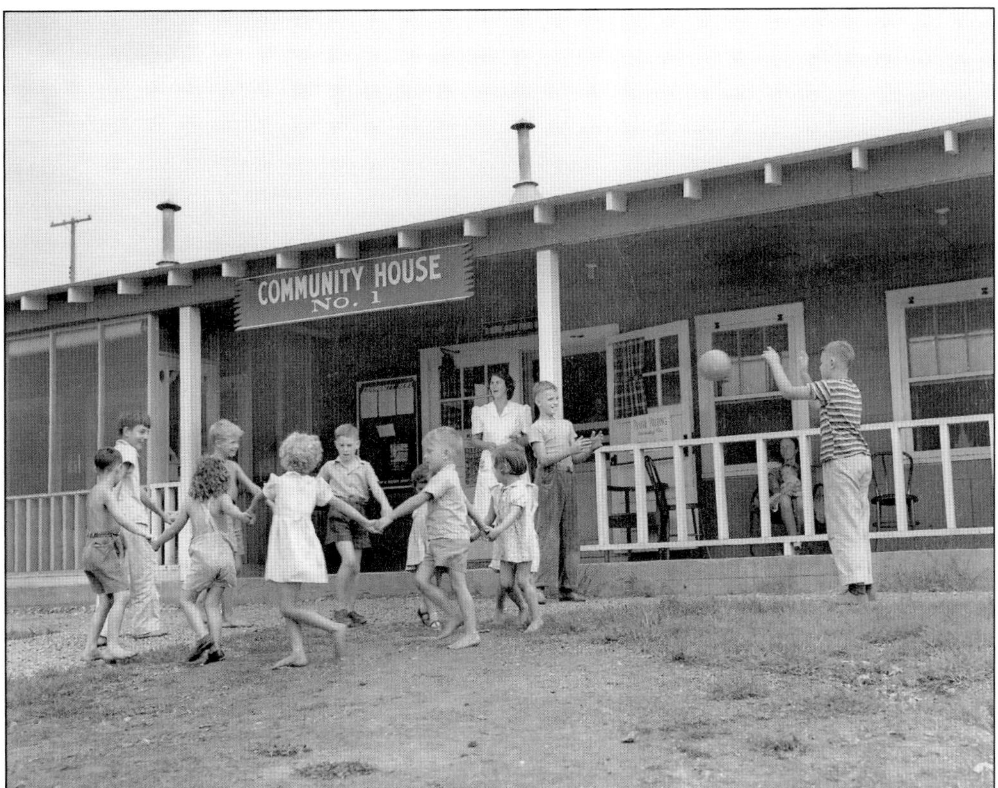

Community House No. 1. Children of the Happy Valley trailer camp are playing games at summer day care while their parents are at work. All age groups of children attended during the summer months. Construction had begun in this area on the K-25 Plant.

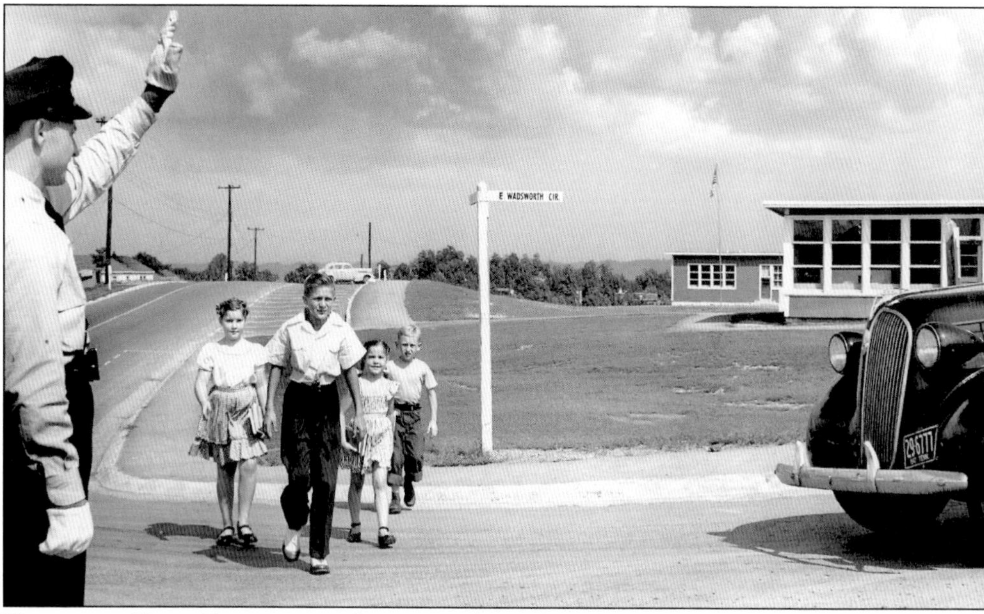

HIGHLAND VIEW ELEMENTARY SCHOOL. The Oak Ridge schools were fully accredited and compared favorably with the national standard. Highland View was the fifth school built and had an enrollment of 1,349 by end of the 1946 school year. Students are shown walking home after a school day.

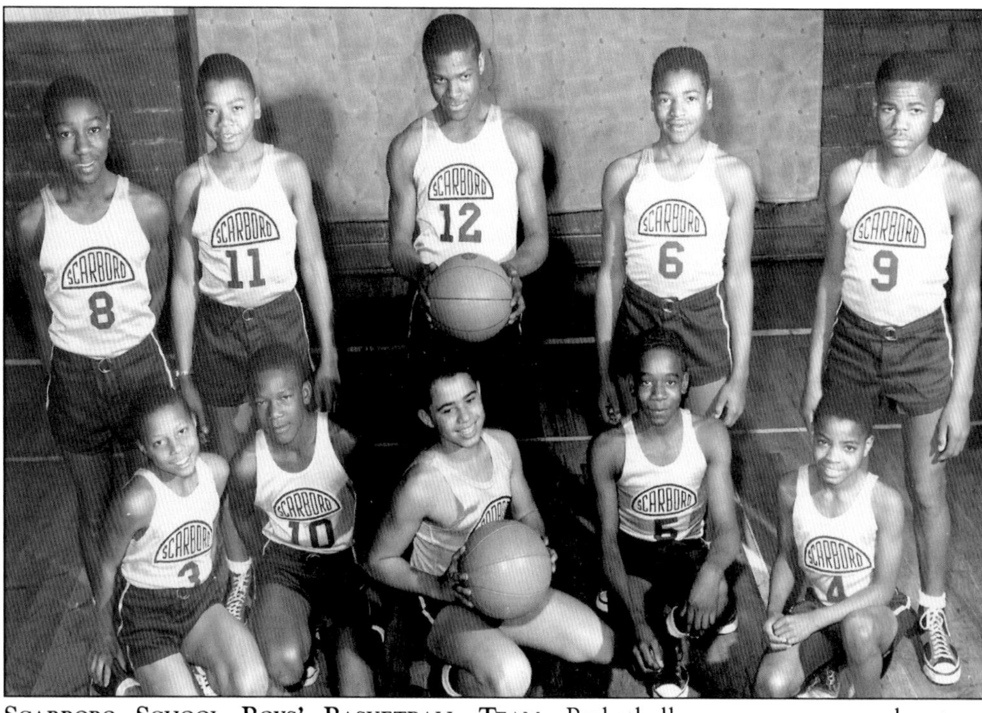

SCARBORO SCHOOL BOYS' BASKETBALL TEAM. Basketball was a very popular team sport that uplifted the spirit of the youth during the building of Oak Ridge. It provided a challenging exchange for elementary school teams to interact with each other in a structured and competitive environment.

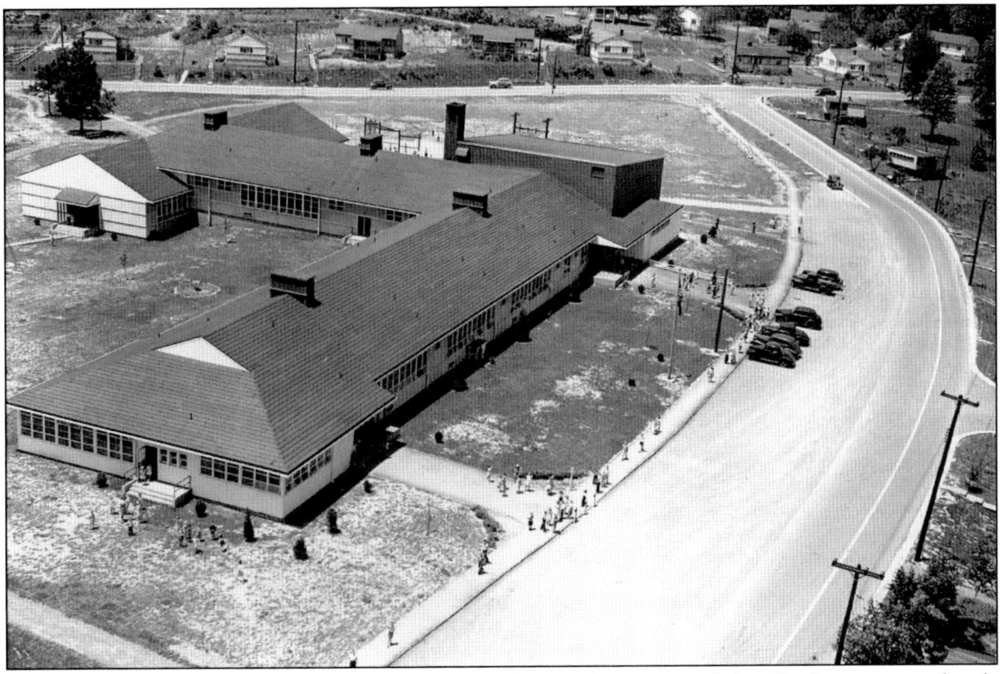

Cedar Hill Elementary School. This aerial view shows one of the 10 elementary schools located within the reservation. This school had 18 classrooms, an art room, a library, a music room, a gymnasium, and 2 kindergarten rooms. Constructed as a one-story, wood-and-cemesto-board building, it contained 34,190 square feet.

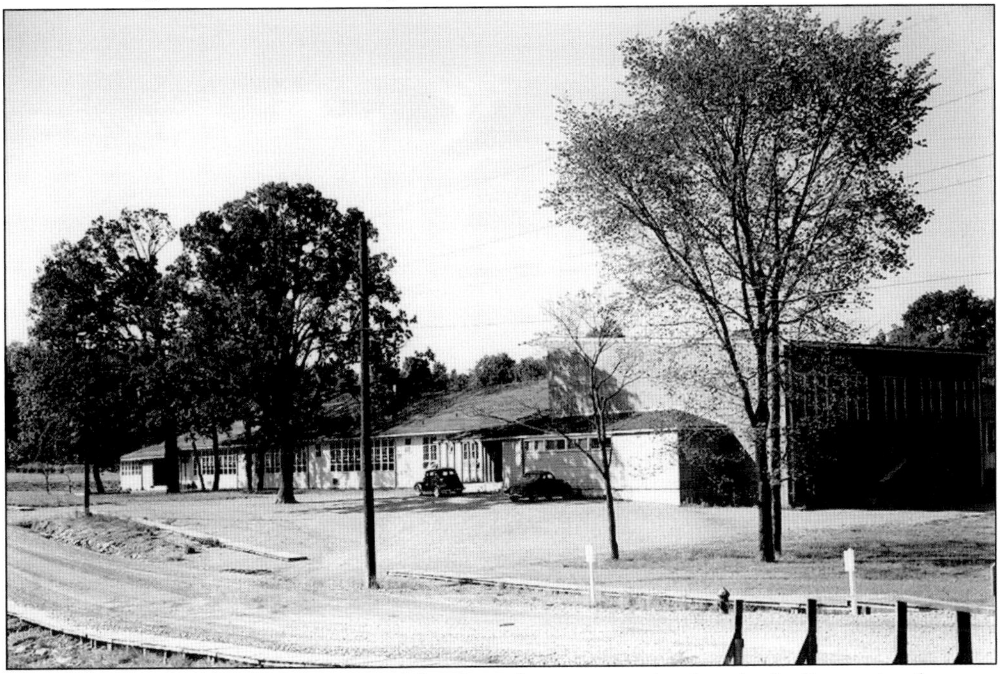

Elm Grove Elementary School. The first elementary school to be built was in the area known as Elm Grove. This wood-and-cemesto structure was 32,220 square feet and held 14 classrooms. Buses transported the children to class from the area neighborhood.

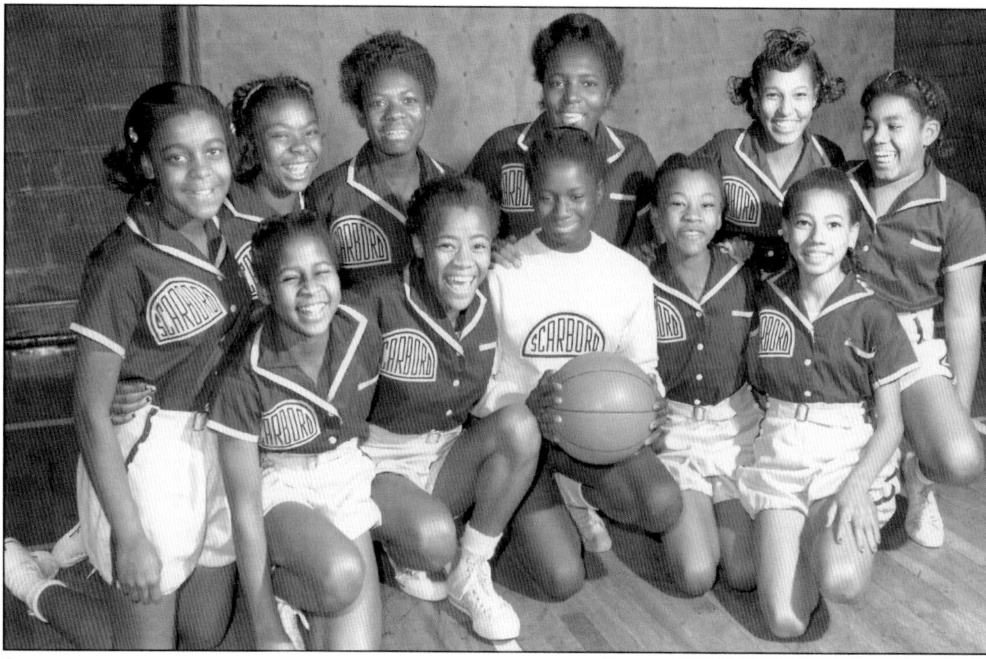

SCARBORO SCHOOL GIRLS' BASKETBALL TEAM. This group of elementary-school girls made up an exceptional basketball team in their segregated black school. Pictured from left to right are (first row) Dorothy Allen, Mary S. Steele, Mary E. Berry, Maggie Carter, and Bobbie W. Caldwell; (second row) Connella Steele, Emma D. Allen, Maude L. Williams, Addie R. Berry, Bobbie Young, and Shirley Bowie.

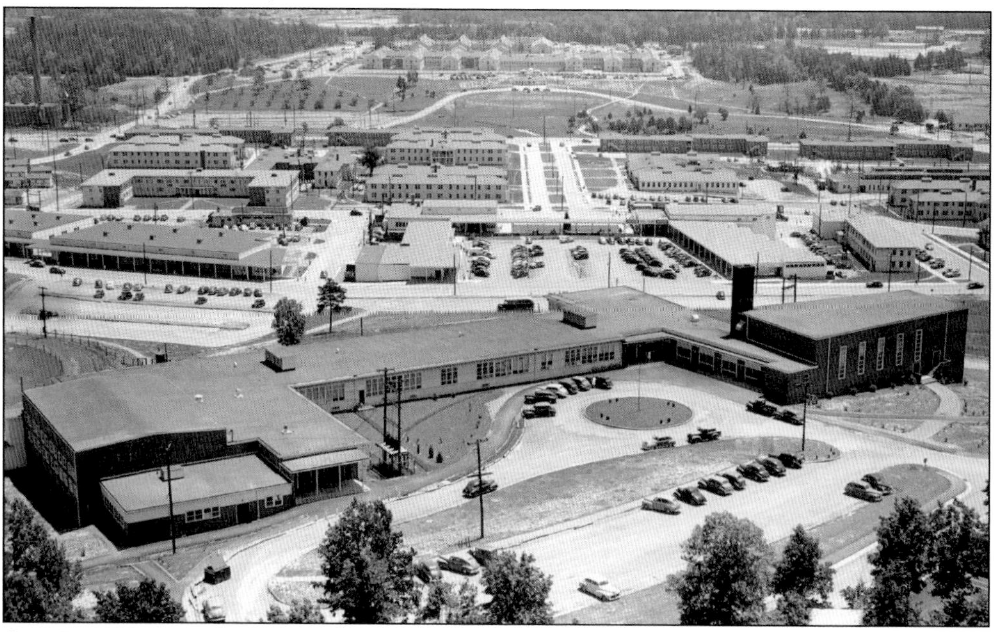

OAK RIDGE HIGH SCHOOL. On October 4, 1943, the first session of high school began with an enrollment of 830 students. This wood structure, sitting on a hill overlooking the Townsite Shopping Center, dormitories, and the administration building, held 30 classrooms. The first superintendent was A. H. Blankenship, a graduate of Columbia University.

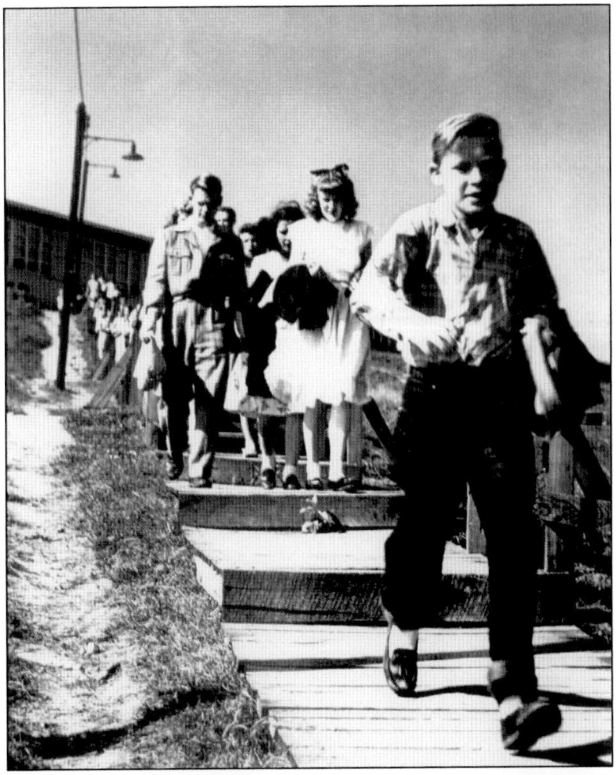

School Is Out. These high school kids are coming down the boardwalk steps after a day of learning. The boardwalks were a necessity for all early Oak Ridgers. The run-off to the left would turn into a fast-running stream during heavy rains, adding to the mud at the bottom of the hill.

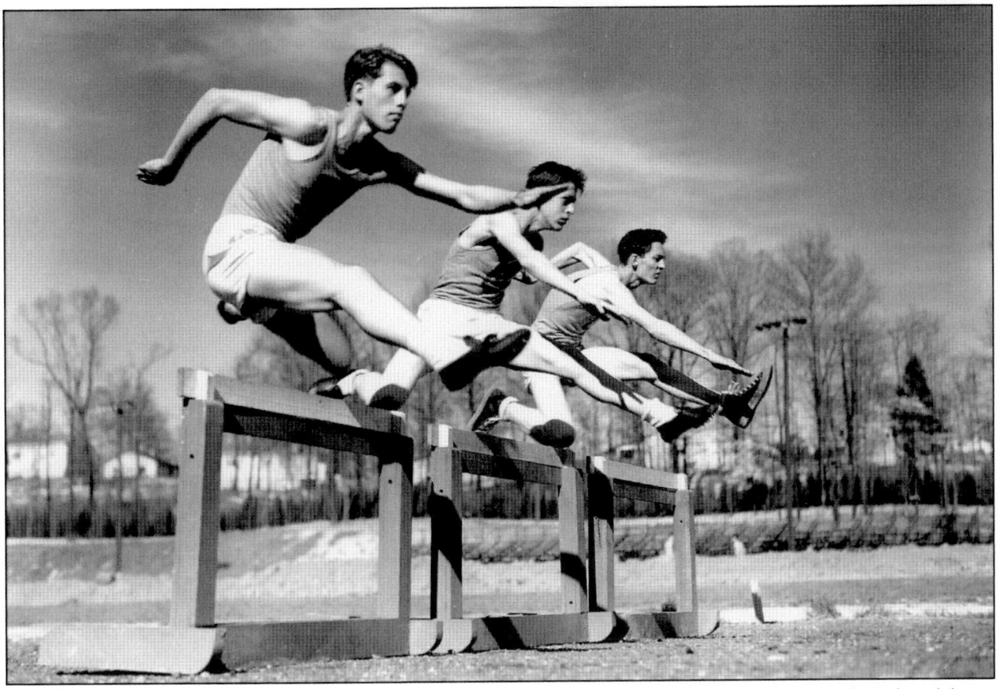

Up and Over the Hurdles. During physical education class, Oak Ridge High School boys are running track at the Blankenship athletic field and are jumping over hurdles, practicing for a track meet. In the background, some cemesto homes are visible.

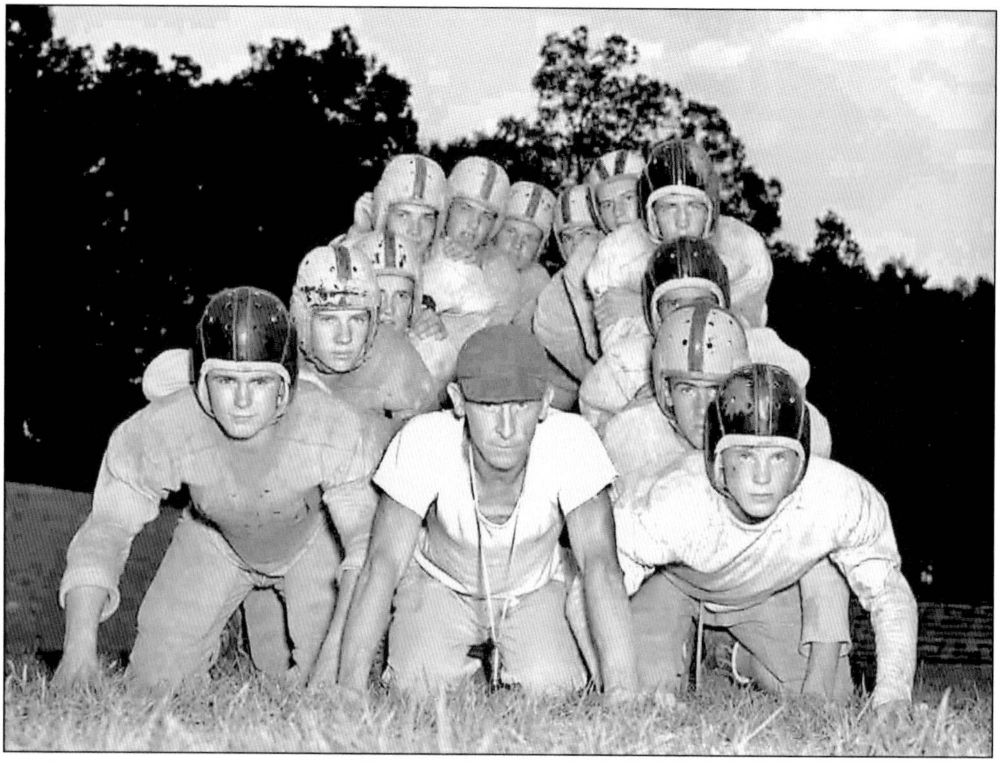

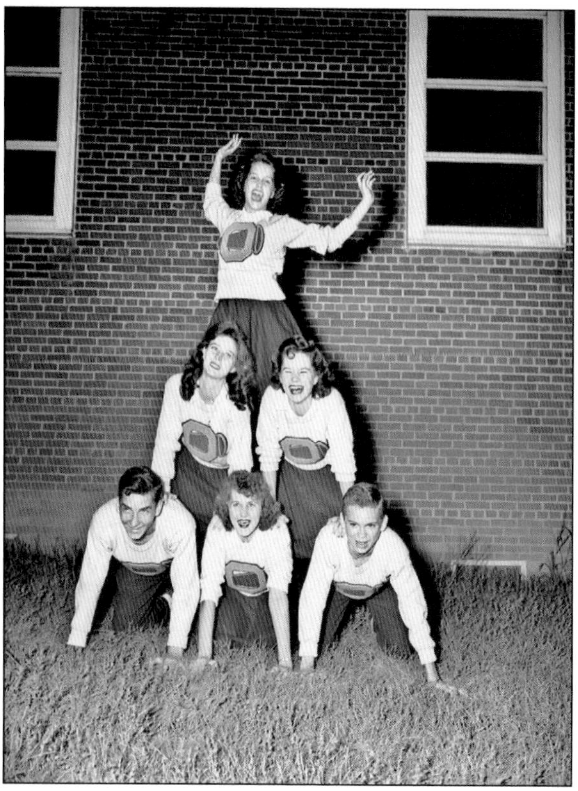

HIGH SCHOOL FOOTBALL TEAM. Primitive football equipment was used during a practice session. Helmets were made of leather with no face guards, and uniforms had very little padding. Ben Martin, center, was coach and physical education teacher for the Oak Ridge Wildcats. Forming a "V" for victory are players Johnson, Corry, Lusk, Osborn, Crigger, Larson, Brown, Zirkle, Chapman, Hawood, Scroggins, and Meed.

WILDCAT CHEERLEADERS. These young, energetic Oak Ridge High School noisemakers are practicing a cheer for an upcoming football game. They are, from left to right, (first row) Bill Taylor, Kitty Thomas, and Jack ("Flattop") McGuire; (second row) Pat Johnstone and Tee Whittlesley; (third row) Judy Gregory.

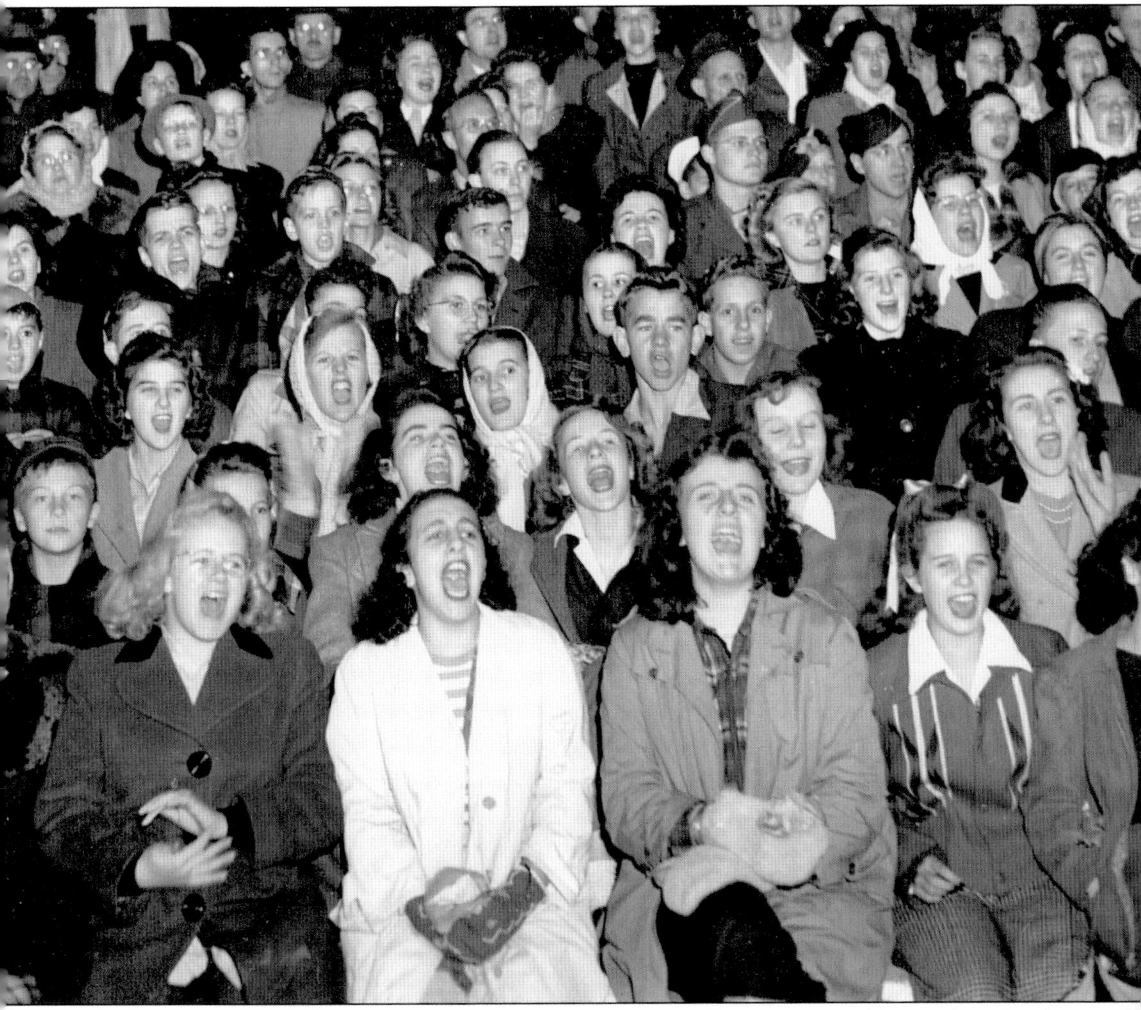

LET'S ROLL, WILDCATS, ROLL. These fans are cheering during an Oak Ridge High School football game at the Blankenship athletic field. You can almost hear them singing the school song as they encourage the team on for a touchdown. Team spirit was at a high point for Oak Ridgers and their new city.

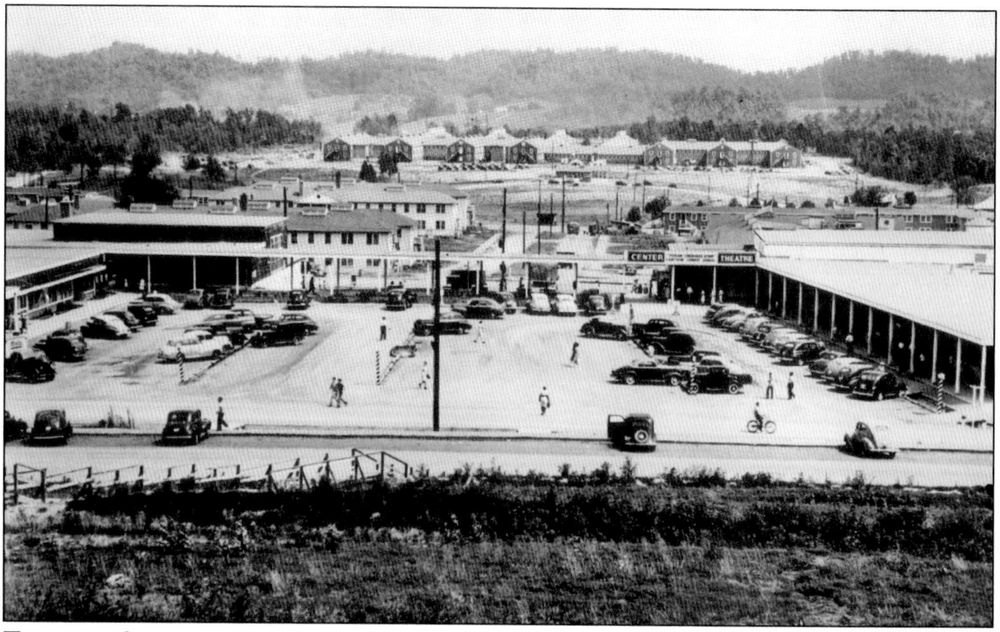

TOWNSITE SHOPPING CENTER. In the foreground is a view of the centrally located hub of daily business. It consisted of six buildings housing most of the commercial shops needed to support the town. In background on the hill is the Manhattan District administration building.

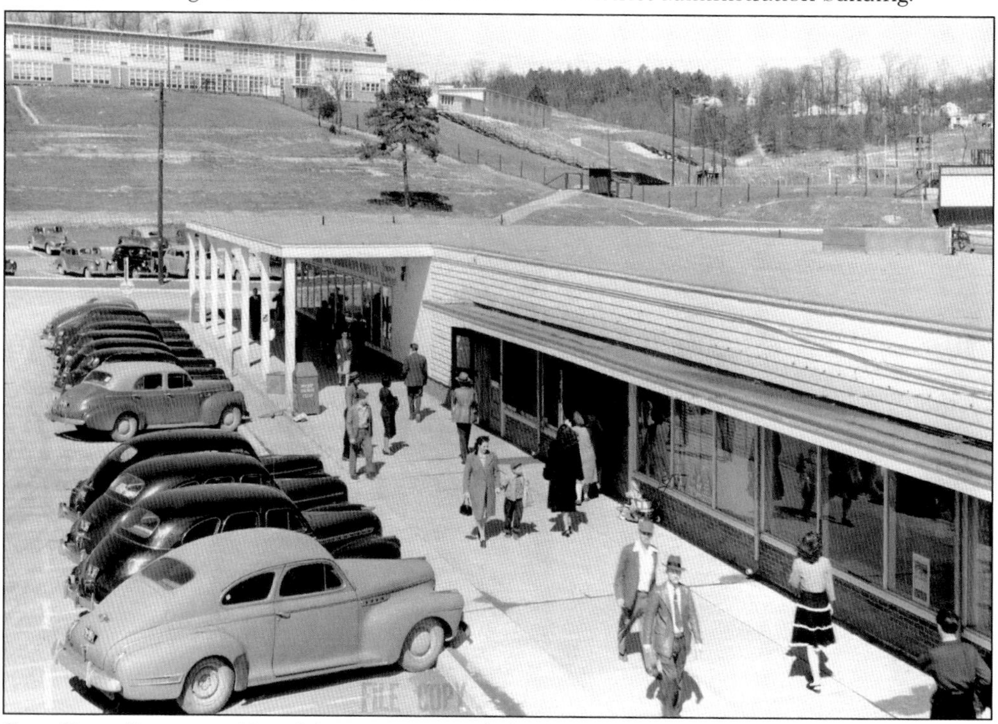

SEMI-BUSY SHOPPING DAY. Men, women, and children stroll by the shops located within the Townsite shopping center. In the background on the left is the Oak Ridge High School; on the right is the Blankenship athletic field. At far right in the background are the cemesto homes of one of the neighborhoods.

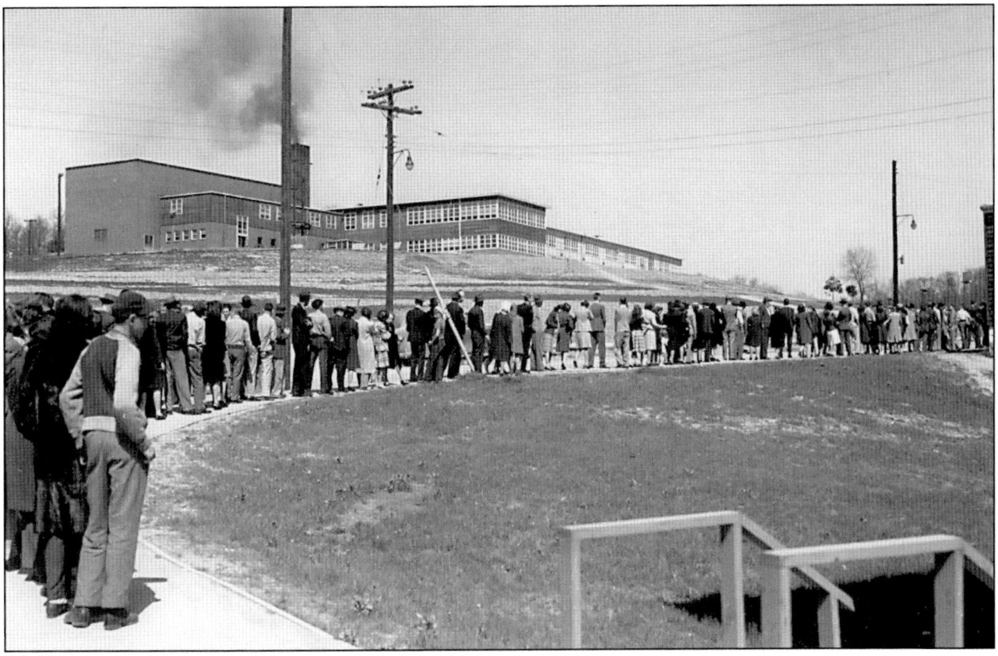

Smoke Like a Chimney. The supply of cigarettes was rationed by the government along with many other commodities. Residents are waiting patiently in line hoping to receive cigarettes issued from Williams Drugstore in Townsite. The building in the background is the Oak Ridge High School.

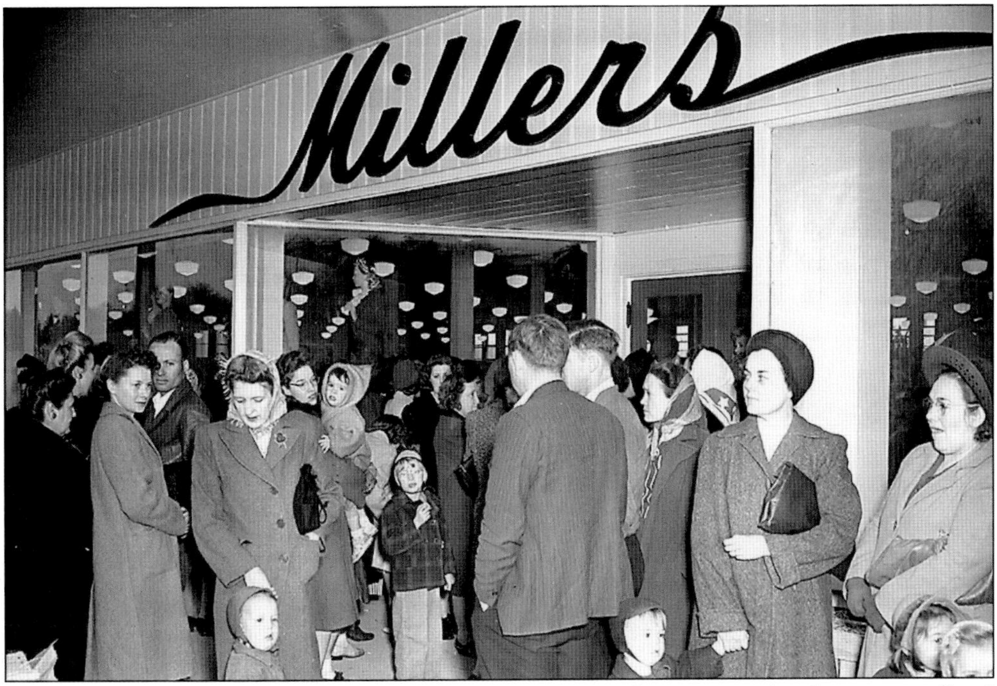

Department-Store Shopping. Located in the center of Townsite, this busy area offered residents a variety in shopping. Department stores, jewelry stores, shoe shops, markets, and drug stores dotted the landscape with necessity items and a few luxury sales.

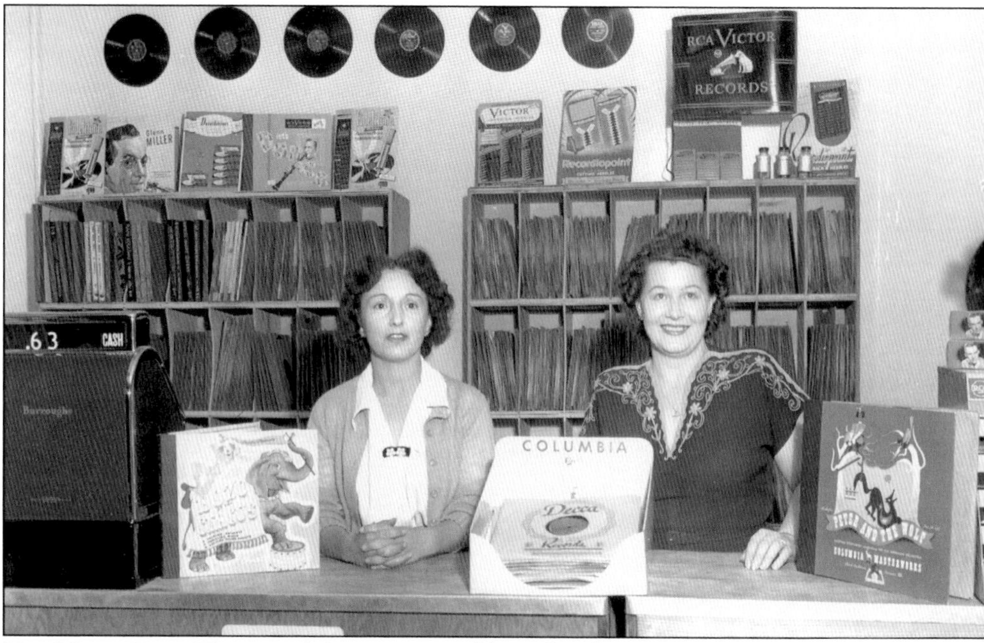

THE MUSIC BOX. This record shop, co-owned by Bill Pollock, provided Oak Ridgers with their first opportunity to purchase records in the early days. On November 19, 1944, Pollock piped the first music over telephone lines from Ridge Hall to the new Grove Hall for a Tennessee Eastman Training Department party. In December, he added Jefferson, Central, and Middletown Halls, followed by the Army Post Exchange and Gamble Valley in March 1945.

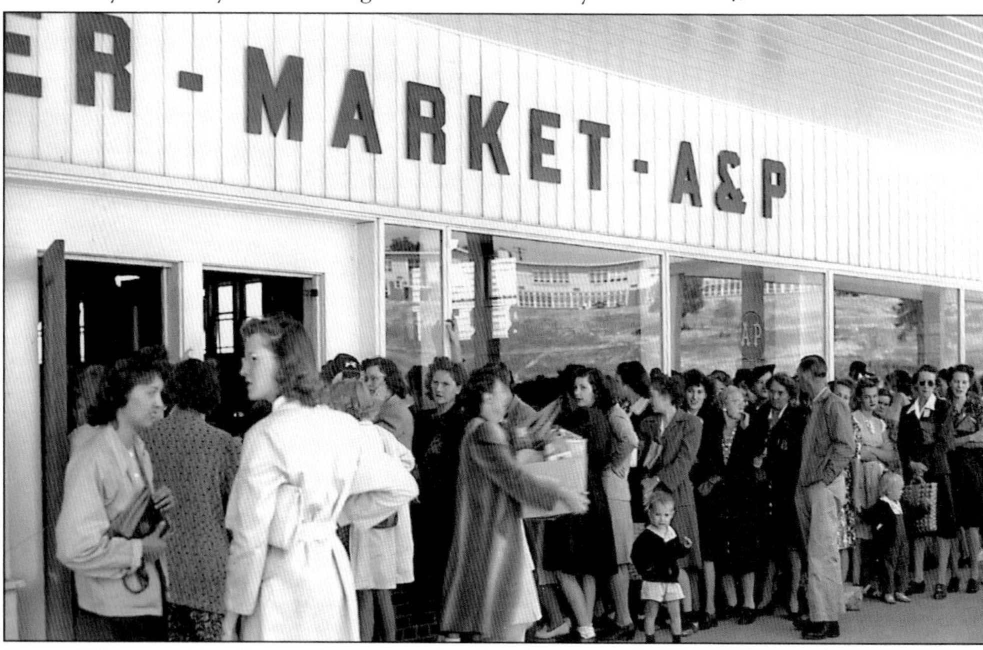

SUPER MARKET. Standing in line seemed to be the norm, as shoppers wait their turn to buy groceries at the market located at Town Center II. Residents were given ration stamps to purchase certain food items. This was one of many markets located in Oak Ridge providing food for the shoppers.

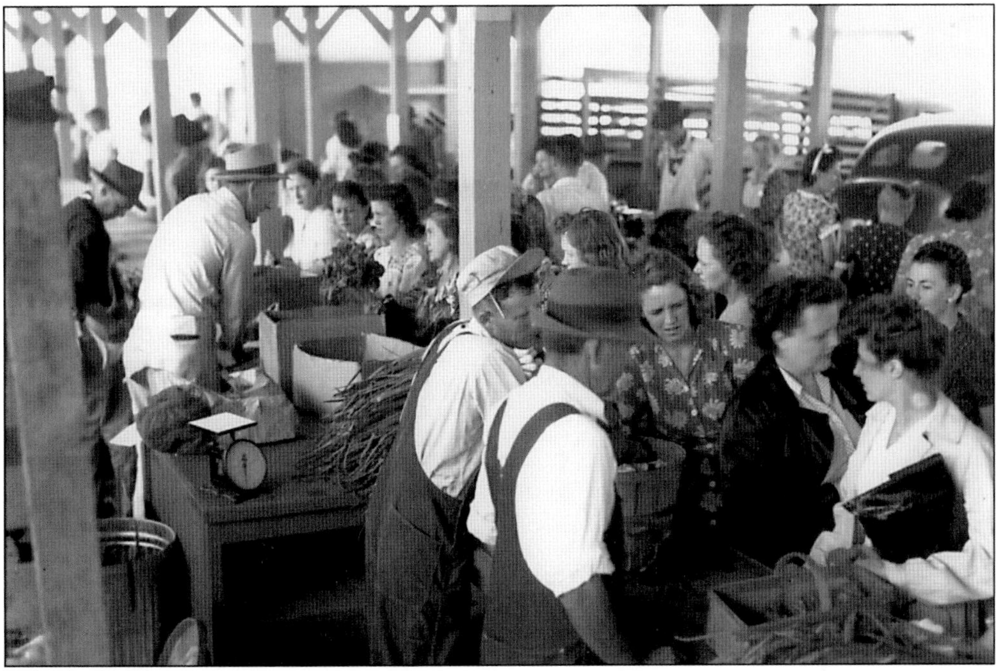

FARMER'S MARKET. Farmers from surrounding areas brought their fresh produce into Oak Ridge to sell to the residents. This open wooden structure, located on Fairbanks Road, was a source of fresh vegetables grown by farmers that had been relocated to nearby counties when the government bought their land to build the "secret" city.

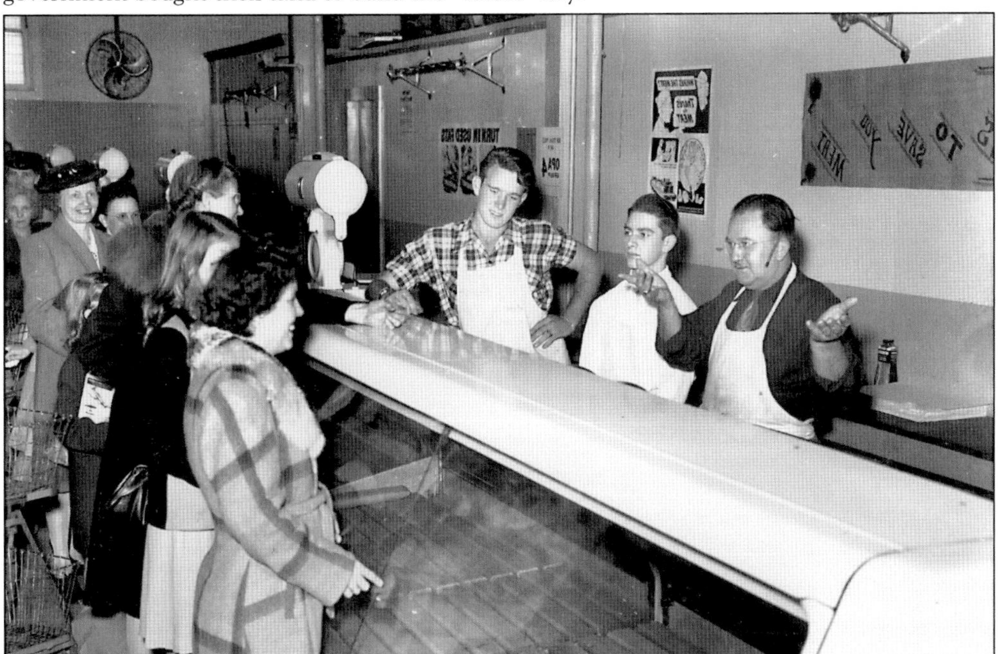

SOLD-OUT MEAT COUNTER. A&P grocery store butchers tell waiting customers that there is no meat today. The store first went into operation on August 4, 1943, and made its first sale before the construction crew could get the door mounted.

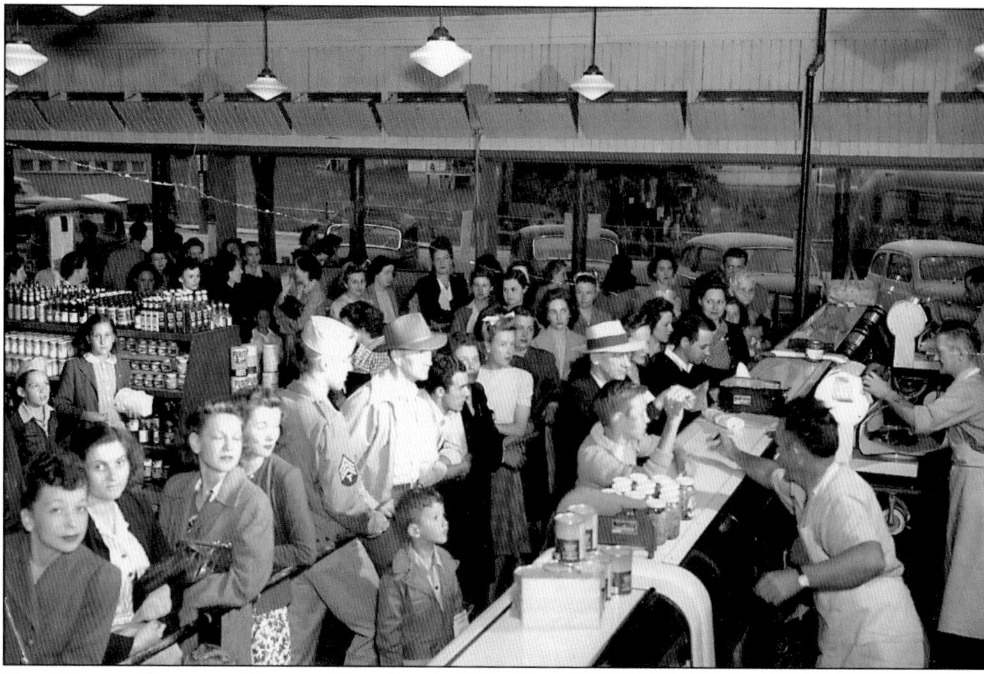

ELM GROVE GROCERY STORE. Standing in line to purchase groceries was the one thing Oak Ridgers could be sure of. Although time-consuming, it provided a time for socializing and getting to know your neighbors. Food selection was limited, and many late-day shoppers met with empty shelves.

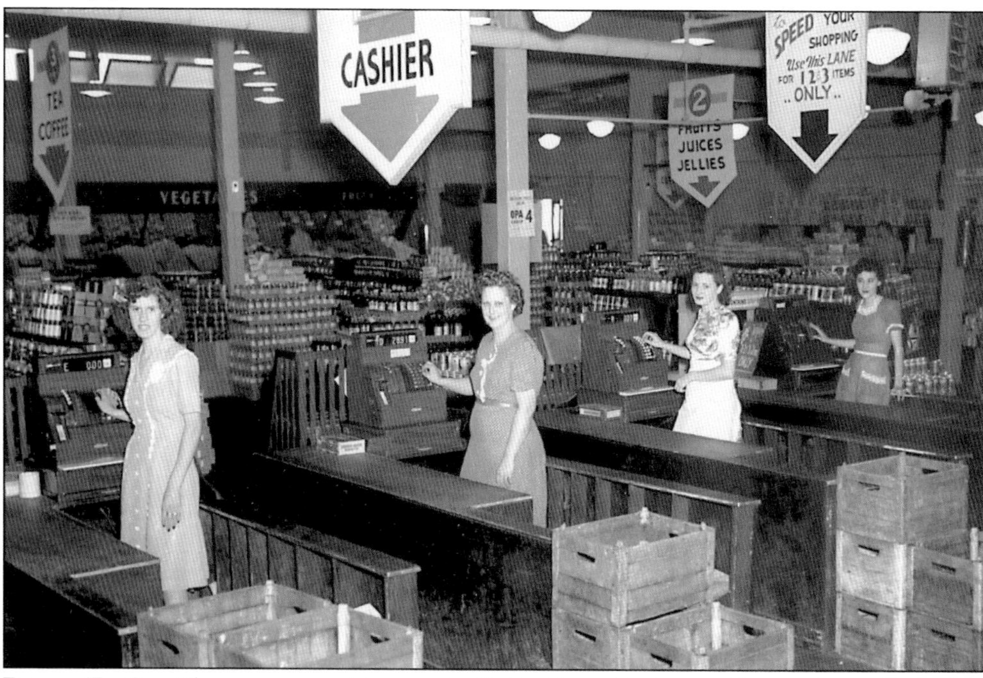

READY TO GO. These pretty cashiers at the Tulip Town Market in Grove Center have their work cut out for them at this soon-to-be very busy store. Do you think they could conceive the modern methods used in today's marketplace?

CHILLING NEWS AT HILLTOP MARKET. These two Hertzell brothers were on the cutting edge of technology. Their store was the first to have a deep-freeze. It was installed on July 12, 1947, and introduced a new way of storing and preparing food in the hot summer months.

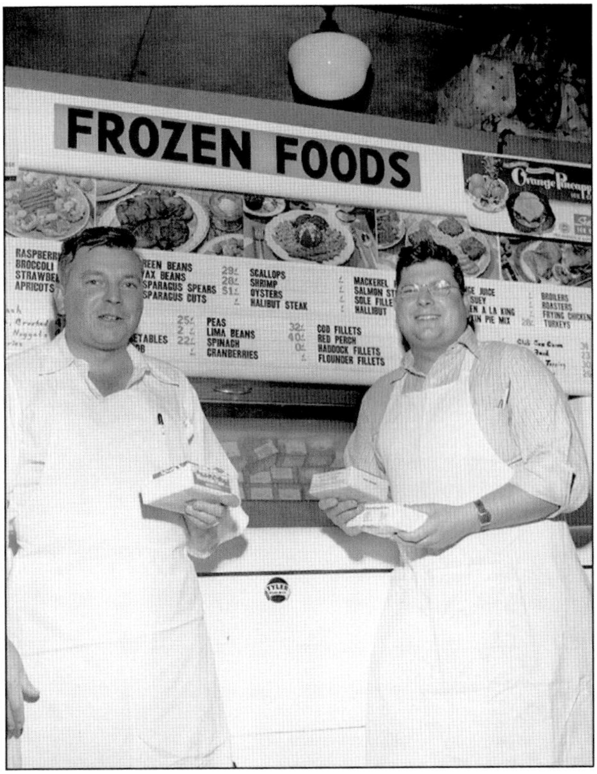

TULIP TOWN MARKET AT GROVE SHOPPING CENTER. Ladies at left "ham" it up for the photographer at this busy general store. A variety of food and household products could be purchased here: Pet milk, Carnation milk, jams and jellies, Purina dog food, and meat from the butcher shop. The grocer, at center with hands on hips, is supervising the operation.

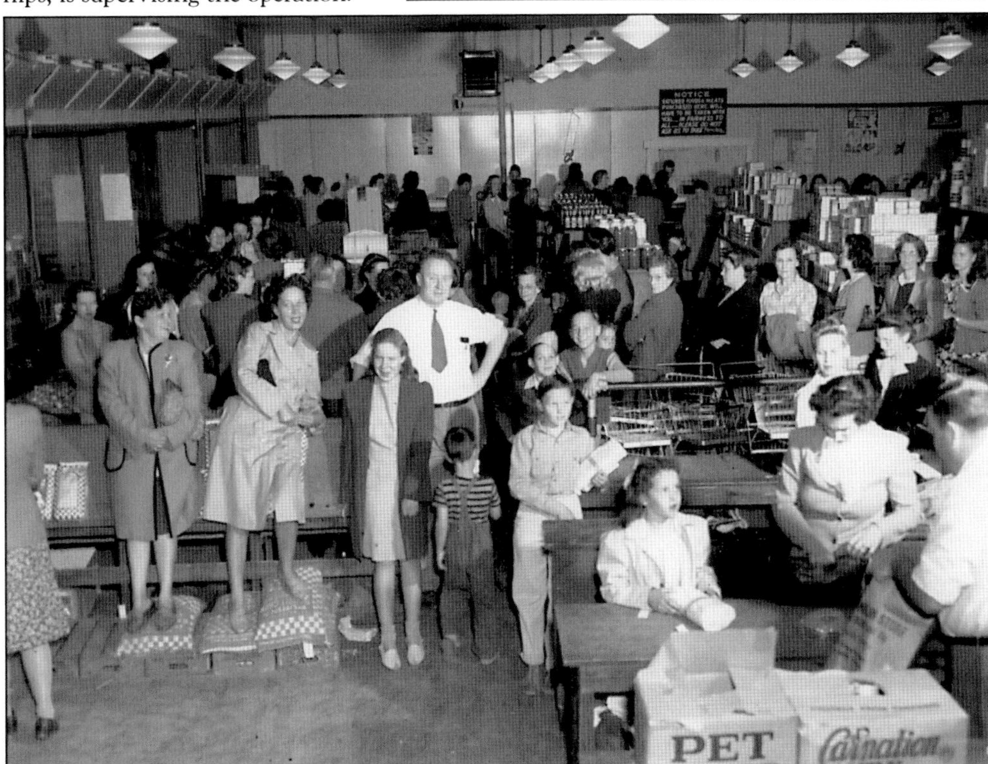

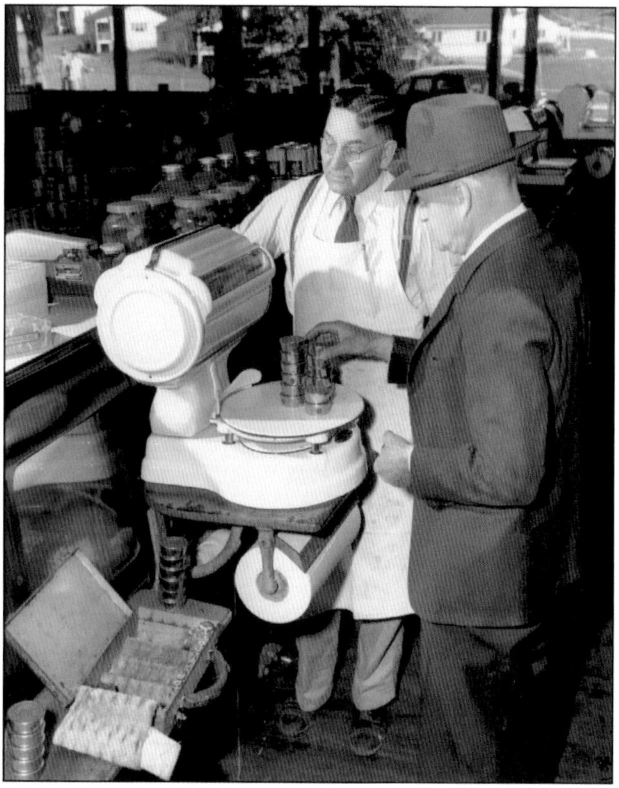

WEIGHTS AND MEASURES. Due to the rationing of meat, a government official calibrates a butcher shop scale to ensure the populace gets a square deal. The weight standards are being used as the grocer looks on. This store was located at Elm Grove Market. Cemesto houses can be seen through the windows.

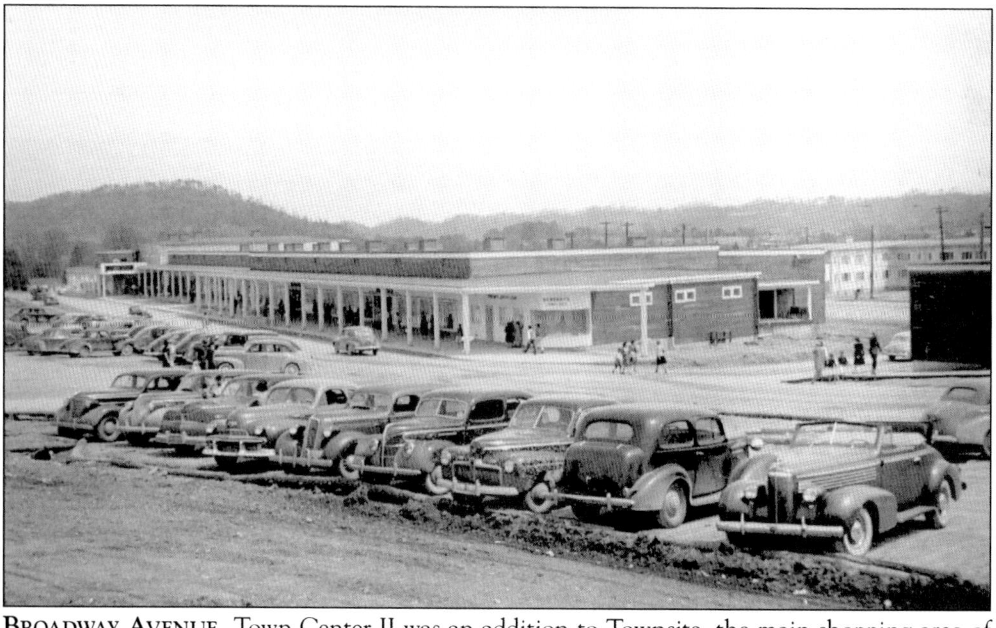

BROADWAY AVENUE. Town Center II was an addition to Townsite, the main shopping area of Oak Ridge. At the far end is Service Drug Store, Ridge Theater, Jewell Lee Dress Shop, Evelyn's Flower Shop, McCroy's, A&P Grocery Store, Taylor's Department Store, and Henebry's Jewelry Store on the corner. Residents from every state of the union began pouring into the stores before the buildings were completed.

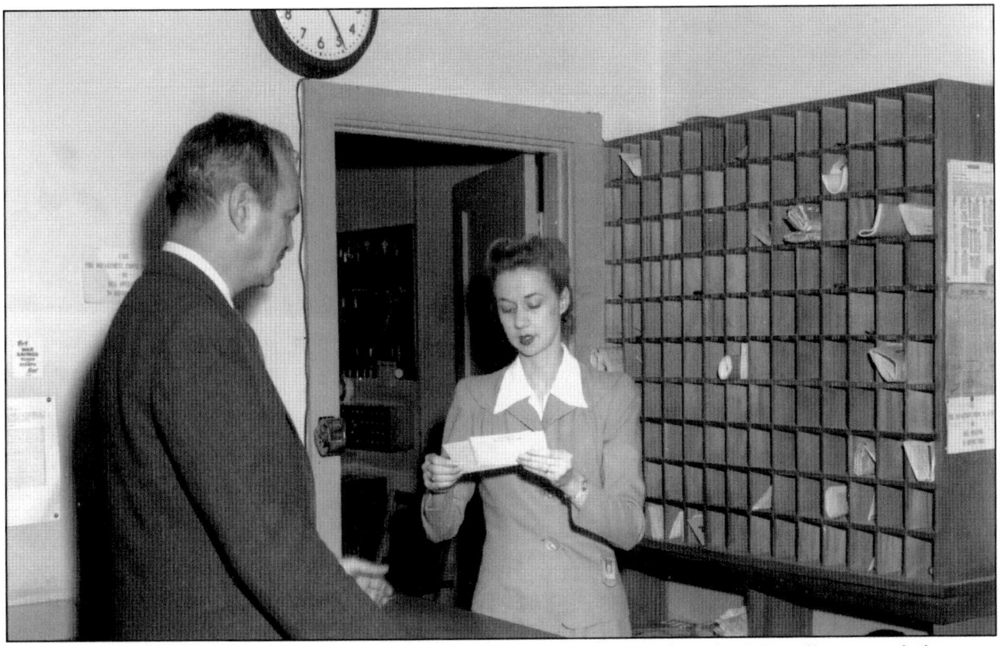

Communication Room in a Residential Dormitory. John O. Merrill, one of the city designers of the firm Skidmore, Owing, and Merrill, stops to retrieve his mail and messages from the dormitory attendant at the end of his busy day. Each dorm was equipped with this system of communication.

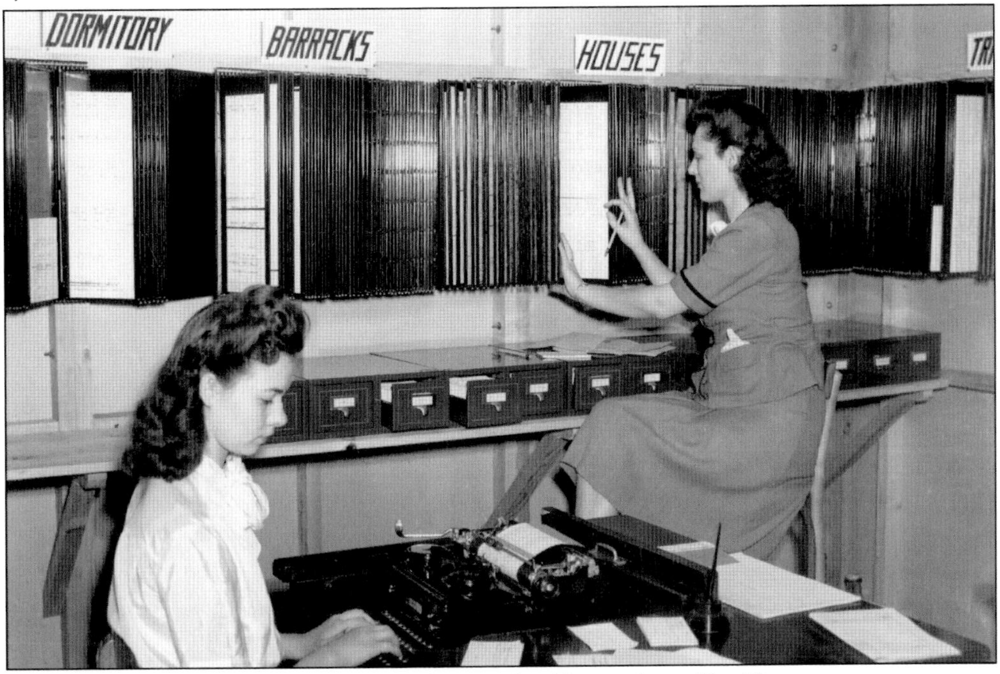

Maintaining the City Directory. A considerable number of buildings were necessary to house the various administrative and service facilities and activities connected with the operation of Oak Ridge. A system was initiated that tracked residents and businesses as they moved about the city as construction progressed and homes and buildings were made ready for occupancy.

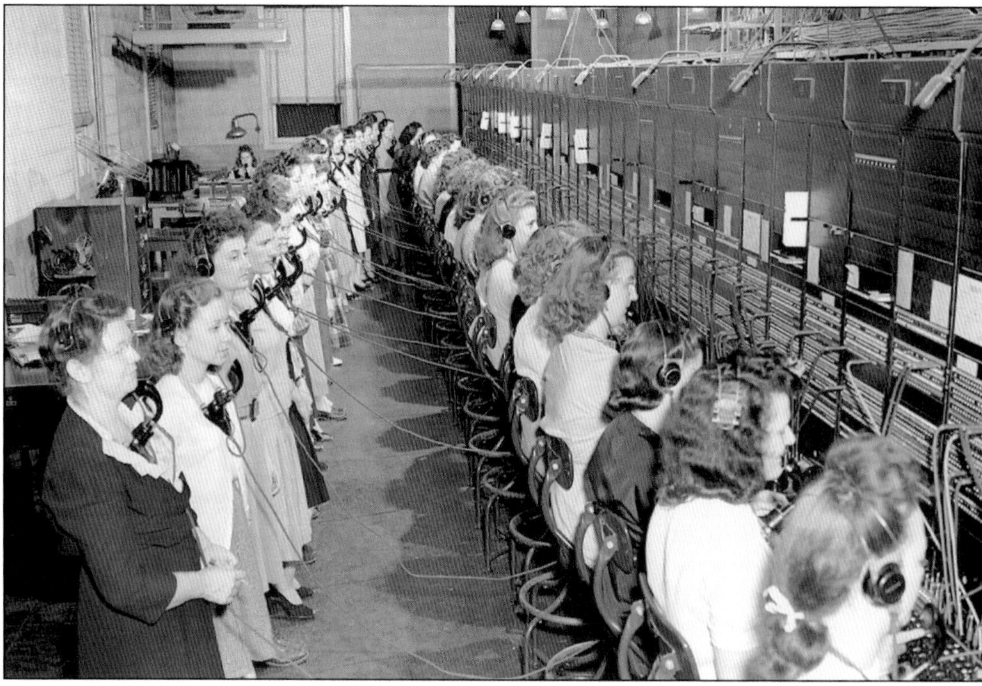

Number, Please. These Clinton Engineer Works operators are standing in line waiting their turn to work the switchboard on the next shift. All phone calls were routed through this switchboard before they had dial telephones. This system was used until late 1943.

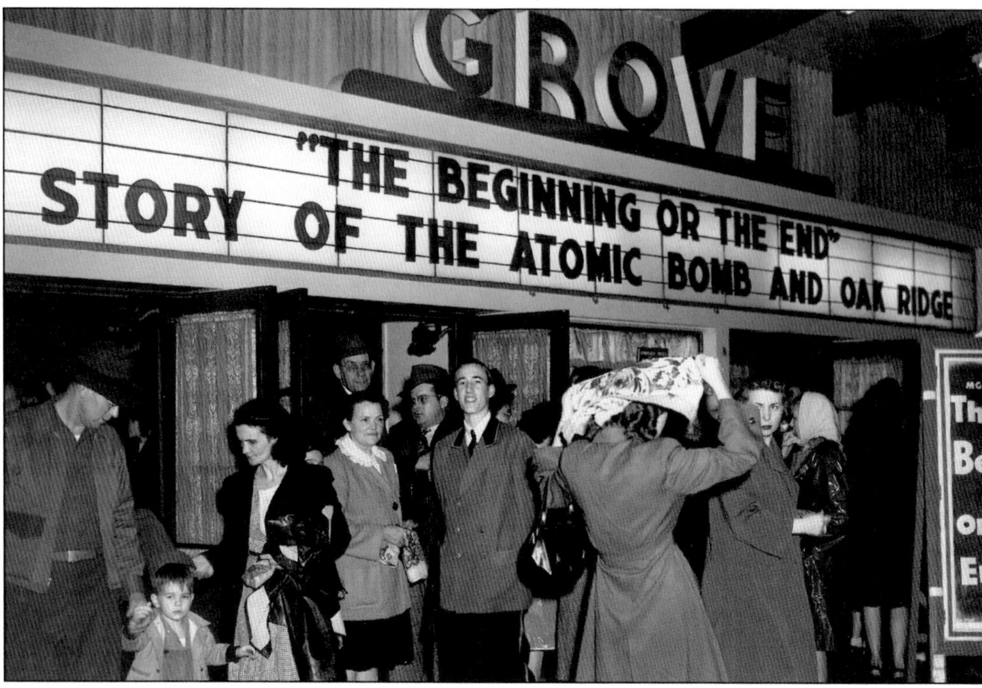

The Beginning of the End. The story of the birth of Oak Ridge was depicted in a full-length movie shown at the Grove Theater in 1947. Some of the cast members were Brian Donley portraying Gen. Leslie Groves and Hume Cronyn as J. Robert Oppenheimer.

MILKSHAKE TIME AT THE SODA FOUNTAIN. Finley King (left) and Russell Poe (right) are enjoying a milk shake at one of the many snack bars dotted throughout the city. Provided by the Recreation and Welfare Association, these gathering places provided a place for relaxation and social exchange. Neighborhood drug stores also offered a chance for a soda and a quick lunch.

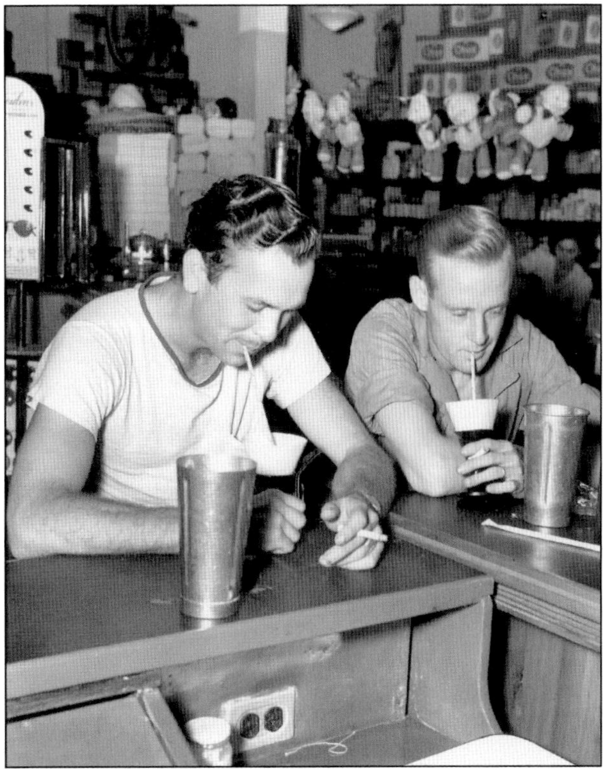

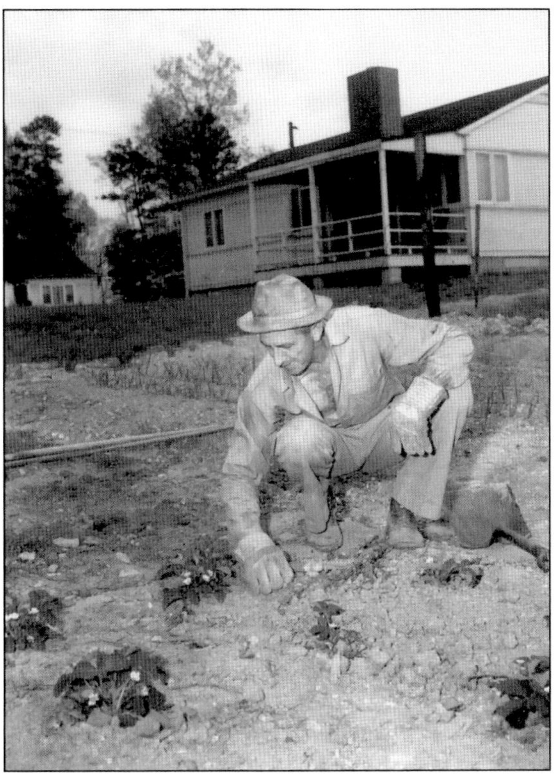

TENDING HIS VICTORY GARDEN. This unidentified man is monitoring the growth of his strawberry plants. Without prior experience working with the combination of clay and chert earth, gardening was difficult. The climate was generally mild, with a mean annual temperature from 59 degrees in January to 75 degrees in July.

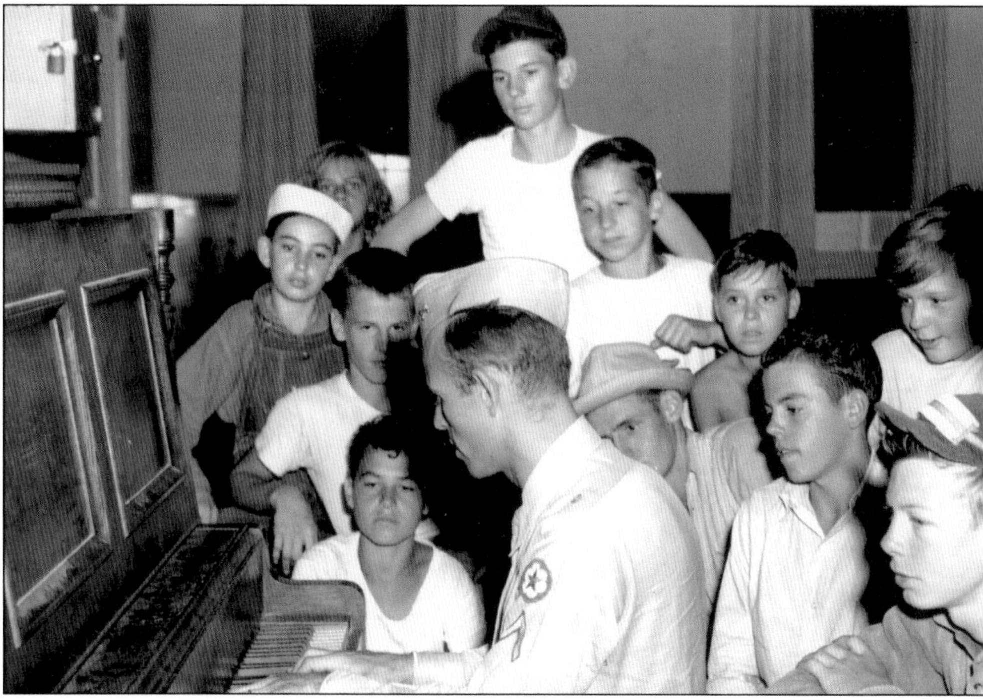

A GI Tickles the Ivories. Pvt. Cullie B. Woodall provides entertaining tunes at the recreation hall. In their off-duty hours, military personnel would often visit the rec halls to blend with neighborhood residents. This would lift the soldiers' spirits and ease the tension of loneliness.

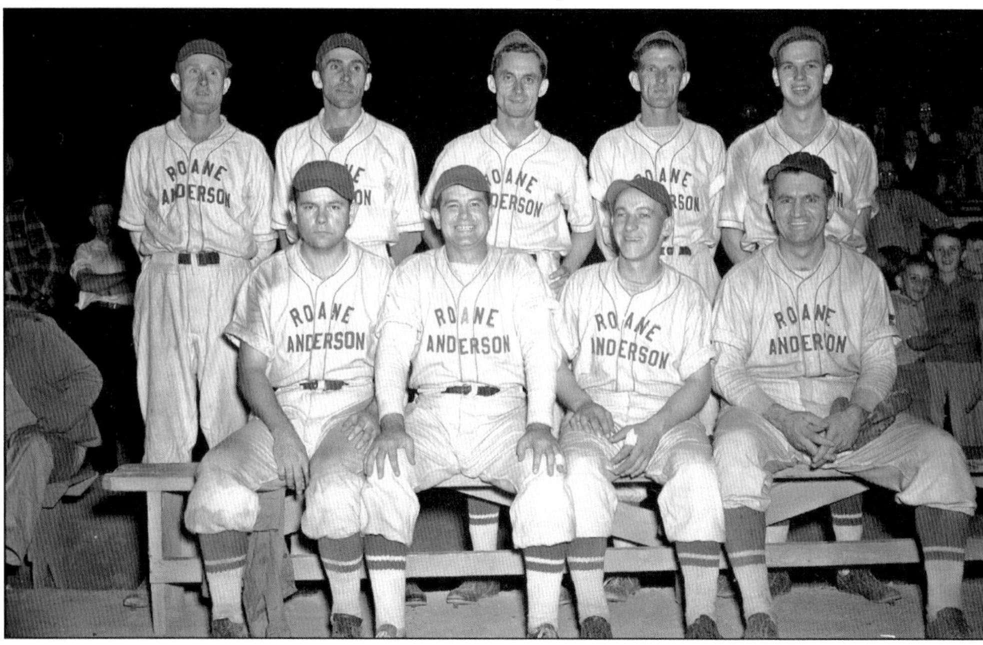

Roane-Anderson Baseball Team. Shown here is one of the many baseball teams that participated in league play. Members of this team worked for the company that first operated the town facilities. The company name was derived from the two counties that comprised the Manhattan District Project, Roane County and Anderson County.

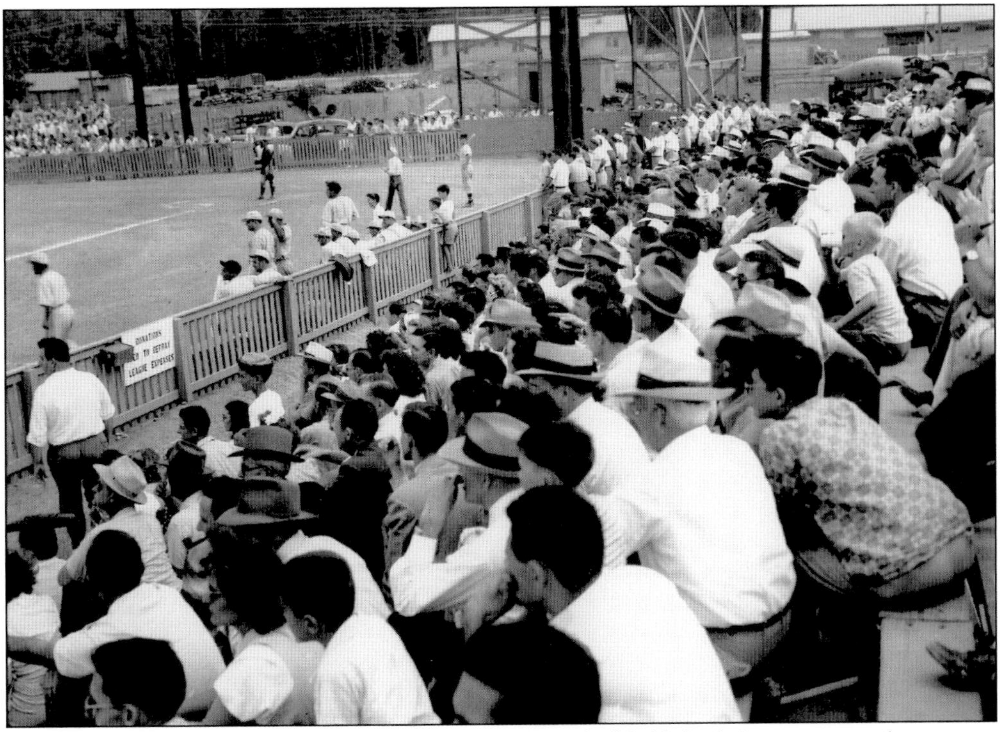

Baseball Game. Oak Wood Park was one of the many ballfields built for recreational activities. Spectators view a game between the Army Cards and Moore General Hospital. Teams outside the restricted area were invited to participate in league activity.

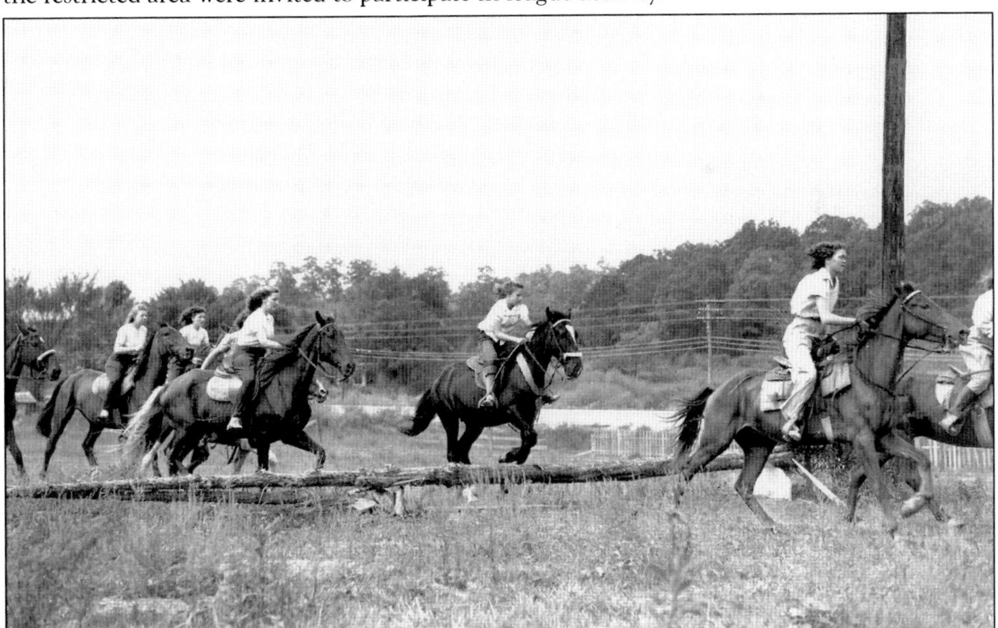

Horseback Riding Club. Young ladies participate in a riding event at the government-built stables. Horsemanship was taught at the club, and various contests were held. The stables were built by the Manhattan District Project for their use as well as to be used by the residents.

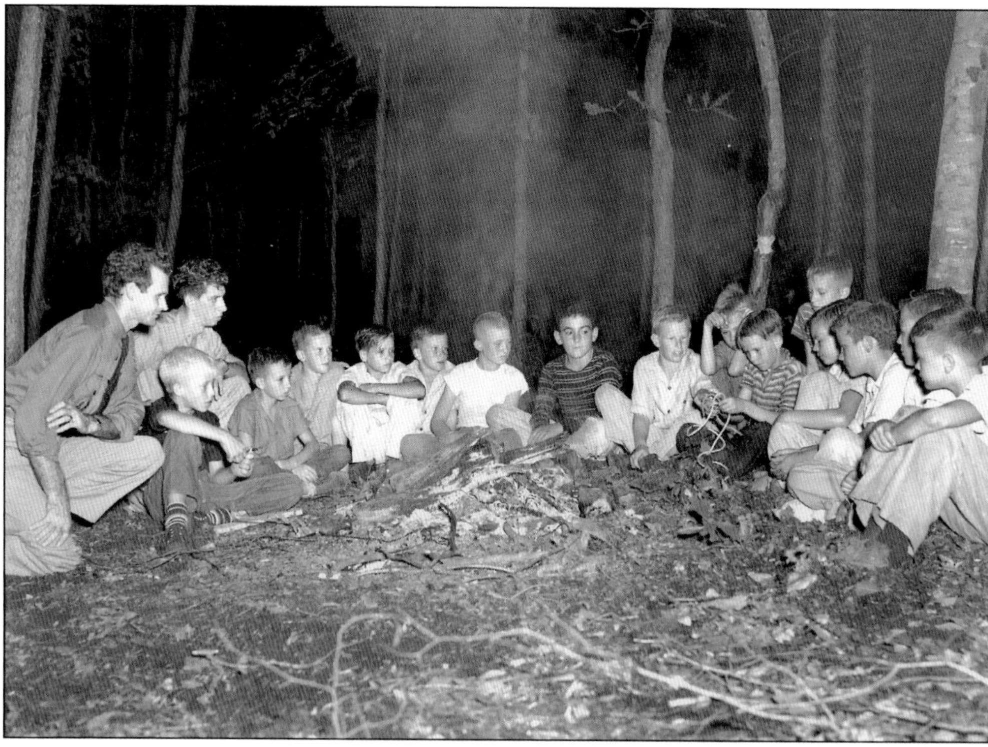

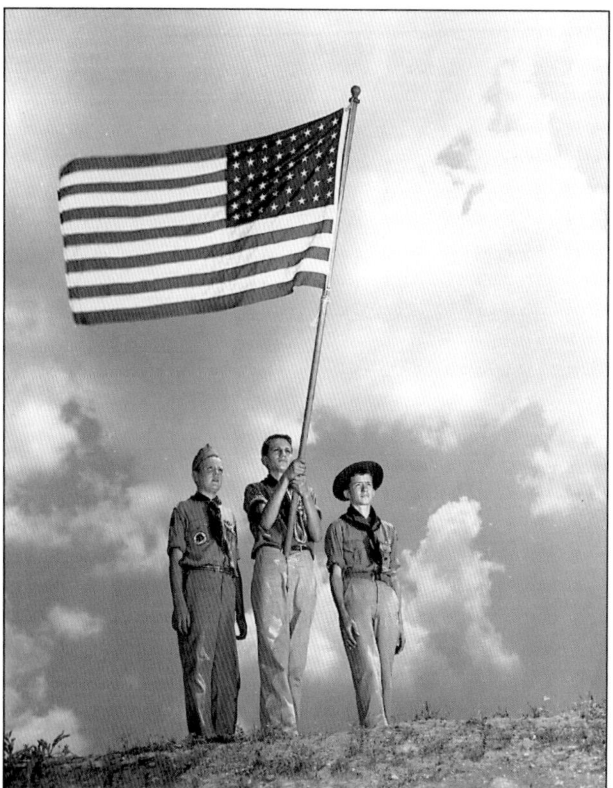

CUB SCOUTS ON AN OUTING. Two scoutmasters are observing youngsters' progress in knot tying. Outdoors was plentiful in the fenced-in city, providing a safe haven for camping activities. Fathers also enjoyed these outings, for they got a break from working six days a week.

BOY SCOUTS HONORING THE AMERICAN FLAG. Boy Scouts who will take part in flag exercises on July 4, 1946, are shown here during a drill session. Scouting was appealing because of the values it stood for. Pictured from left to right are Henry King and Bill Trimby, both of Troop 129, and Bob Livesey, Troop 327.

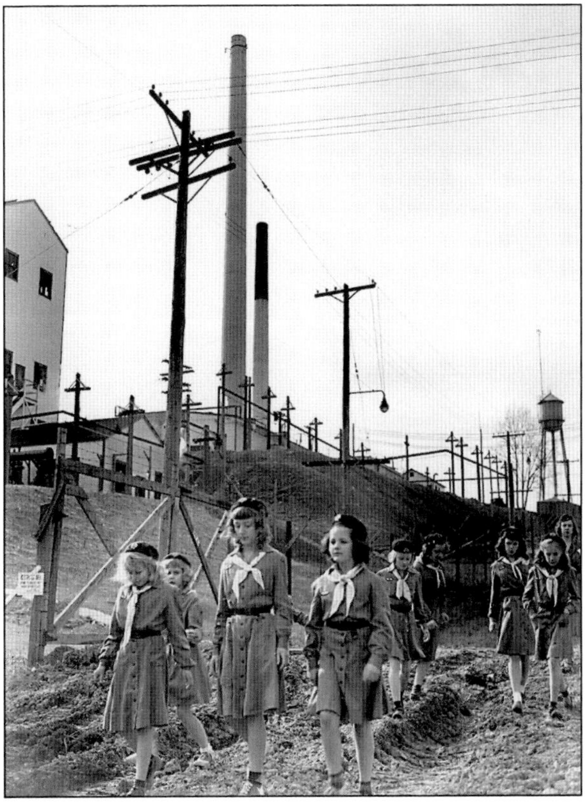

Girl Scouts on a Field Trip. An outing to the Graphite Reactor, now a historical landmark, helped the Scouts understand the work that was performed there during wartime. Parents were now able to discuss some details of working in such a secret plant.

Girl Scouts Raising the American Flag. The Girl Scout Day Camp was dedicated to the girls of Oak Ridge on July 13, 1945, and given the name "Camp Trefoil." The campers chose the name, which was taken from the shape of the Girl Scout pin. The program included songs, crafts, dramatics, and games.

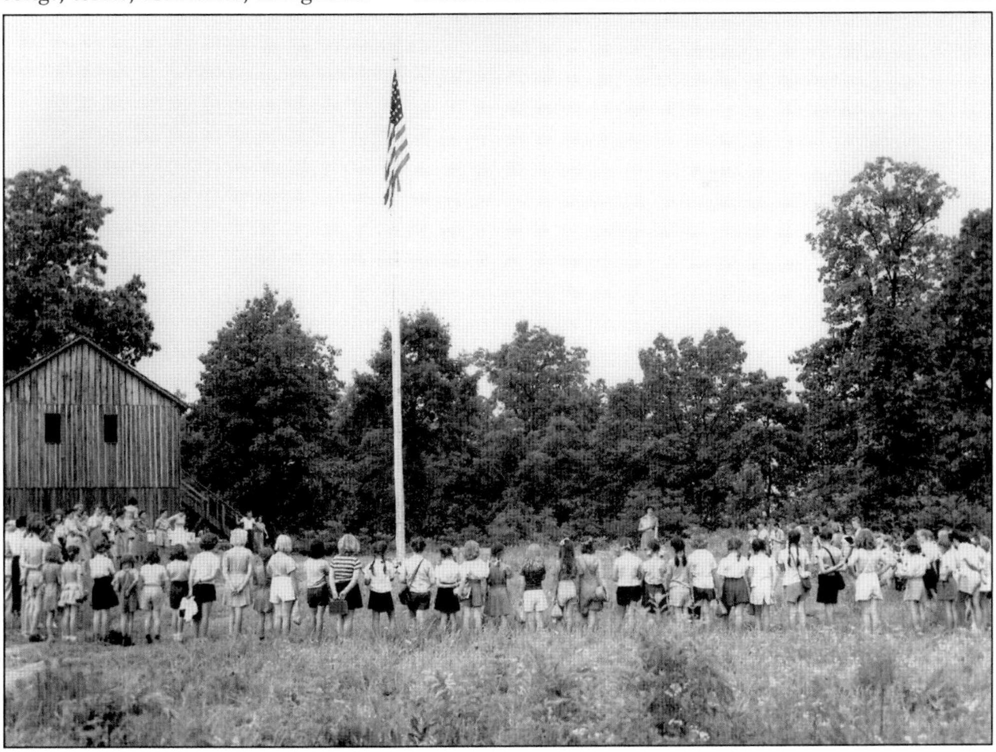

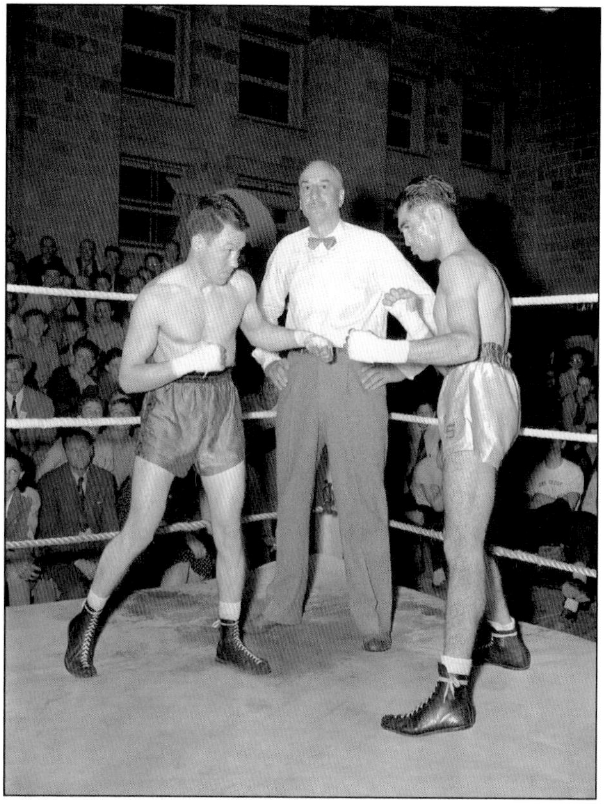

SIZING THEM UP. Referee Gene Demont stands in the middle but not in the direct line of fire as two boxers, Jimmy Maddox (left) and Sammy West, square up. Events like this were attended by folks eager to be entertained. Boxing matches were always a crowd pleaser.

TEENAGERS PLAYING PUTT-PUTT GOLF. These high school youth are enjoying one of the many recreational activities sponsored by the city recreation and welfare division. The city did not have a golf course, so a makeshift putting green was provided.

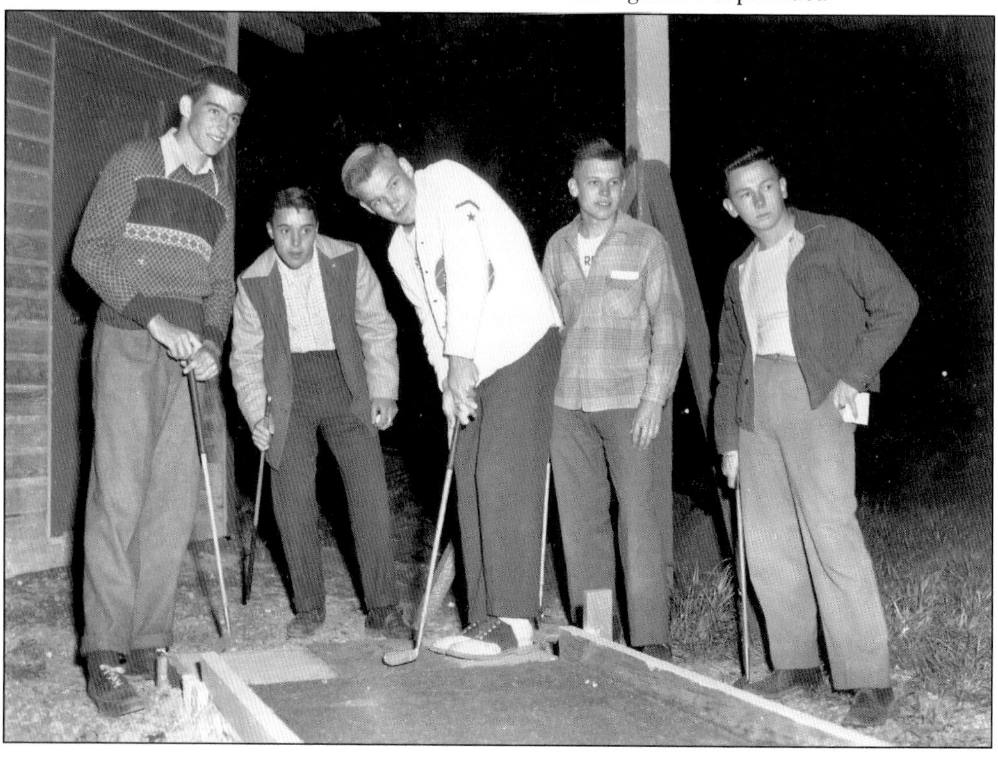

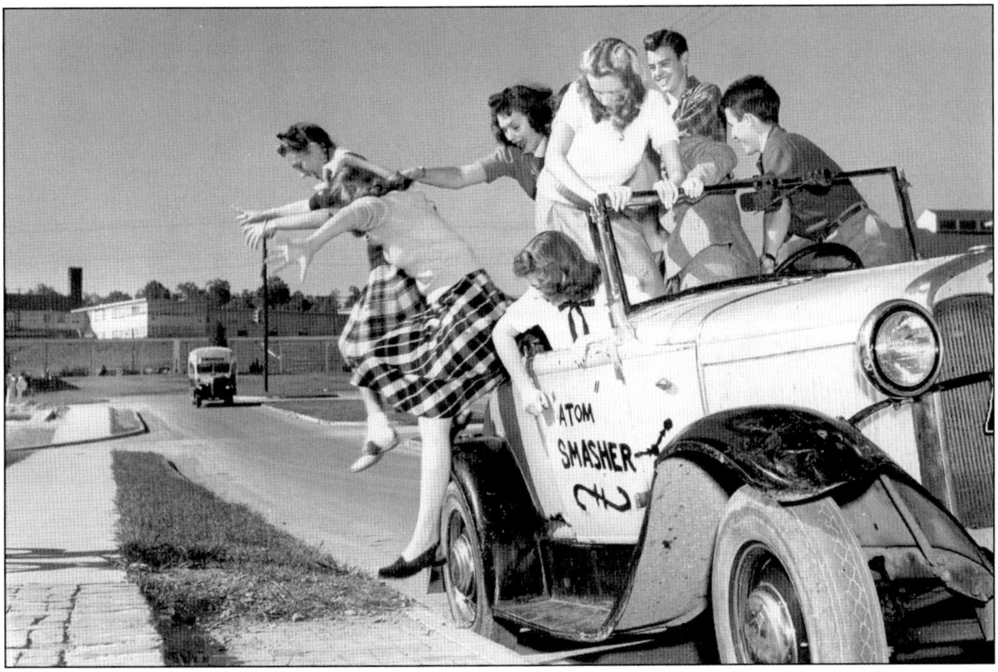

Jubilant High School Students. These students are enjoying the after-school activity of gathering at the Central Cafeteria on Central Avenue. Socializing was an important pastime, and automobiles were scarce. These students decorated their car with the name "Atom Smasher" in remembrance of the successful war effort their parents participated in.

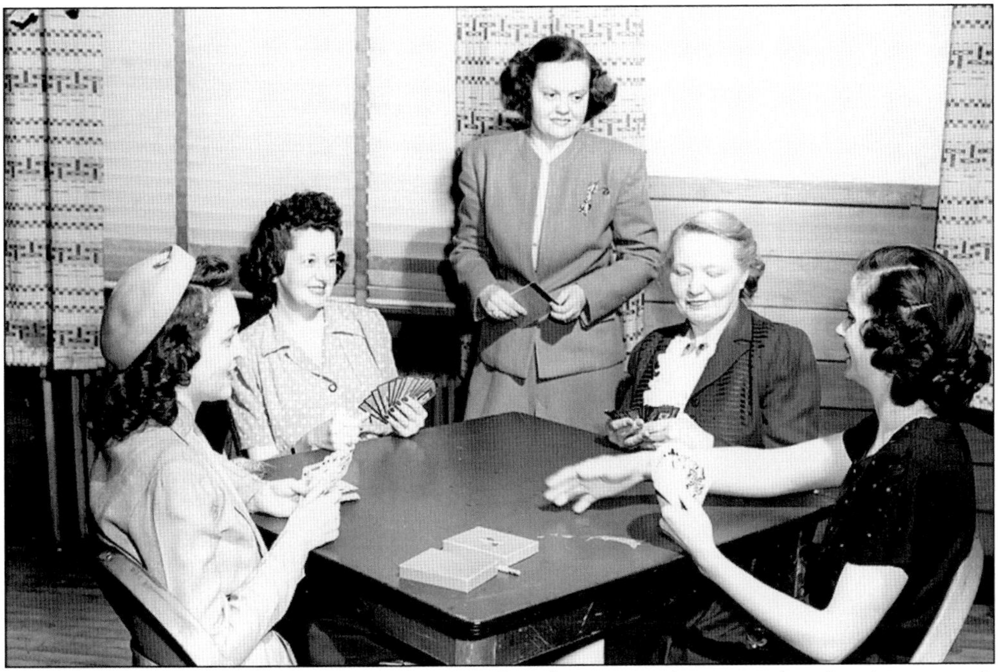

Ladies Bridge Club. Oak Ridge ladies loved to dress up and get together for playing cards and exchanging family news. The club officers organized these games, which took place in the recreation halls in addition to small groups meeting in individual homes.

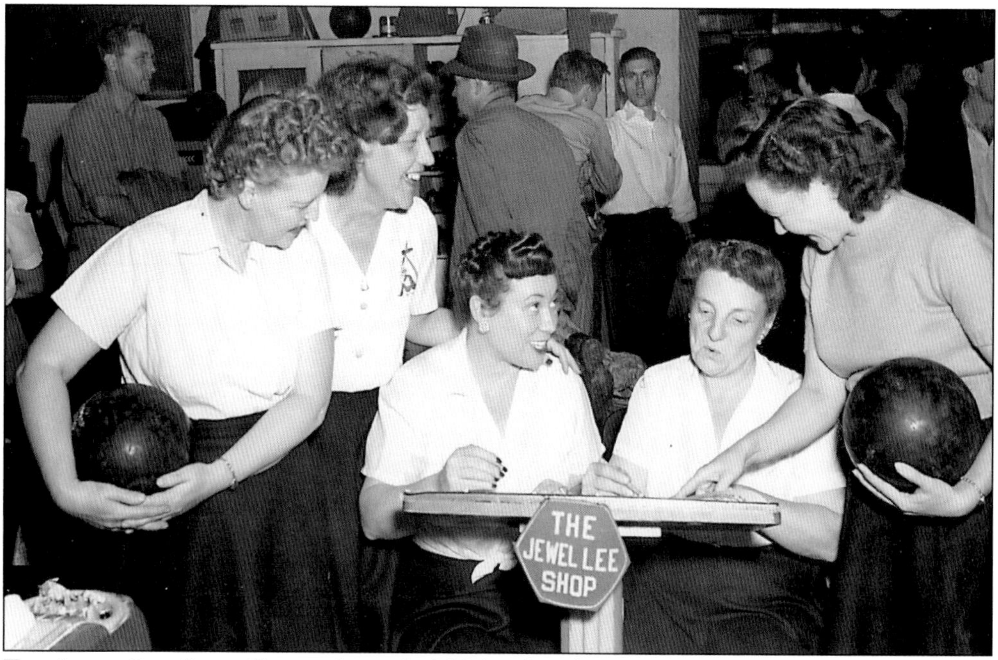

THE JEWEL LEE SHOP GIRLS. A total of 38 bowling lanes existed in Oak Ridge. Central in Townsite, Oak Terrace in Grove Center, Paragon in Jefferson Shopping area, and one in Middletown provided league competition for residents. The team from the Jewel Lee Shop, a women's clothing store, turned heads with their fashionable attire.

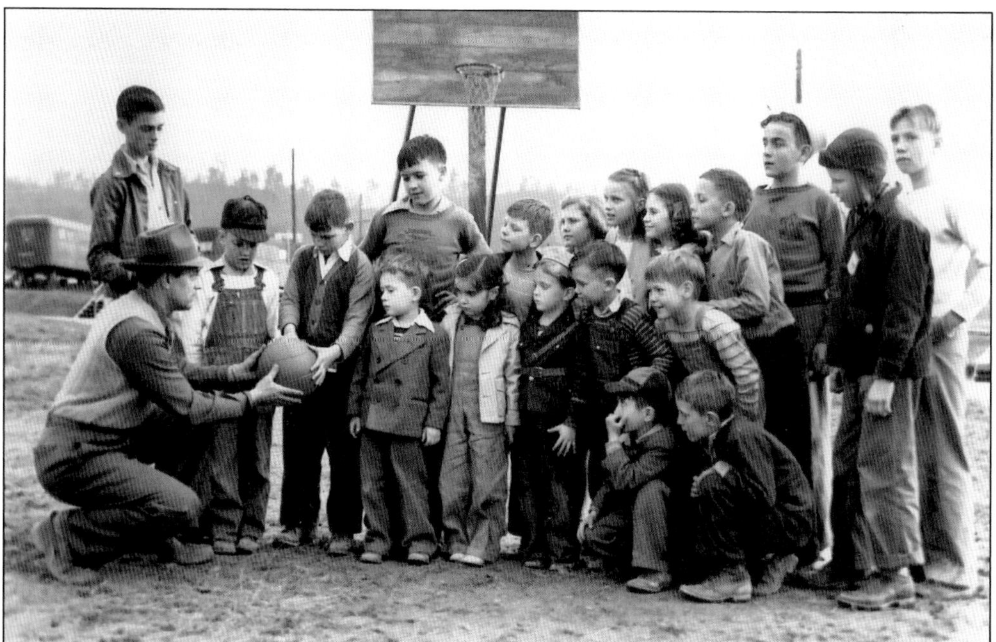

BASKETBALL INSTRUCTIONS. Shep Lauter, from the Recreation and Welfare Association, captivates youngsters with stories of games he has coached. The association was activated on July 21, 1943, with 230 employees supervising social welfare and recreation activities encompassing a diversified range of activities.

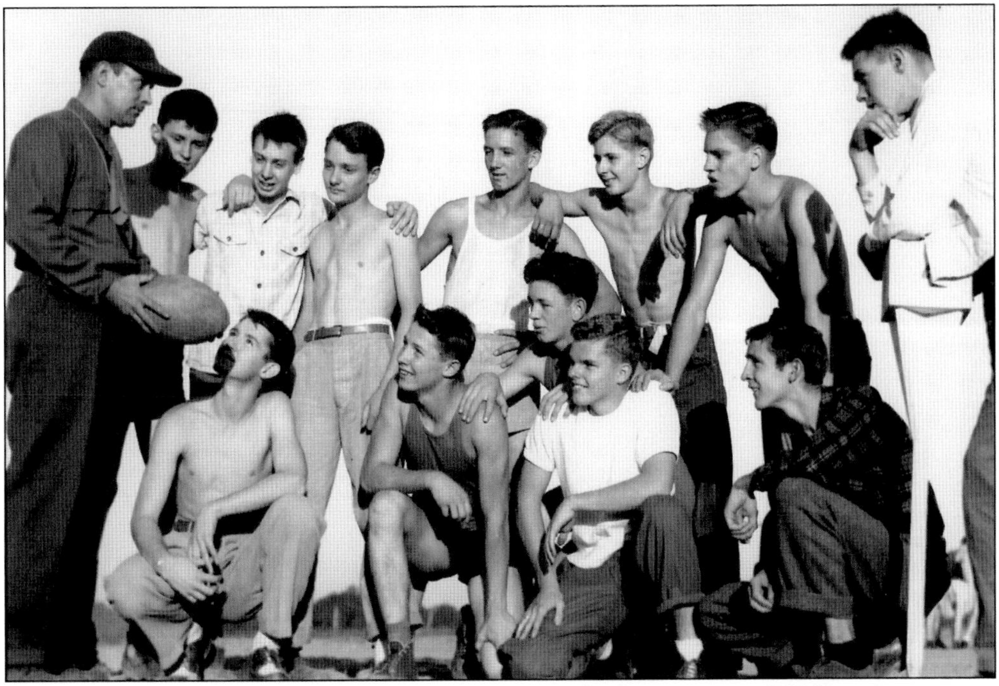

DISCUSSING FOOTBALL STRATEGY. Shep Lauter, from the Recreation and Welfare Association, is giving tips to a shirts versus no-shirts touch football game. Shep worked with all ages providing instructions for sports, including sandlot games as well as organized high school competition.

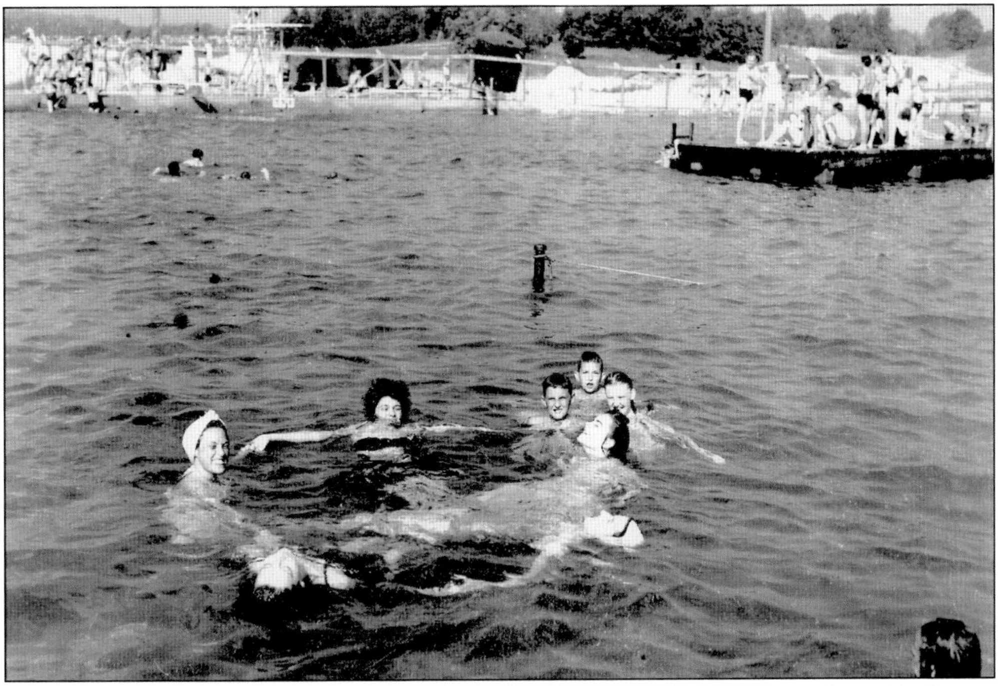

PUBLIC SWIMMING POOL. The pool was located in the Grove Center area and was the largest outdoor public swimming pool in the eastern United States. A local spring provided the water. The depth of the pool ranged from 2 feet to 12 feet.

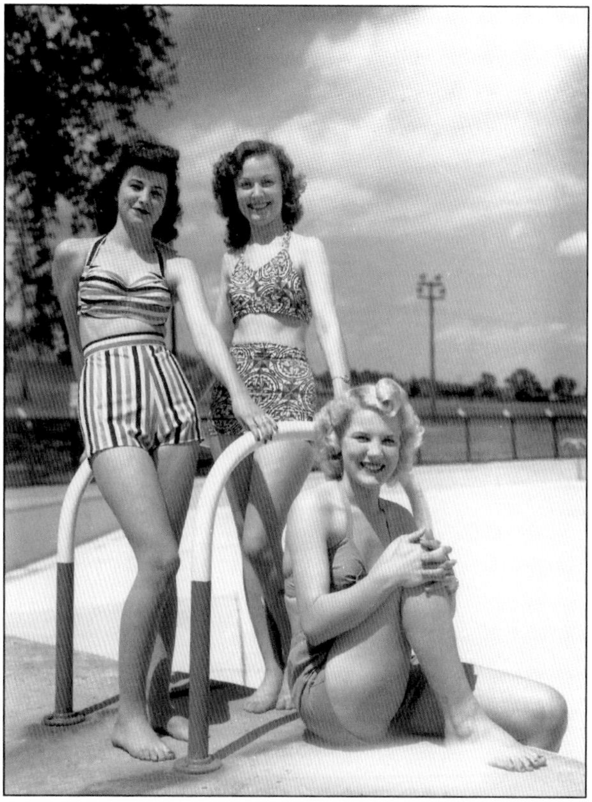

Swimming Pool Opens. This was one of the toughest assignments photographer Ed Westcott ever had. Usually it takes him about five minutes to get a picture, but he worked for an hour and a half getting this one. The girls are, from left to right, Marilyn Angel, Louise Cox, and Velma Strange.

Model Airplane Club. Young members are eagerly receiving detailed directions from instructor Alvin Orville on building wooden gliders and gasoline-powered airplanes. Children during the wartime were very interested in the types of planes that were used in the war. Pictured from left to right are (first row) Jim Brown, Art Morley, Sidney Thomas, Richard Mattice, Alvin Orville, Frank Bryant, Robert Mattice, Pete Preston, and Donald Shephard; (second row) Joe Culver, Dick Culver, Billy Smith, Frank Morgan, Frank Dunkley, and Bruce Farwell.

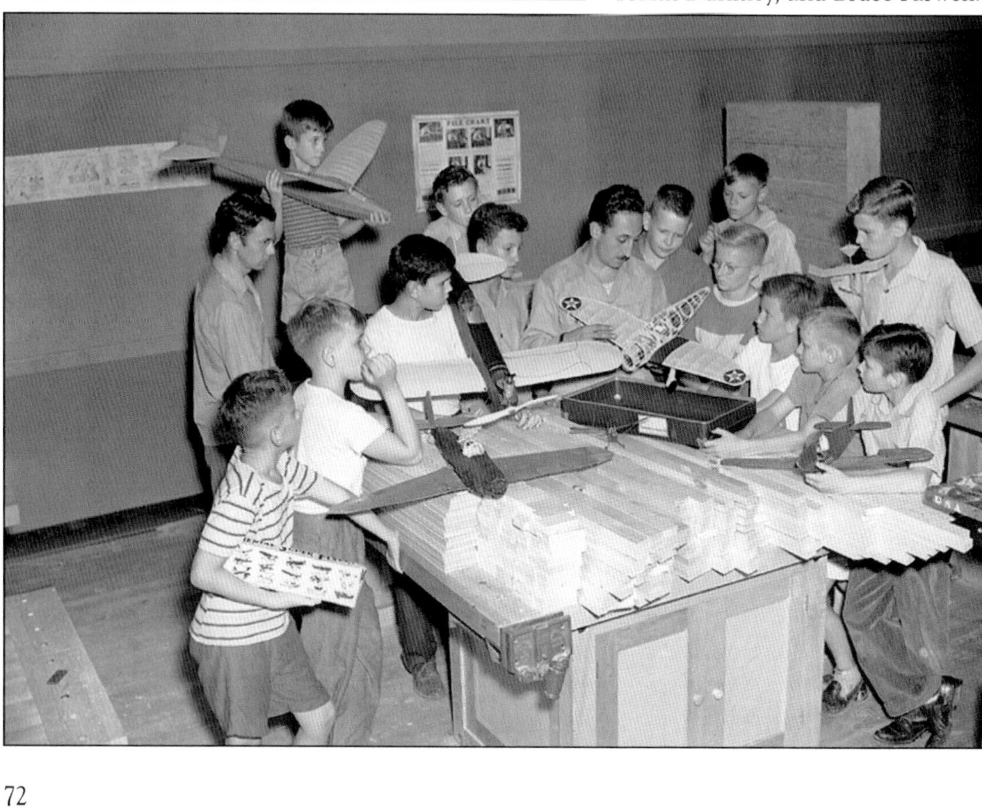

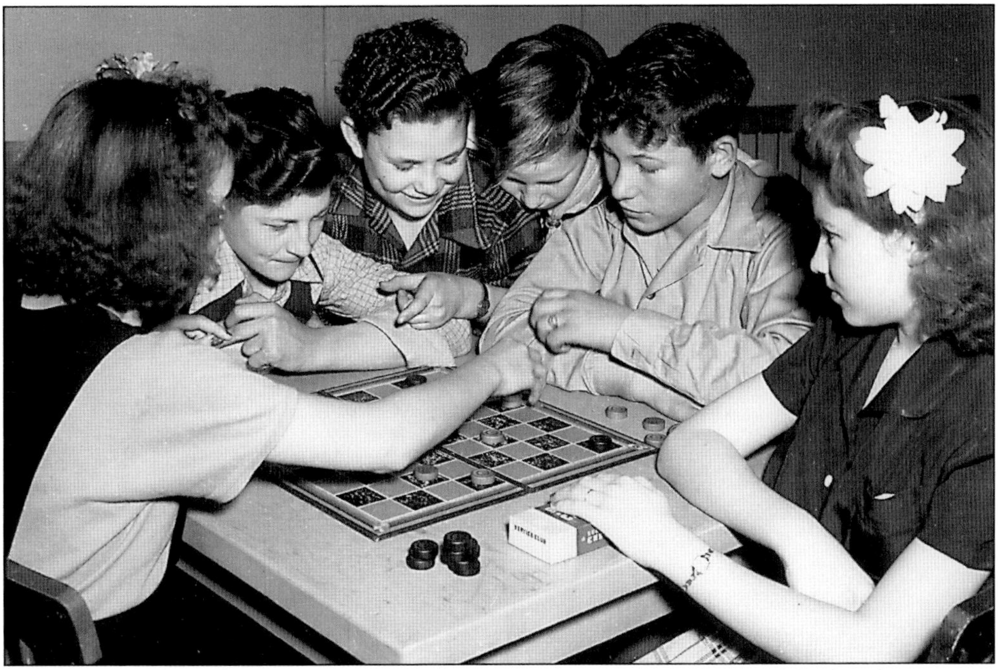

Making the Moves. Youths enjoy a friendly checkers game at their neighborhood recreation center. The young lady on the left, Wanda Francis, is going in for a king as onlookers are amazed at her mobility and control of the board. This activity was a regular event that kept the children occupied indoors during rainy weather. From left to right are Wanda Francis, J. W. Gilliam, Bill Donahue, Jack Berry, Harold Berry, and Wanda Robinson.

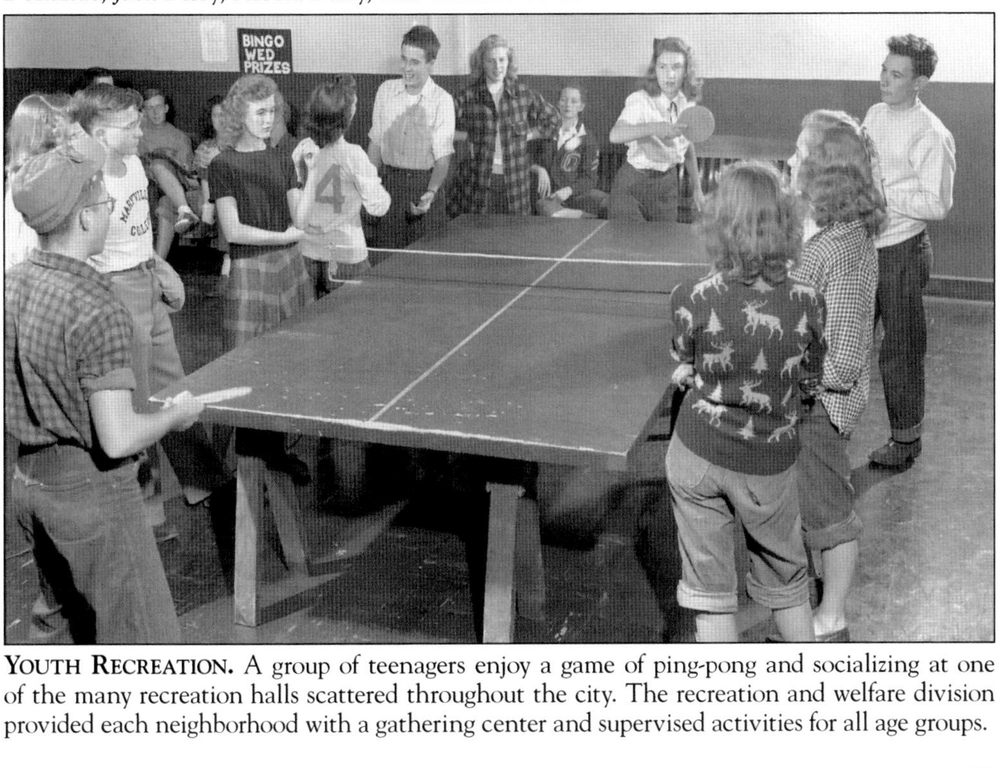

Youth Recreation. A group of teenagers enjoy a game of ping-pong and socializing at one of the many recreation halls scattered throughout the city. The recreation and welfare division provided each neighborhood with a gathering center and supervised activities for all age groups.

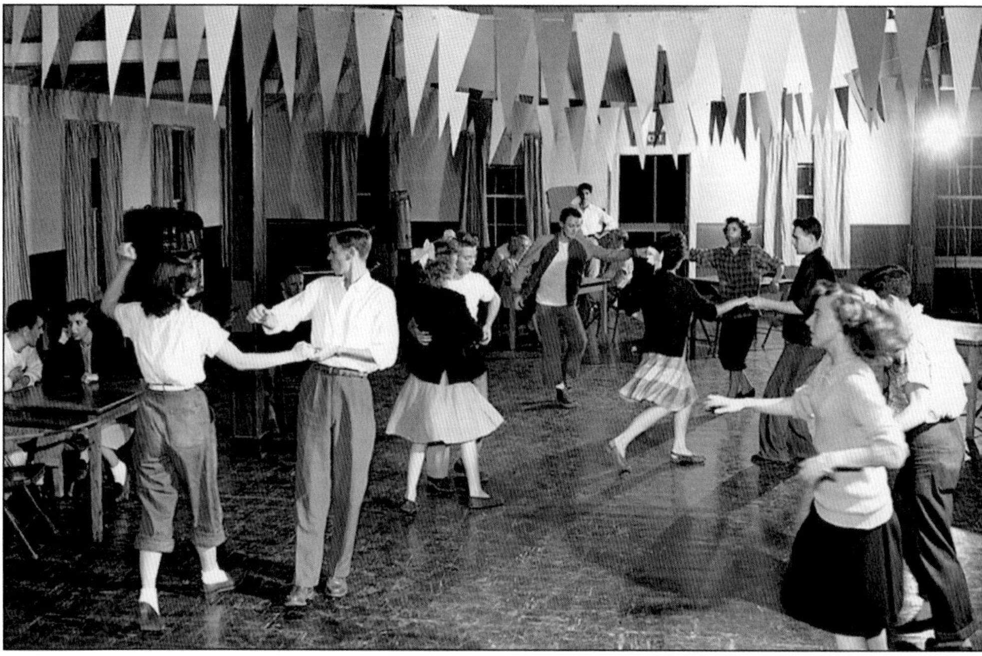

DANCING AT THE WILDCAT DEN. Teenagers dance to a Wurlitzer jukebox as Tommy Dorsey's music fills the air. The Den was located in a room inside Central Cafeteria. The room was decorated with the Oak Ridge High School colors of red and gray. Dances were held every Saturday night.

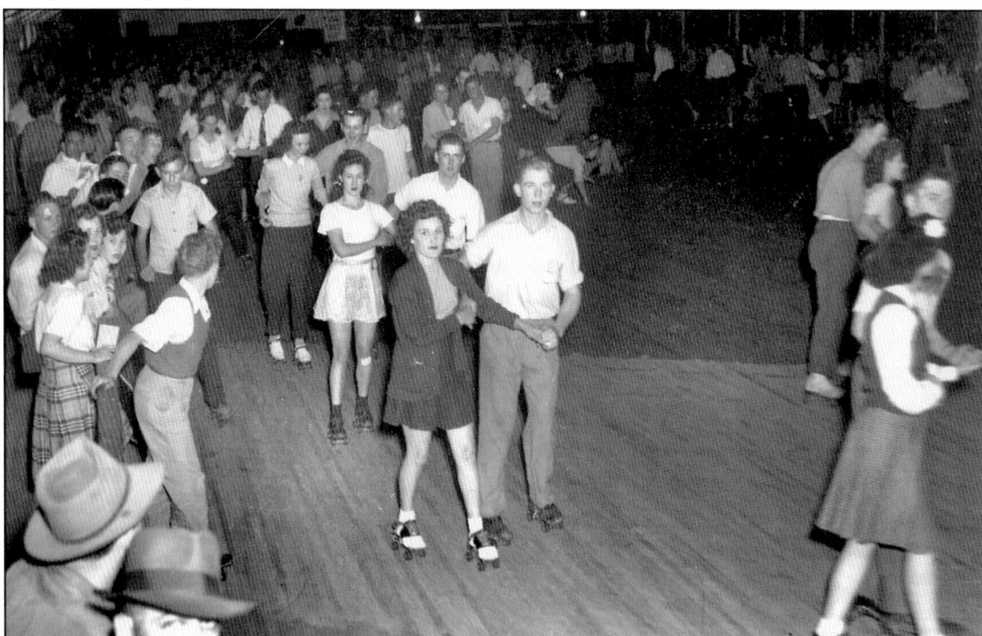

ROLLER SKATING. Couples take the floor to show off their skills on skates. The wooden floor in the skating rink made gliding across the floor enjoyable, even though the skates were primitive compared to present-day skates. The cadence was set by the booming sound of the Wurlitzer organ.

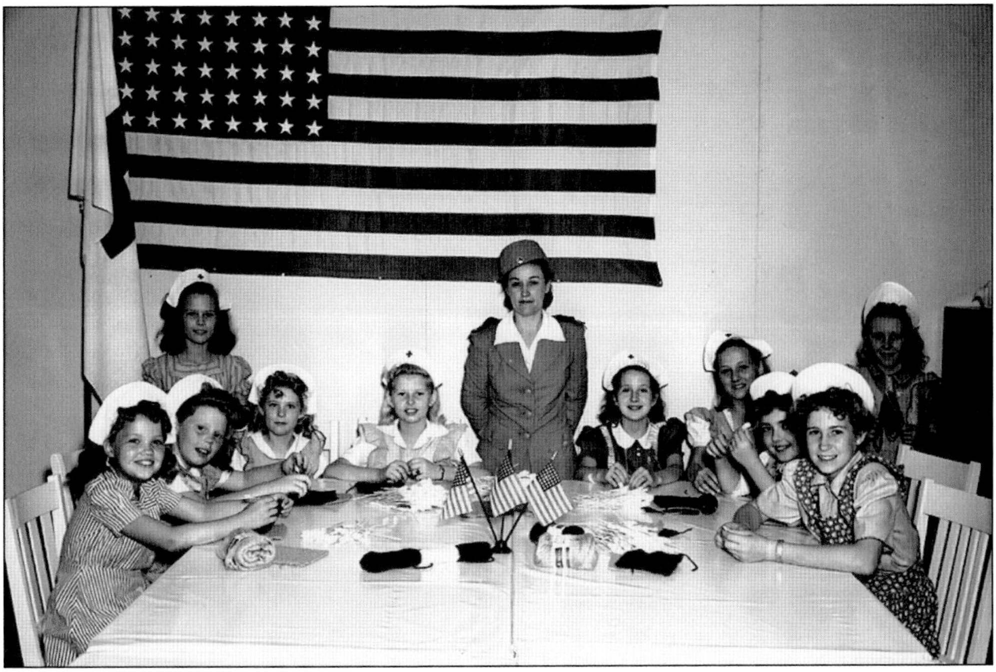

Learning to Care for Others. A Red Cross leader, center, teaches first aid. These young girls are learning the necessary art of dressing a wound with a bandage. Volunteers would step up gladly to do what they could in the way of helping out.

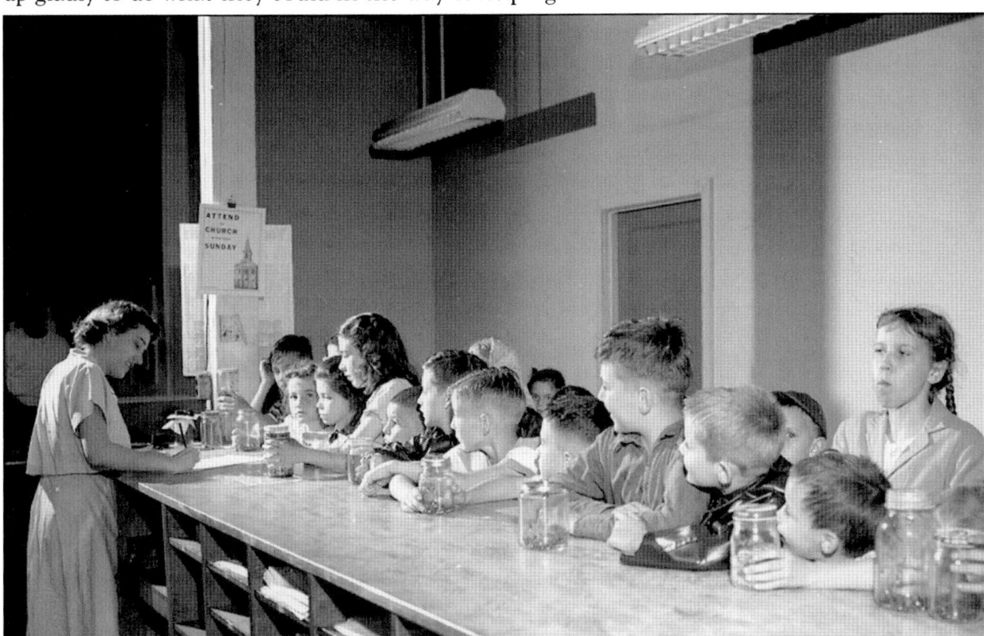

An Annual Summertime Event. Children are lined up at the counter in the *Oak Ridger* newspaper office to sell their week's collection of lightening bugs. A scientific lab purchased the bugs and used them in research projects—for example, to improve food safety by detecting bacteria in food.

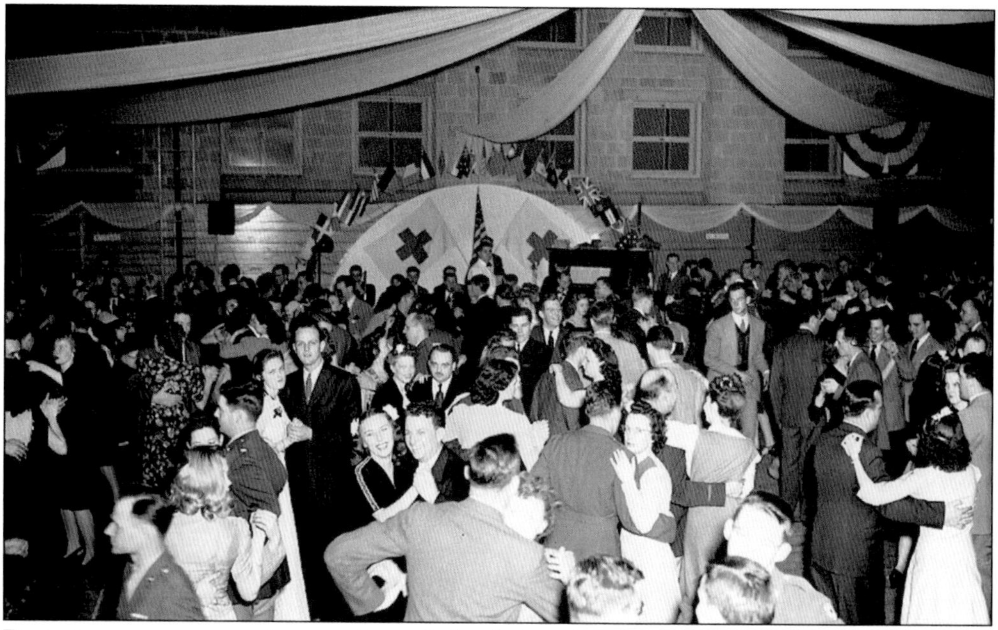

DANCING UNDER THE STARS. Beneath brightly colored streamers and a showing of the American flag, residents enjoyed an evening of community recreation sponsored by the American Red Cross. Oak Ridgers were happy to contribute to the causes of the Red Cross during wartime, knowing that their sisters, brothers, husbands, and wives were fighting to win the war and return home.

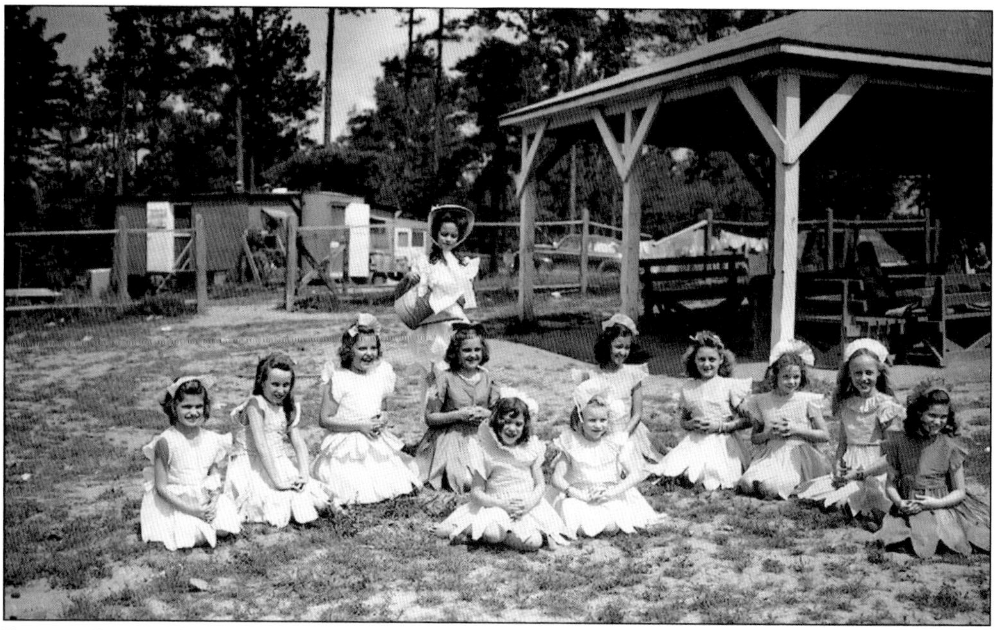

PRETTY LITTLE GIRLS. These little ladies from Gamble Valley trailer camp are participating in one of the many summer recreation programs that were presented by the Welfare and Recreation Association. Dressed in costumes to look like lovely flowers, they presented a play for their parents and friends. The programs gave the children a variety of activities to keep them busy over the summer months.

A True Beauty. Winner of the Miss Oak Ridge beauty contest for 1944 was Miss Claudia Bussler. Seen here in a stylish costume, she defeated 14 other lovely ladies entered in the pageant. The show was held in the Oak Ridge High School auditorium to a packed crowd that cheered loudly for the winner.

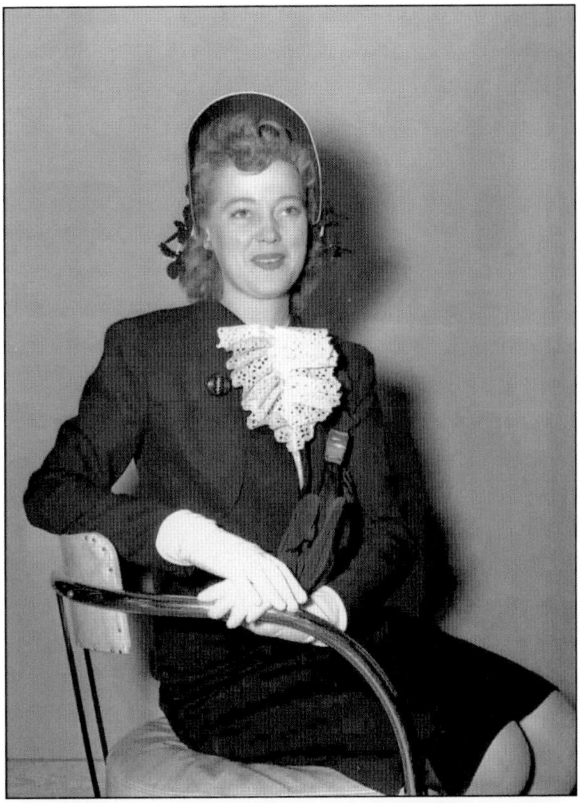

Watering Hole. The Crossroads Tavern, located behind the Grove Center shopping area at the intersection of Raleigh and Robertsville Road, was a favorite gathering place for Oak Ridgers. Beer, soft drinks, and short-order food were available. This tavern continued to operate into the early 1990s.

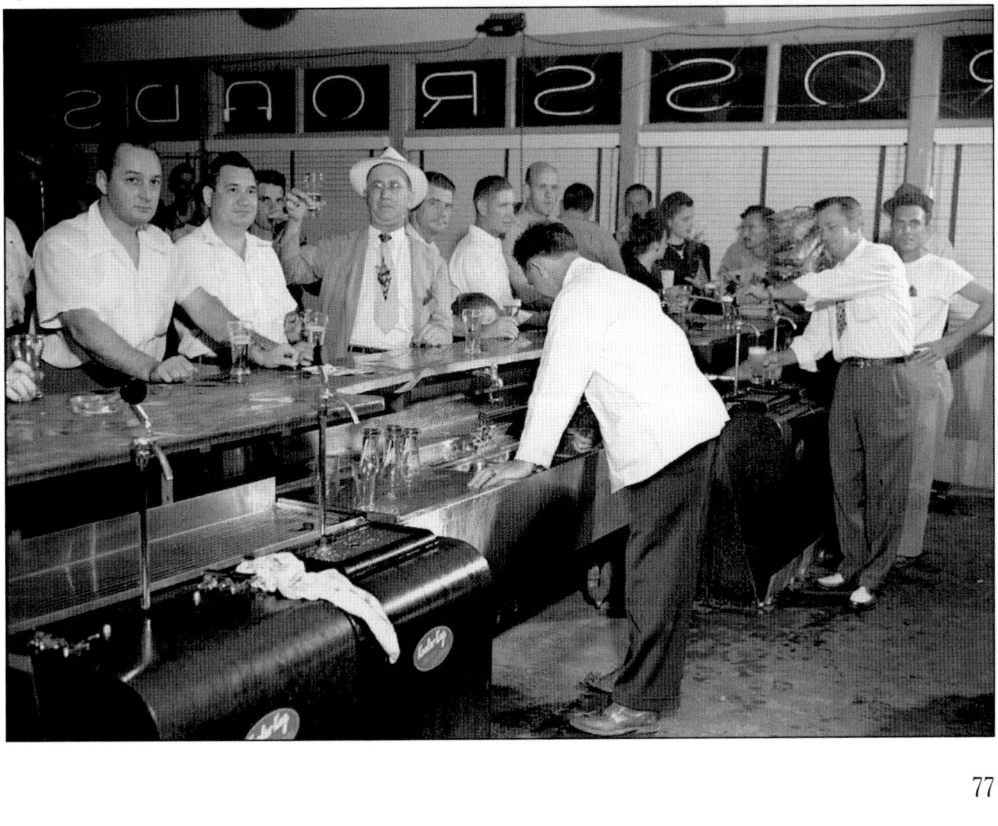

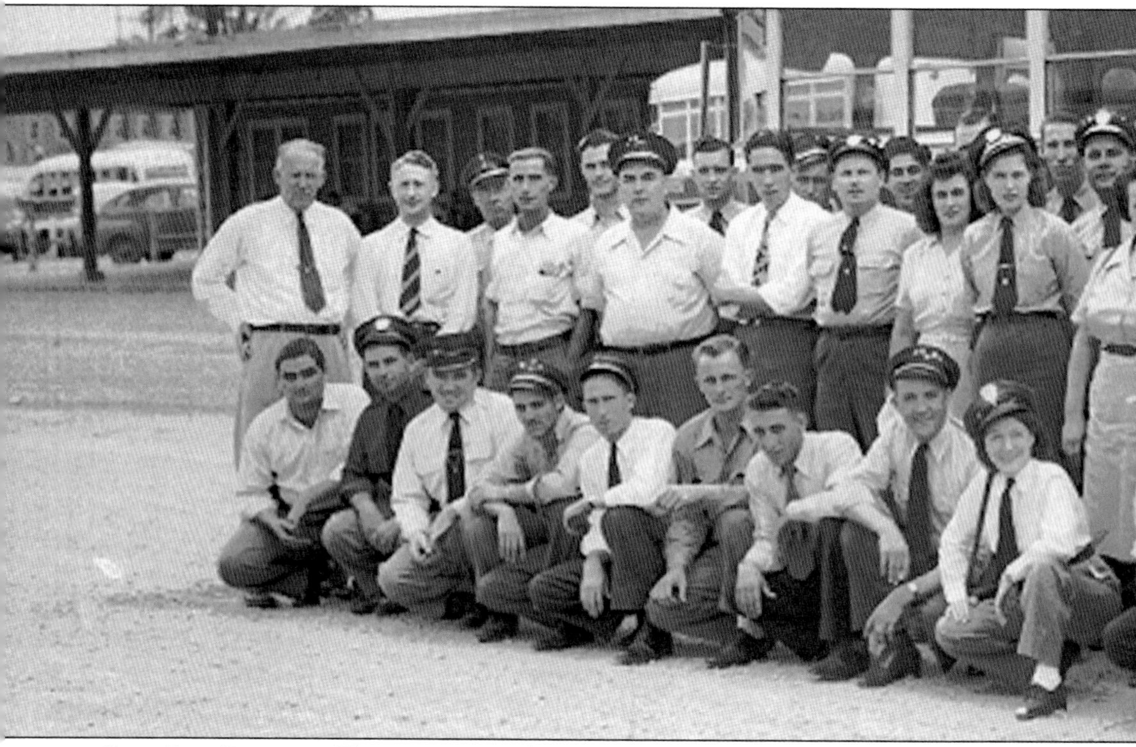

City Bus Drivers. These transit workers had their work cut out for them. Each driver was a vital part of the mass transit system, getting citizens transported in a timely and safe

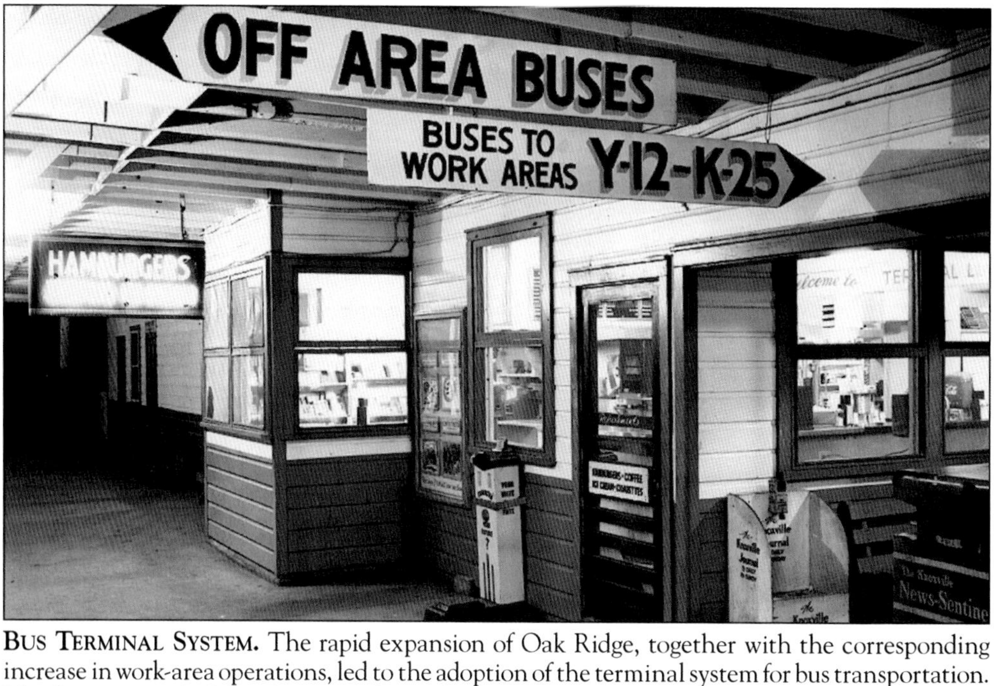

Bus Terminal System. The rapid expansion of Oak Ridge, together with the corresponding increase in work-area operations, led to the adoption of the terminal system for bus transportation. The first terminal, Central Terminal, was located near Townsite and opened in February 1944. With Oak Ridgers working 24 hours a day in the plants, this area was a very busy one.

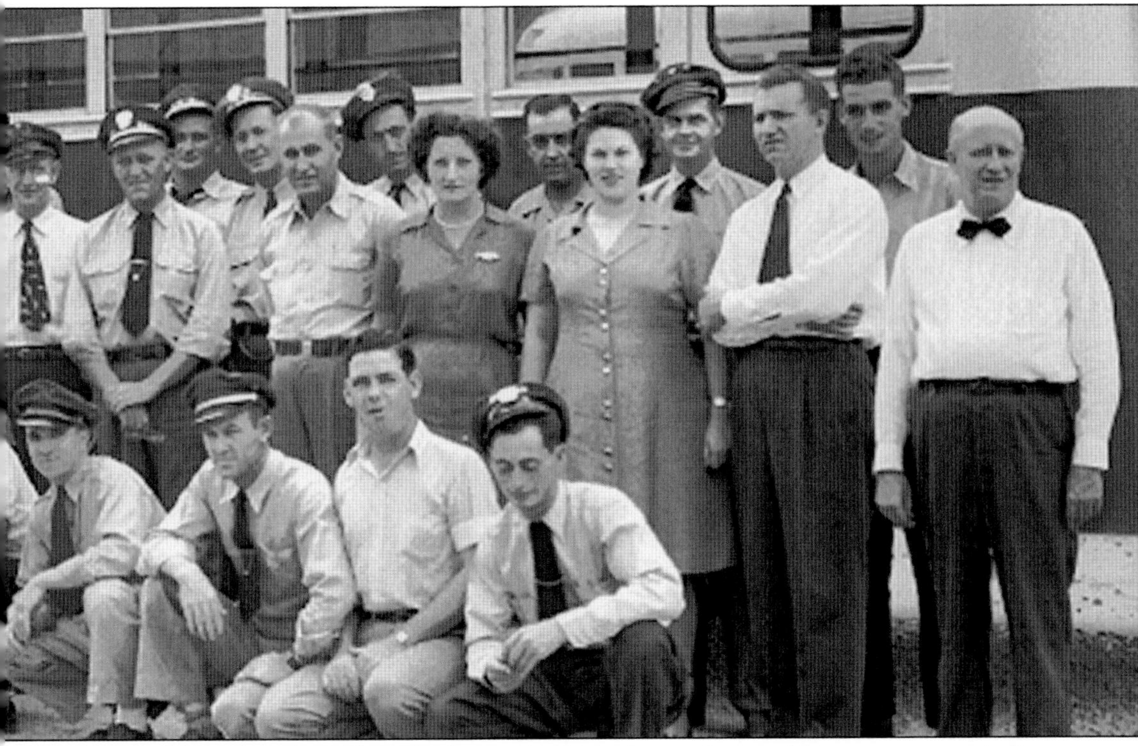

manner. No fare was charged until February 1, 1944, when a charge of 5¢ per person, excluding schoolchildren, was instituted for the Townsite area.

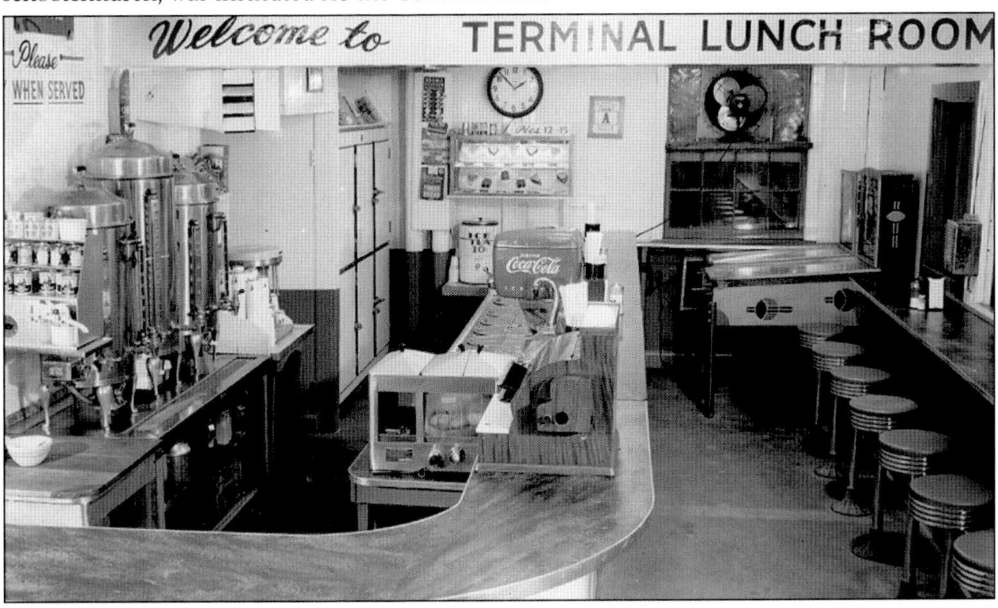

A QUICK BITE ON THE RUN. The Terminal Lunch Room was a great place to grab a quick cup of coffee and a doughnut. All plants worked around the clock, seven days a week. The bus terminal was always busy, with workers coming and going, so the lunchroom got its share of business. Residents also would venture through the lunchroom as they transferred from bus to bus during their travel around the city.

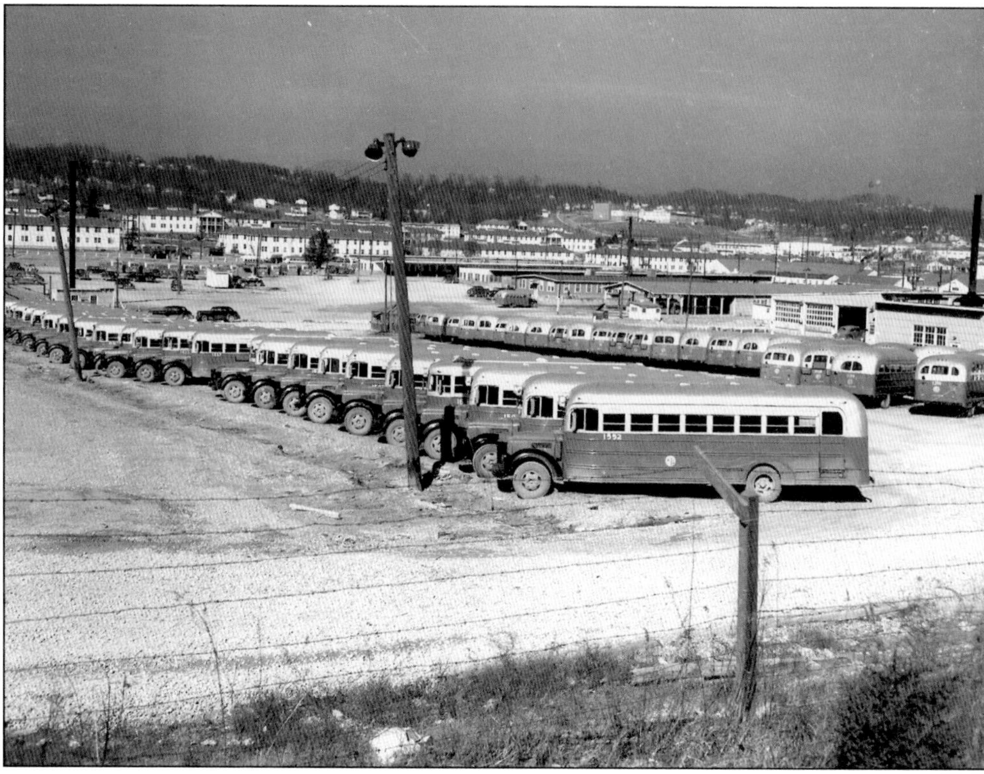

RESIDENTIAL BUS SERVICE. This operation utilized 90 buses to provide regular bus service over 75 miles of streets in the residential area. In March 1944, five Townsite routes were in operation carrying 215,000 passengers. By March 1945, the service had 21 residential routes with a total of 1,335,000 passengers.

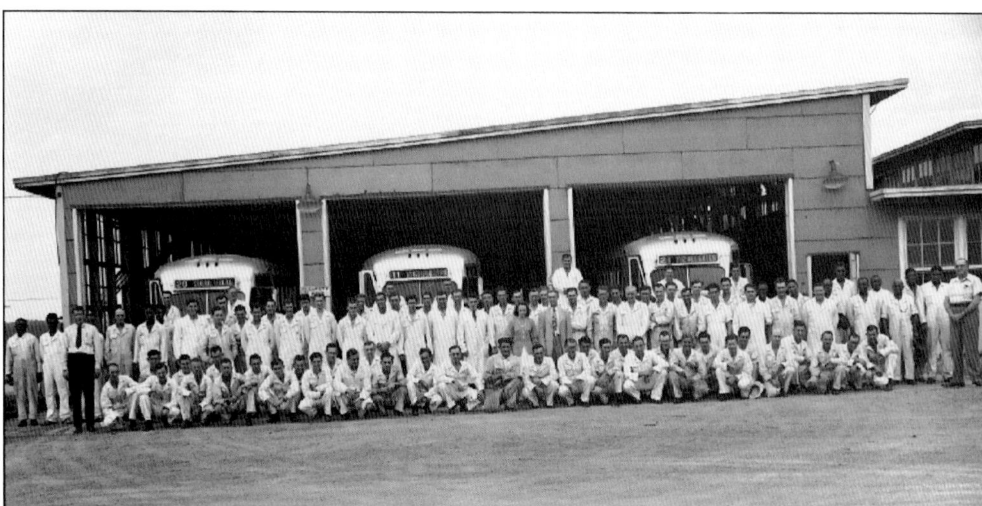

BUS MAINTENANCE CREW. The operation of bus transportation was a crucial part of operating the plants and city. Maintenance and drivers worked around the clock taking vital workers to and from their jobs. In February 1944, the number of passengers that had ridden was 289,465, and at its peak in May 1945, 2,531,281 passengers were transported.

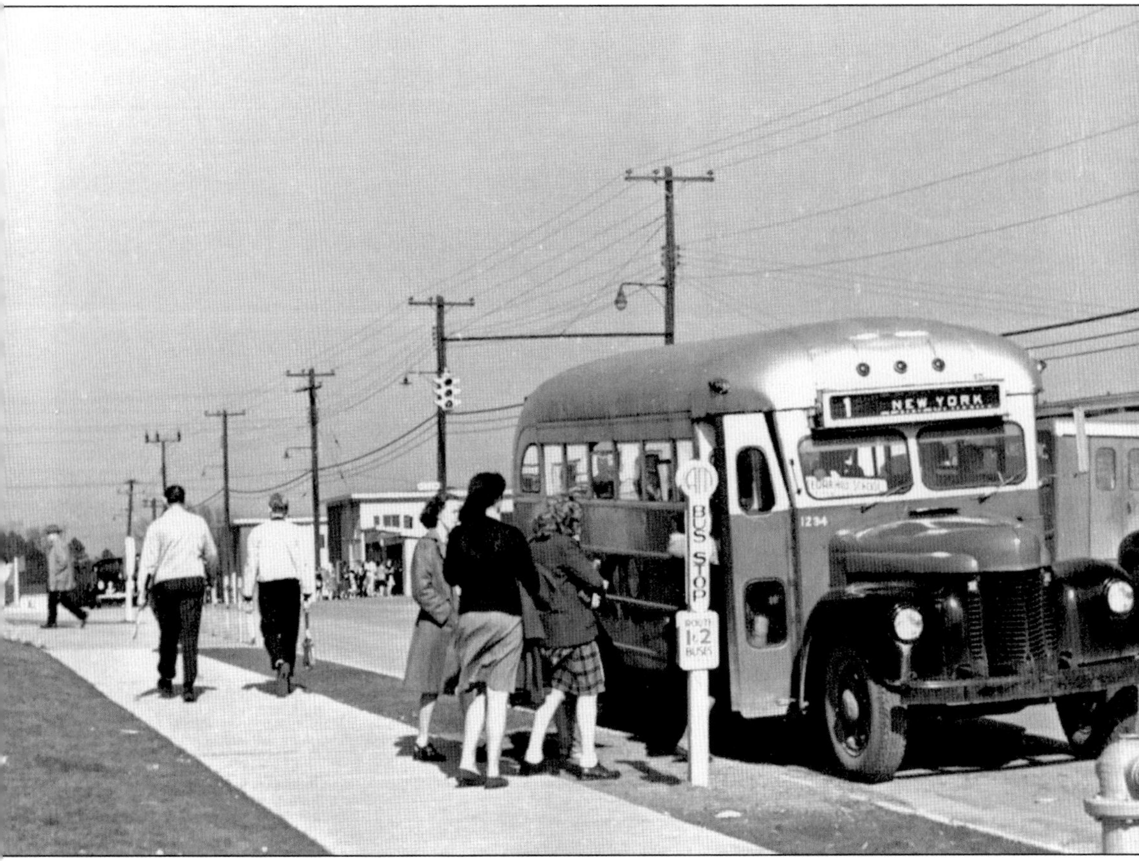

SCHOOL BUS SERVICE. School-bus operations began in the fall of 1943. During the initial period of the school system, this service was performed by the residential-area buses. In March 1944, 500 schoolchildren were transported daily to and from school in buses assigned especially for school transportation. Twelve months later, school-bus traffic had increased to 2,200 passengers daily.

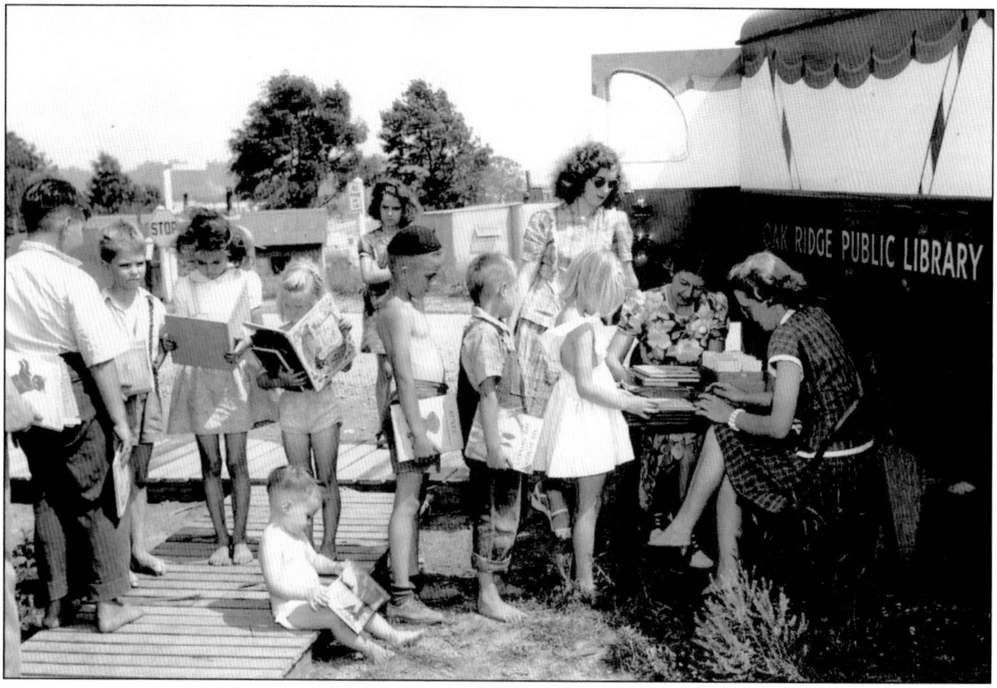

BOOKMOBILE. In this picture, children from the Gamble Valley trailer camp enjoy books from the Oak Ridge Public Library. In summer months, when school was out, the truck would visit the neighborhoods, offering children the opportunity to keep their reading skills keen.

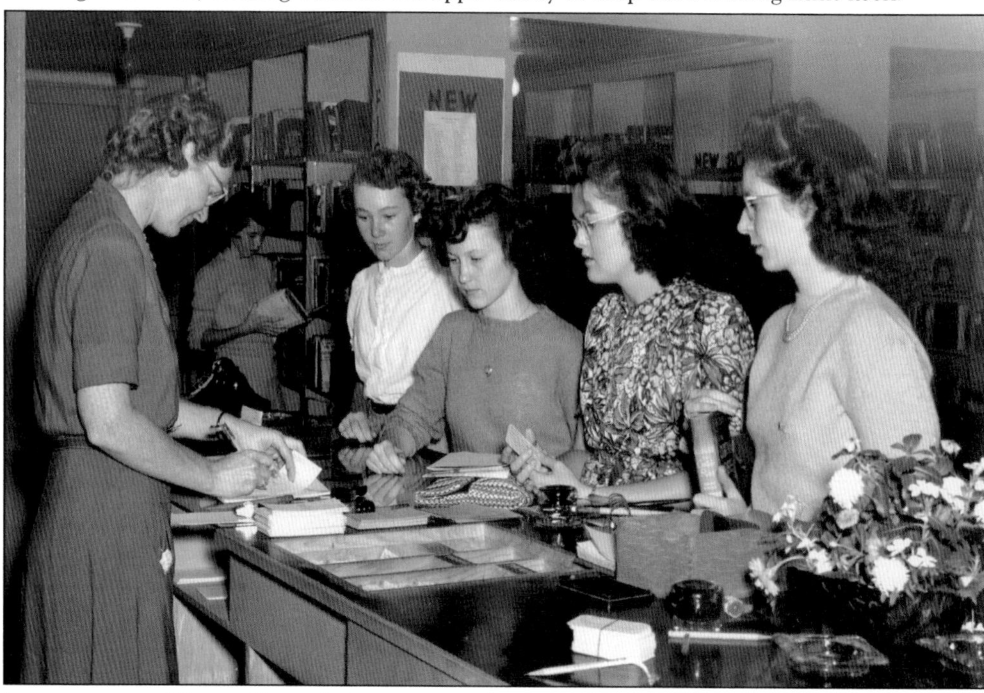

LIBRARIAN AT WORK. Young ladies are completing applications for a new library card at the Oak Ridge Public Library, which was located in Townsite. Students from the nearby Oak Ridge High School would frequent the library for quiet study time and to do research for reports.

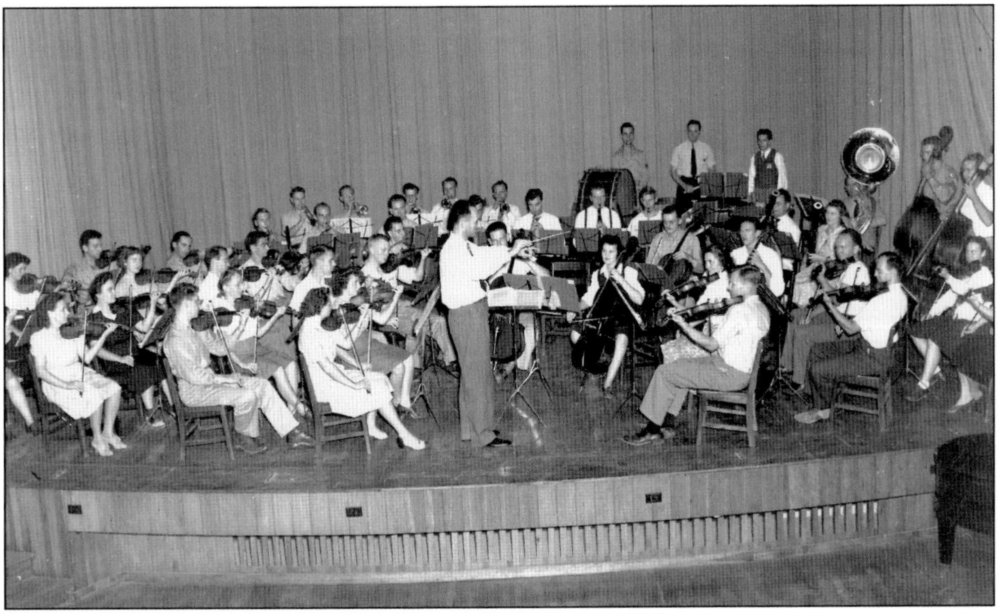

SYMPHONY. Under the baton of Waldo Cohn, the Oak Ridge Symphony presents its first concert, sponsored by the Recreation and Welfare Association. The musical programs were free to the public and held in the Oak Ridge High School auditorium. Ninety members made up the orchestra.

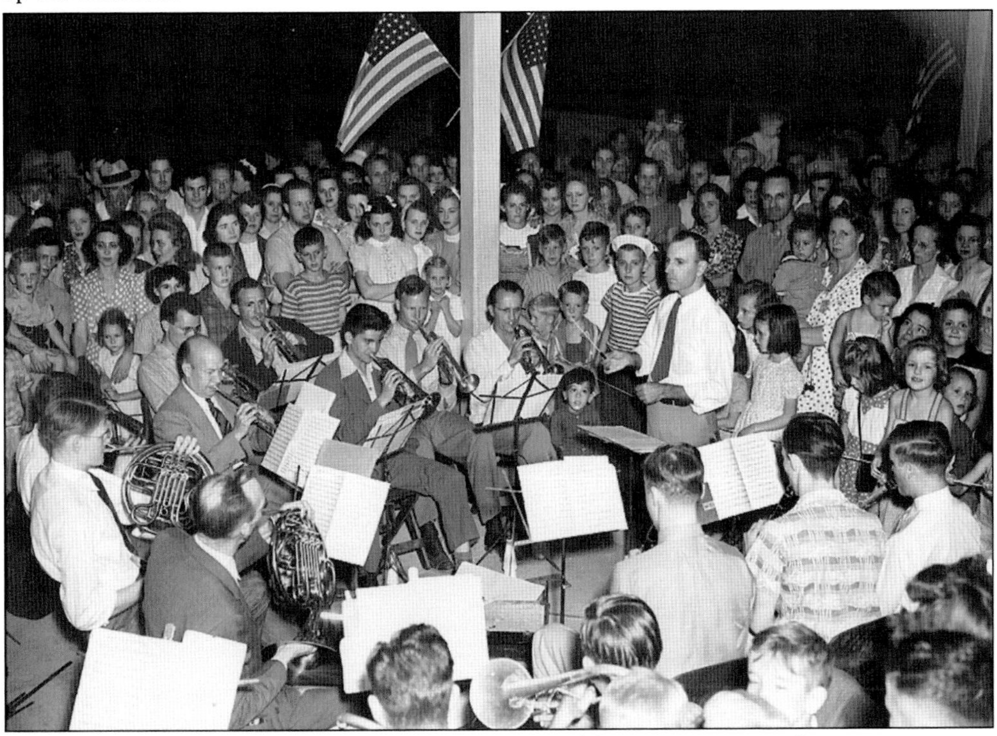

YOU CAN'T BEAT OUR BAND. This July 4, 1944, celebration was one of many community concerts presented by the Recreation and Welfare Association. At right center, bandleader DeForrest Beers leads the players in joyous patriotic songs as the crowd looks on.

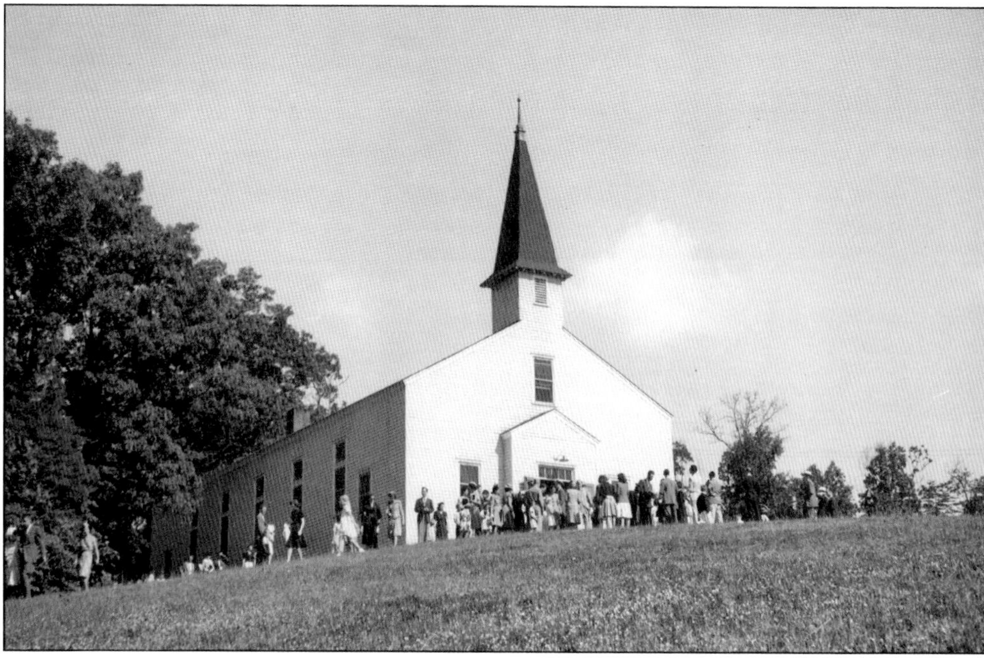

COMMUNITY CHURCH. The Chapel-on-the-Hill, which was the newest church built at that time, was used for all religious denominations. Built by the army, it was dedicated on October 19, 1943. The church was centrally located above Townsite and was attended by families who came to build and operate the plants and the city.

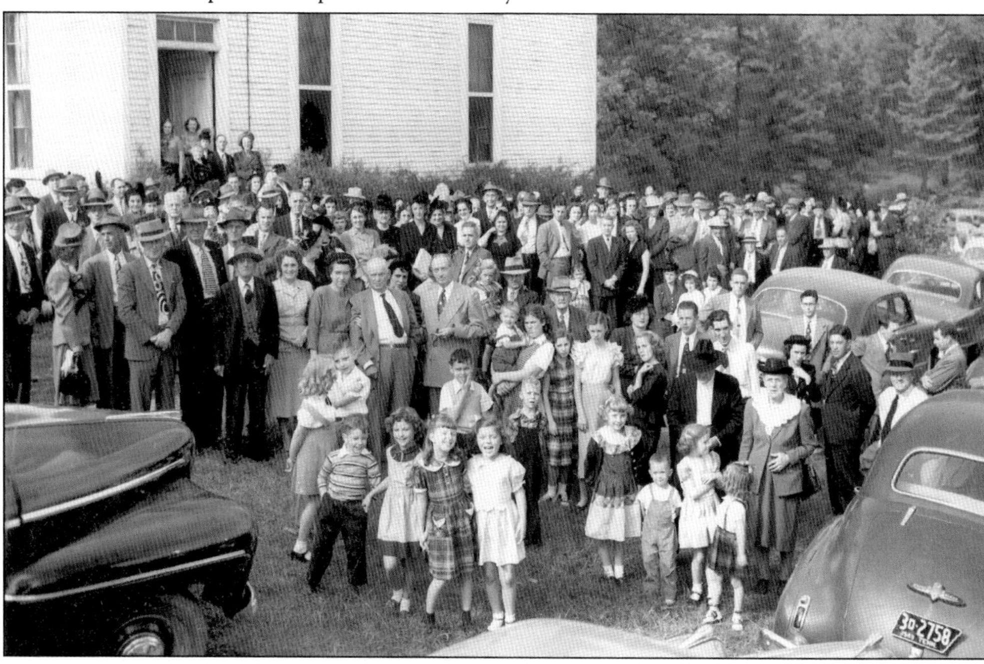

CHURCH REUNION. Members of the George Jones Baptist Church in the Wheat community gather for an annual reunion. Folks gathered from the surrounding area that at one time was prosperous farmland. The government purchased the land to make way for construction of the Manhattan District Project.

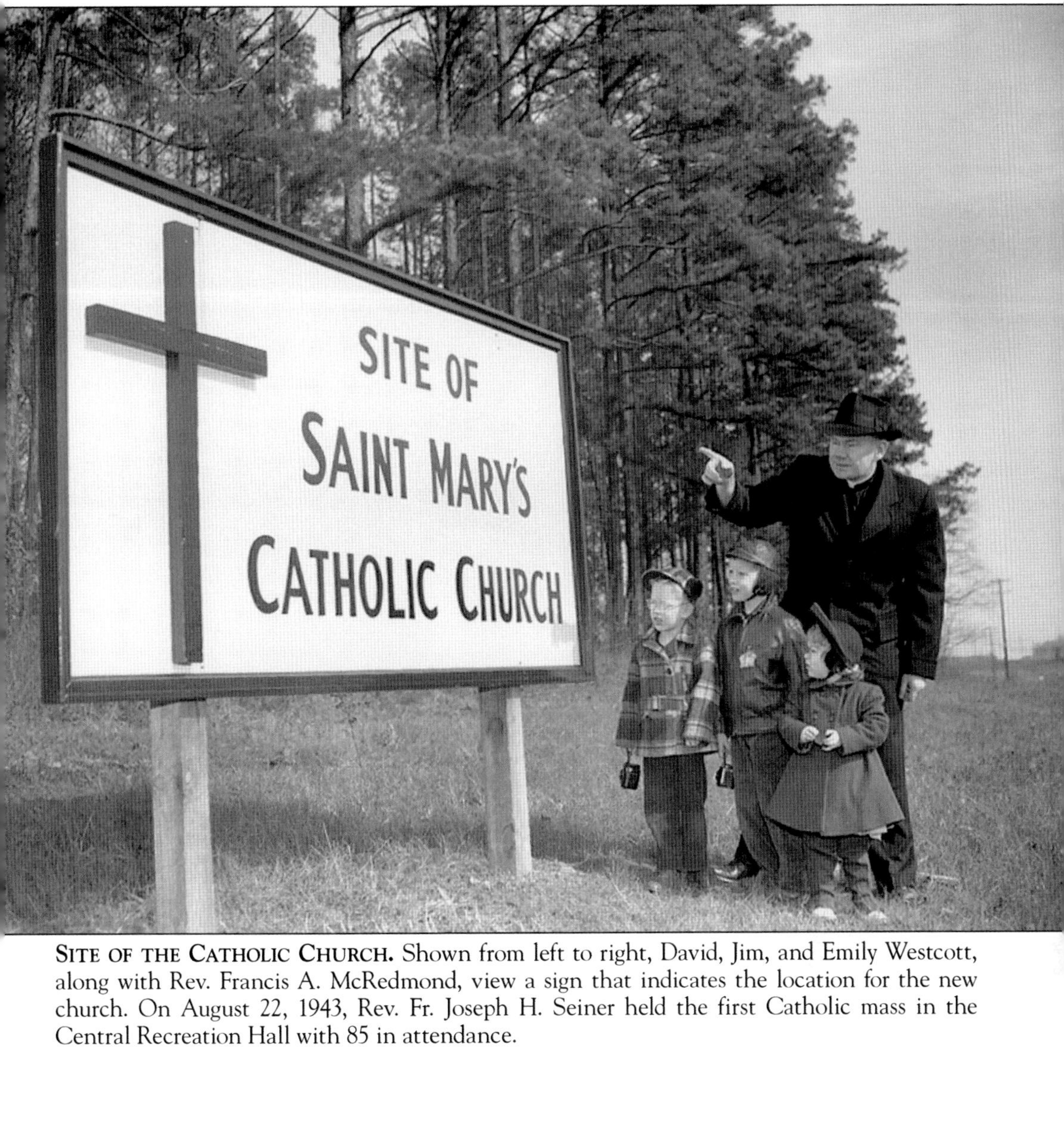

SITE OF THE CATHOLIC CHURCH. Shown from left to right, David, Jim, and Emily Westcott, along with Rev. Francis A. McRedmond, view a sign that indicates the location for the new church. On August 22, 1943, Rev. Fr. Joseph H. Seiner held the first Catholic mass in the Central Recreation Hall with 85 in attendance.

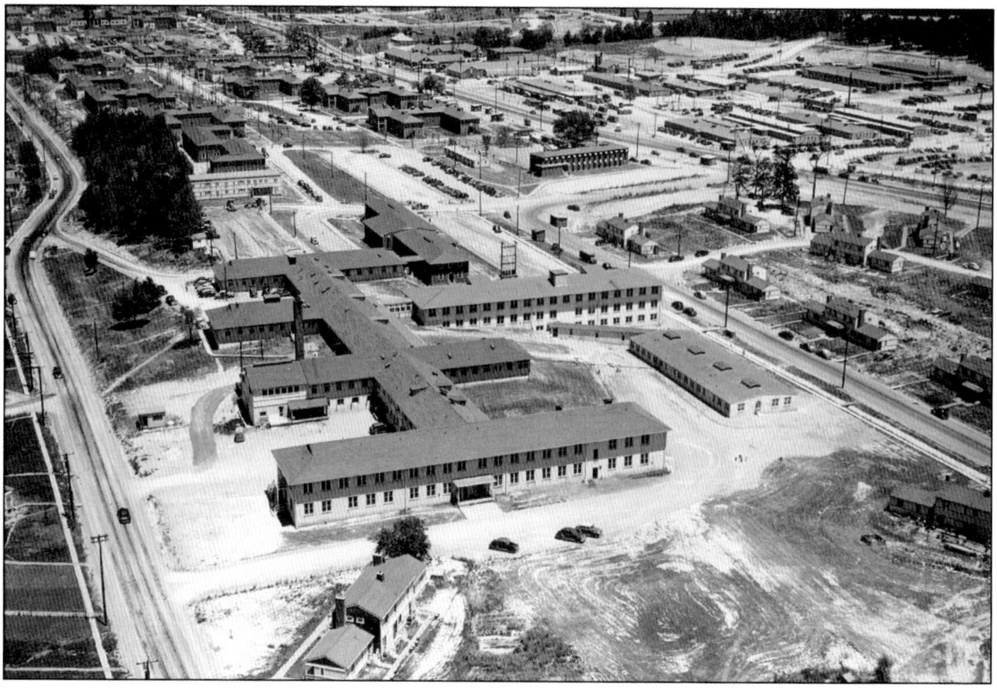

MEDICAL FACILITY. This aerial view looks east. In the spring of 1943, the demand for labor increased, and it became evident that the originally planned medical facility would be insufficient to serve the growing community. Three subsequent additions gradually increased the number of beds to 337. The cost for the fully equipped hospital and its construction came to a total of approximately $1,074,314.

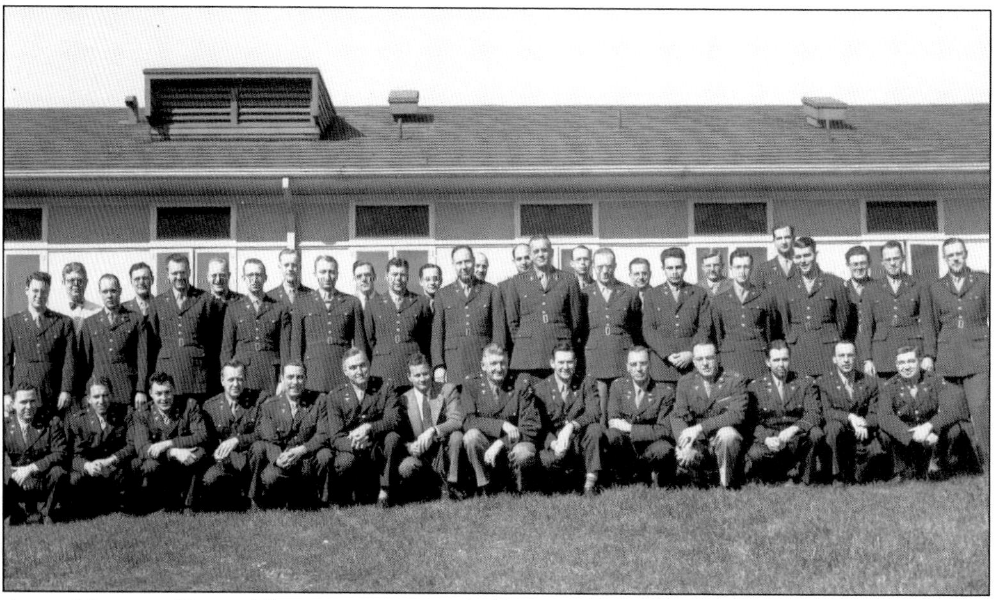

ARMY MEDICAL CORPS. These commissioned officers were selected by the U.S. Surgeon General as the medical force to support the Manhattan District Project. The doctors are standing before the Oak Ridge Hospital, which opened November 7, 1942, with 50 beds. By the summer of 1945, it had grown to 337 beds.

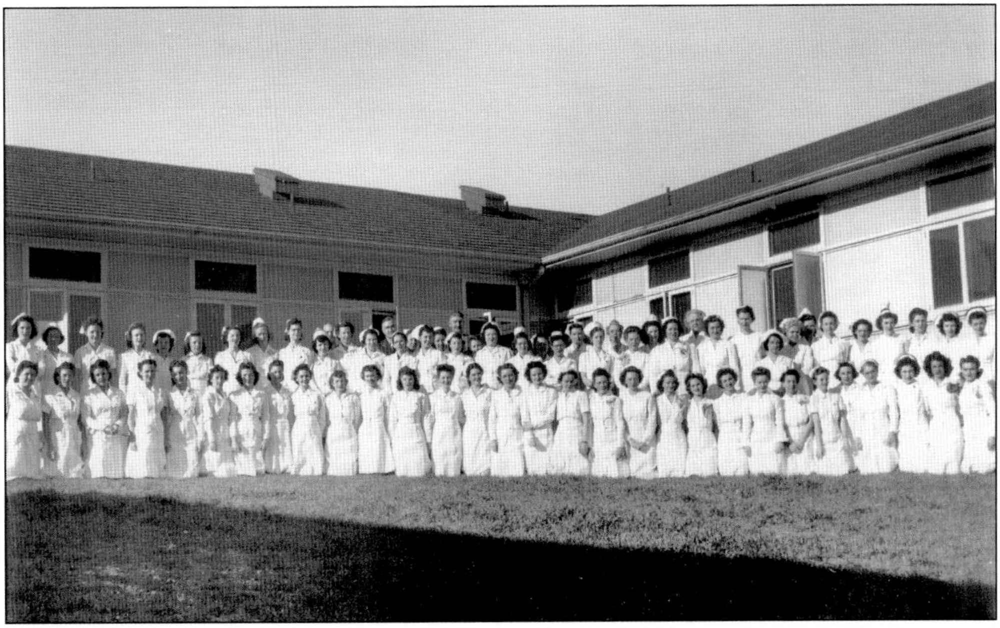

MEDICAL FACILITY NURSES. As the hospital grew from a field hospital provided by Stone and Webster Engineering Corporation to a 337-bed facility, the nursing staff increased steadily. These nurses provided care for patients in the hospital, treated an estimated 6,000 patients per month in the outpatient wing, and provided service to a population of approximately 75,000 persons in June 1945.

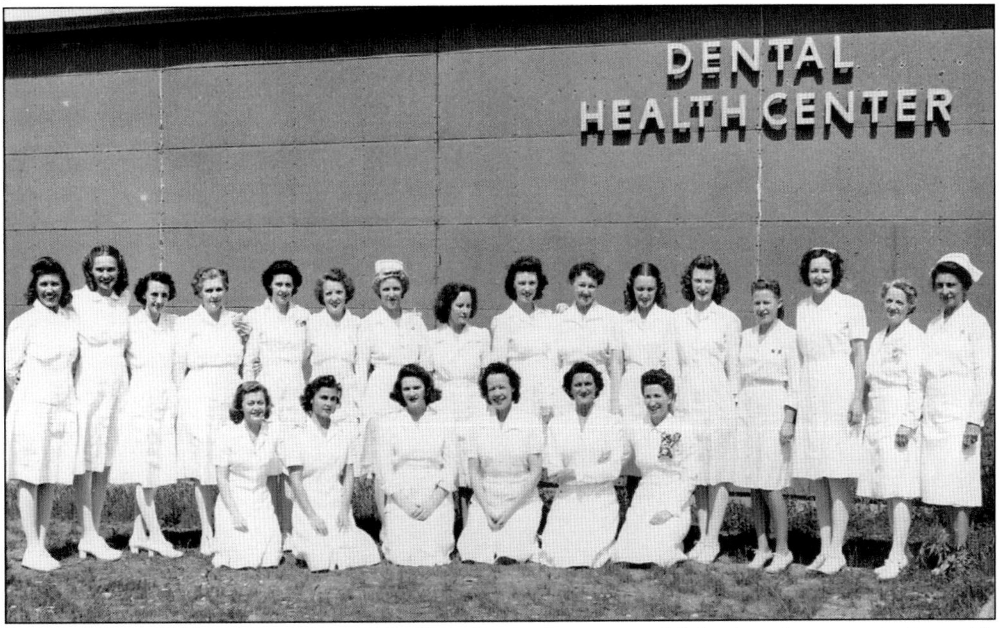

DENTAL HEALTH CENTER NURSES. A dental program was established in close association with the medical program. These women made up the nursing staff required to support the dentists in the community. The dental clinic was a two-story, frame building containing 2 waiting rooms, 21 operating rooms, a large laboratory, 5 small laboratories, 3 X-ray rooms, offices, a record room, a doctors' lounge, a nurses' lounge, and locker rooms.

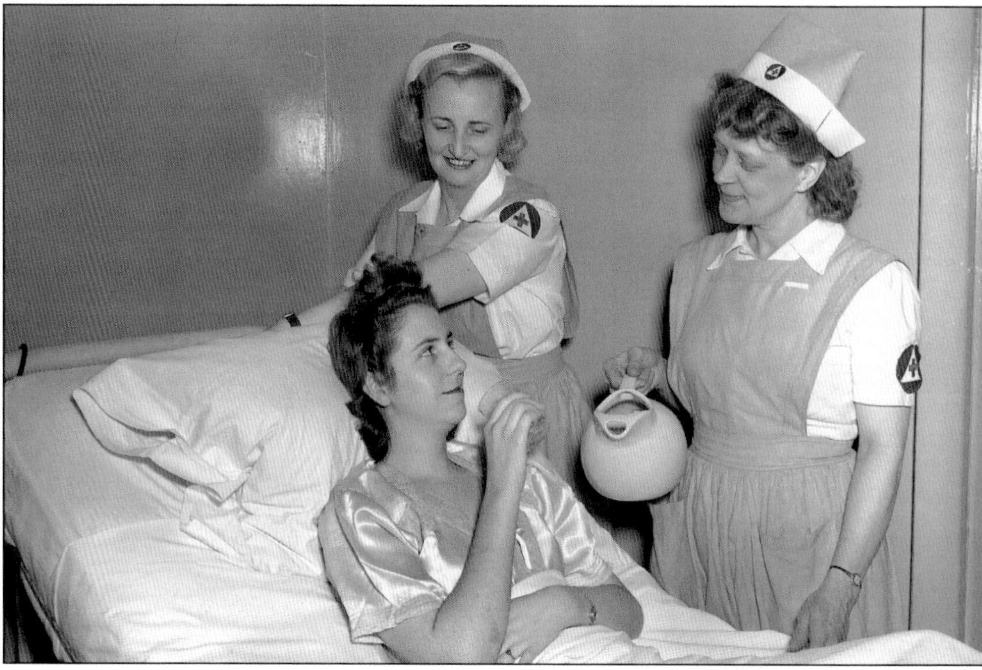

A Typical Oak Ridge Hospital Patient Room. Caring for Mary Jane Plemmons, nurses' aides O. H. Gregor (left) and L. G. De Nagey (right) stand bedside to assist with their patient's every need.

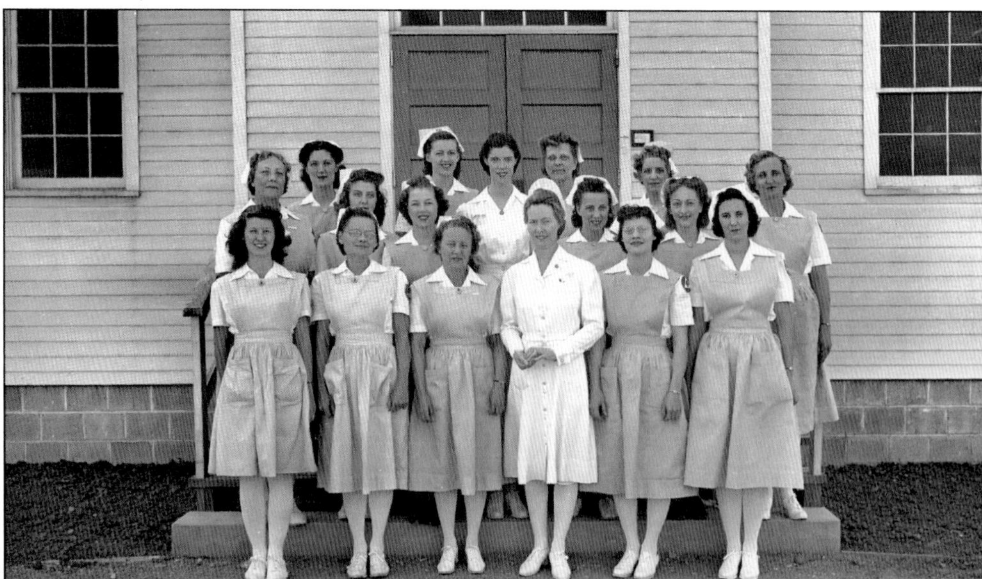

Ladies in Gray. The federal government asked for at least 4,000 Red Cross nurses' aides countrywide. This appeal was succeeded by the following announcement in the February 26, 1944, edition of the *Oak Ridge Journal*: "The call for women to become volunteer Red Cross aides cannot be ignored. With registered nurses leaving each month for the Army and Navy, the shortage of such nurses on the home front is becoming acute." On April 29, 1944, the first class in Oak Ridge of Red Cross nurses' aides graduated.

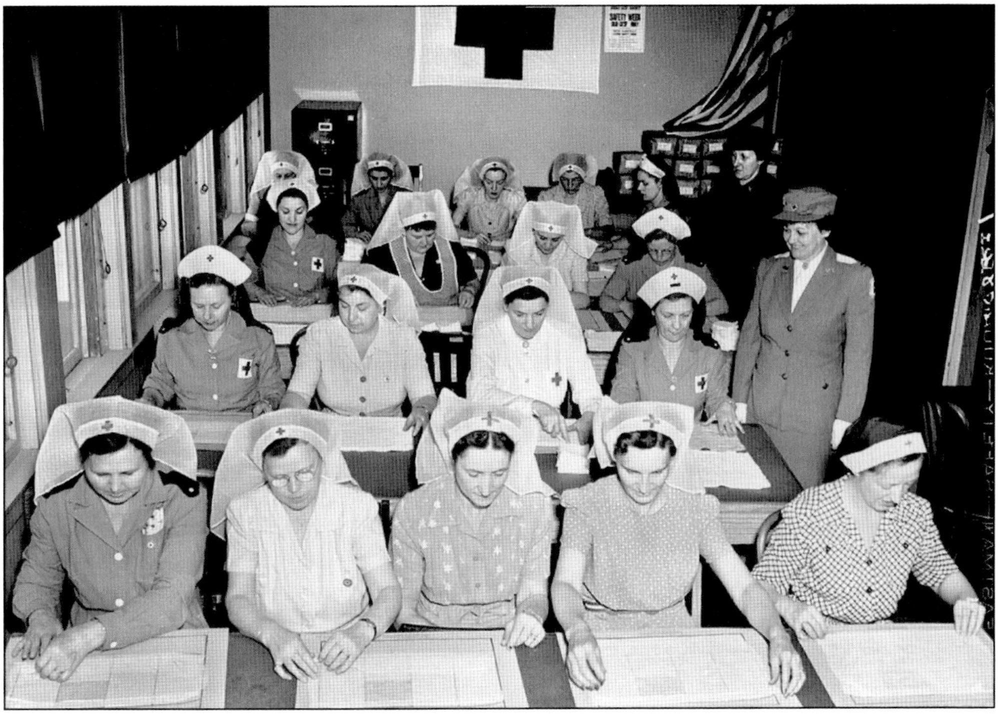

A Call for Help. Not many months after the bombing of Pearl Harbor, the American Red Cross initiated a program to train women to become Red Cross nurses' aides. The purpose of this program was to alleviate the shortage of graduate nurses who left civilian hospitals for service in the armed forces. After 80 hours of rigorous training, they were put to work doing the many routine jobs regularly done by registered or student nurses.

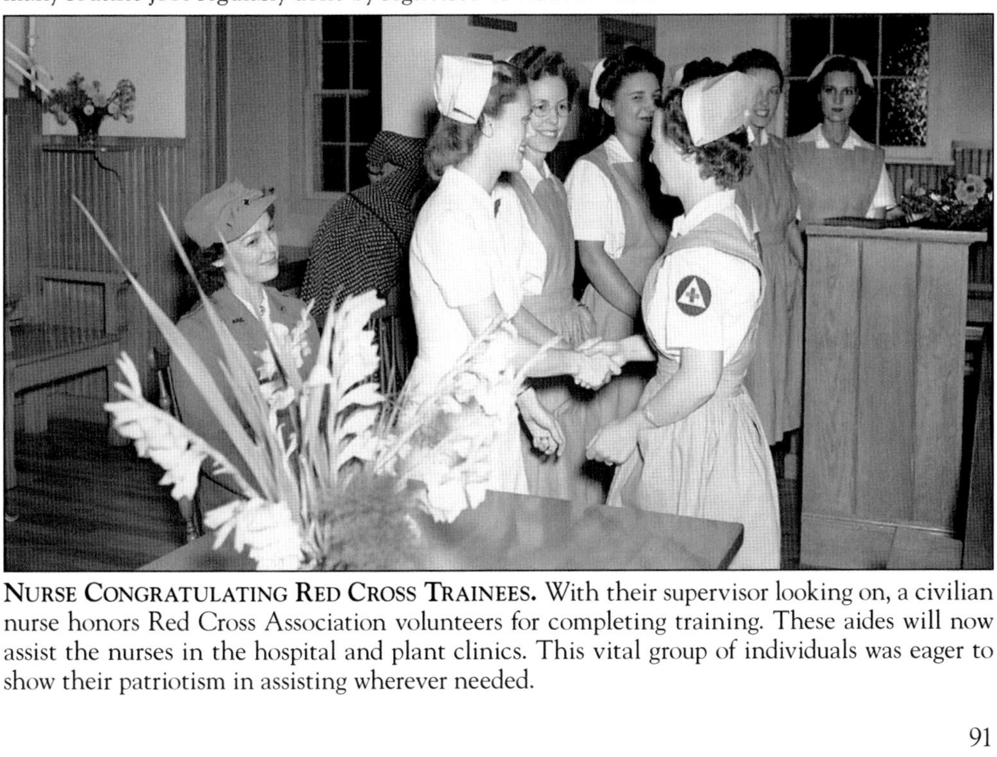

Nurse Congratulating Red Cross Trainees. With their supervisor looking on, a civilian nurse honors Red Cross Association volunteers for completing training. These aides will now assist the nurses in the hospital and plant clinics. This vital group of individuals was eager to show their patriotism in assisting wherever needed.

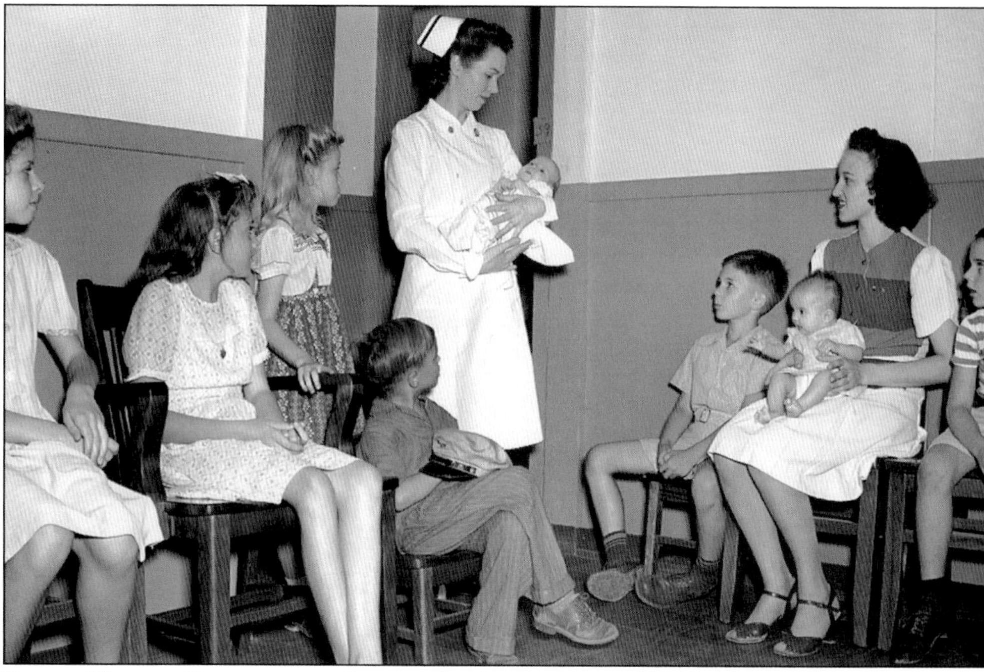

PUBLIC HEALTH DEPARTMENT. Organized in January 1944, the Health Department concerned itself with the usual functions, including area sanitation, purity of milk and water, inspection of food concessionaires, food handlers, and all other matters concerning the health of the community as a whole.

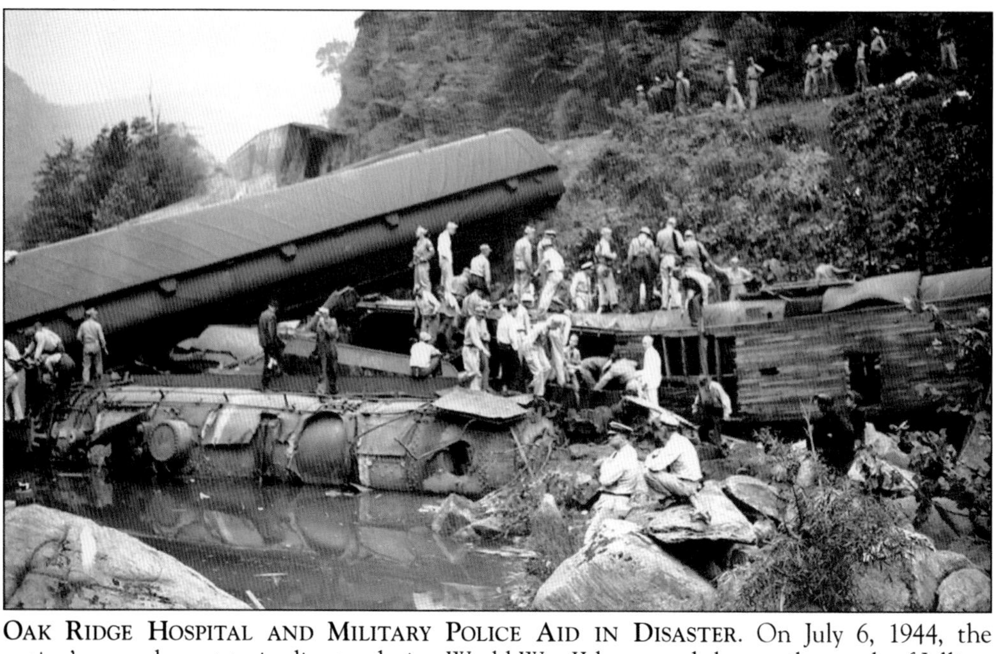

OAK RIDGE HOSPITAL AND MILITARY POLICE AID IN DISASTER. On July 6, 1944, the nation's second-worst train disaster during World War II happened three miles south of Jellico, Tennessee. The military troop train plunged 50 feet to the Clear Fork River, killing 105 and injuring 75. With the assistance of the Manhattan Project Military Police, some of the injured were transported to the Oak Ridge Hospital to be treated by the military doctors.

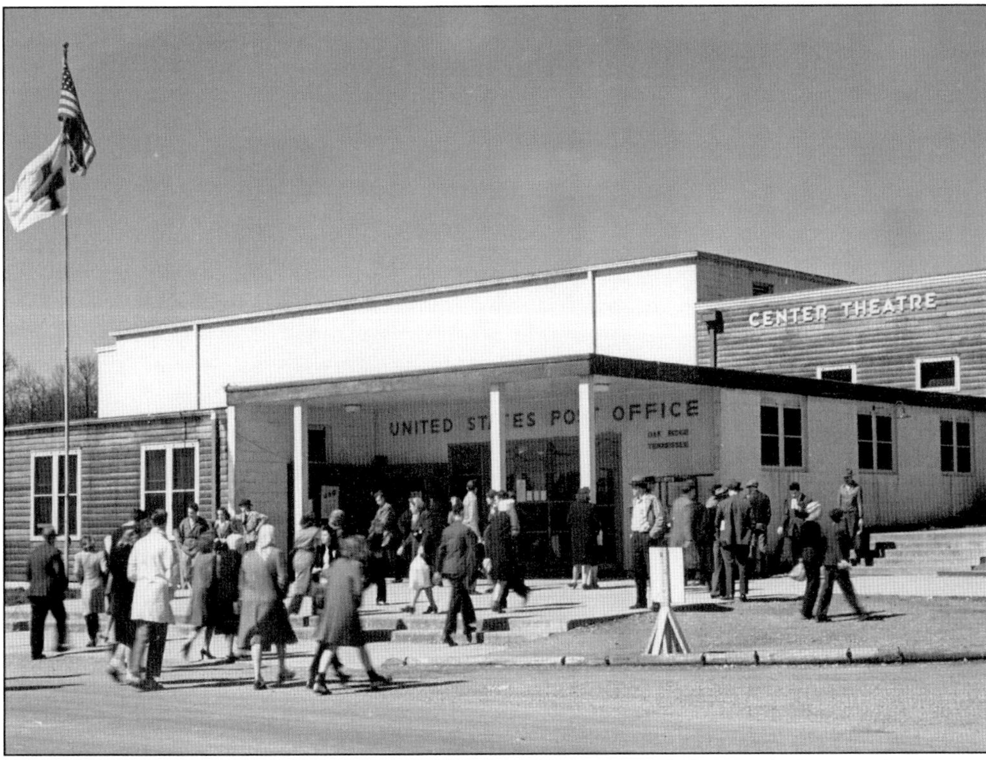

CHECKING THE MAIL. The U.S. Post Office in the Townsite area was always a beehive of activity. One of four on the reservation, it opened on August 15, 1943, with the first postmaster, George E. Bowing, issuing the first letter bearing the Oak Ridge cancellation stamp. On July 20, 1944, the West Village post office opened near the intersection of Raleigh Road and Randolph Road. Floyd Davis was the superintendent of that office.

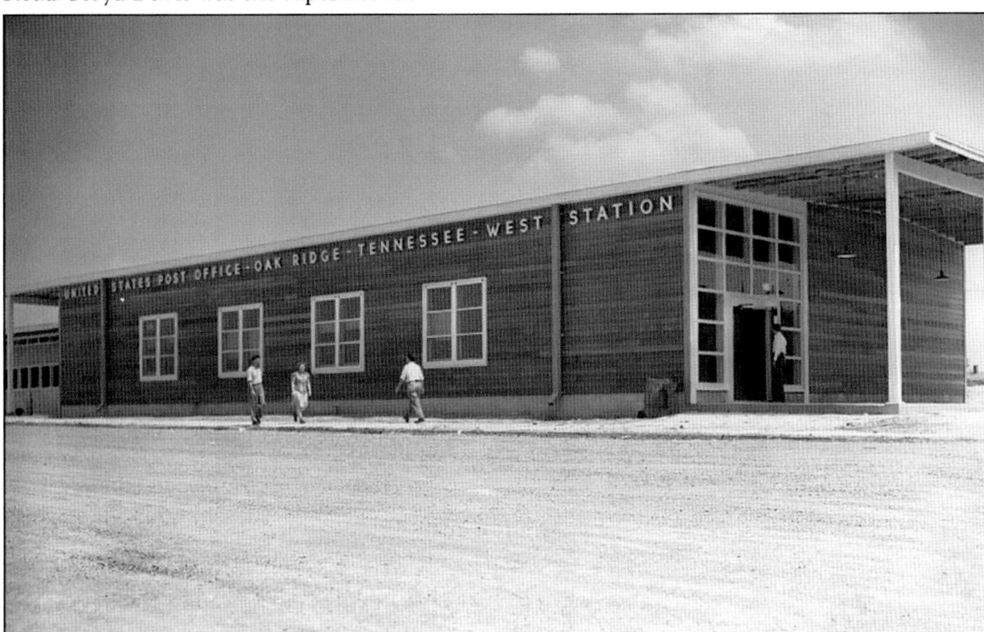

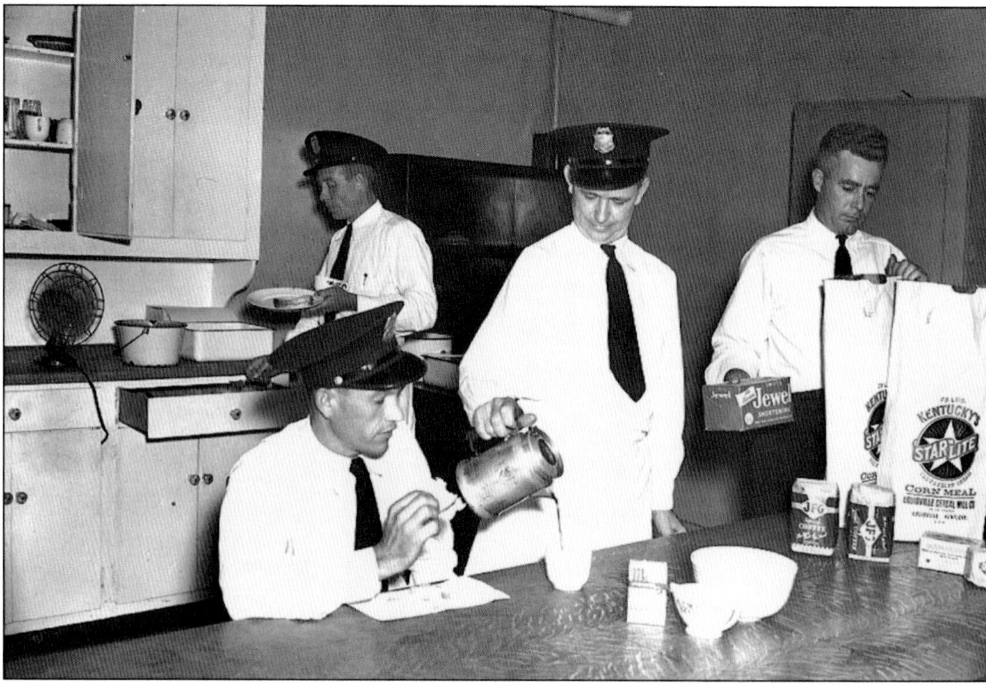

OAK RIDGE FIRE DEPARTMENT. Under fire chief H. H. Maples, a headquarters was set up in an old remodeled barn at Elza Gate. By February 11, 1943, the first fire company, comprised of four men, one 500-gallon-per-minute water pumper, and 1,600 feet of hose, was ready for operation.

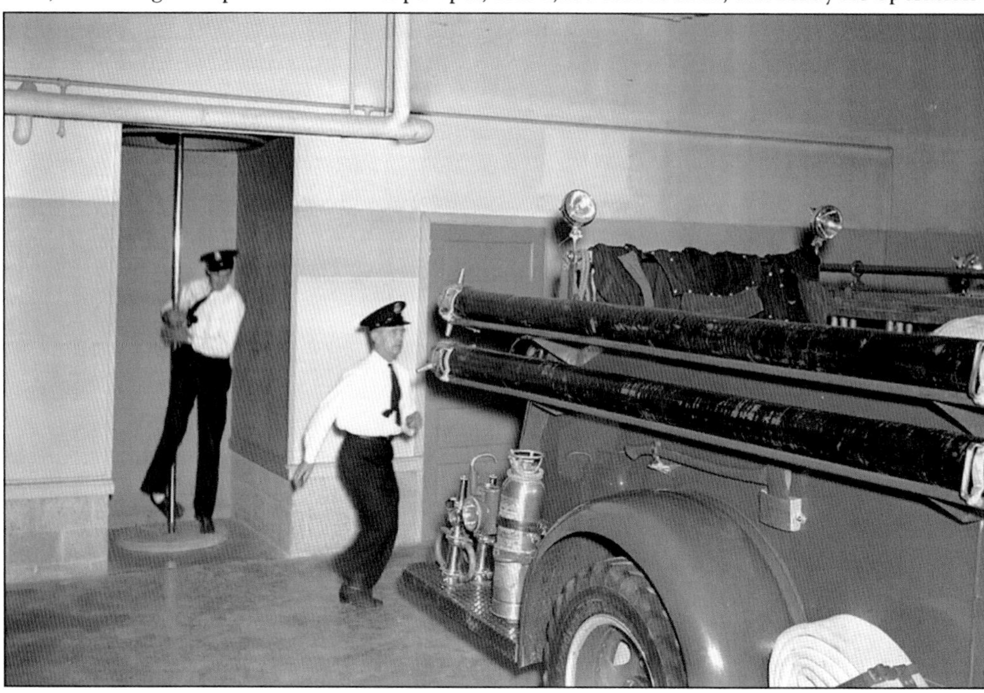

A NEW FIRE HALL. On September 12, 1943, the fire station headquarters was moved to Townsite. At this time, the Oak Ridge Fire Department was the only fire department on the project and served all the restricted and residential areas.

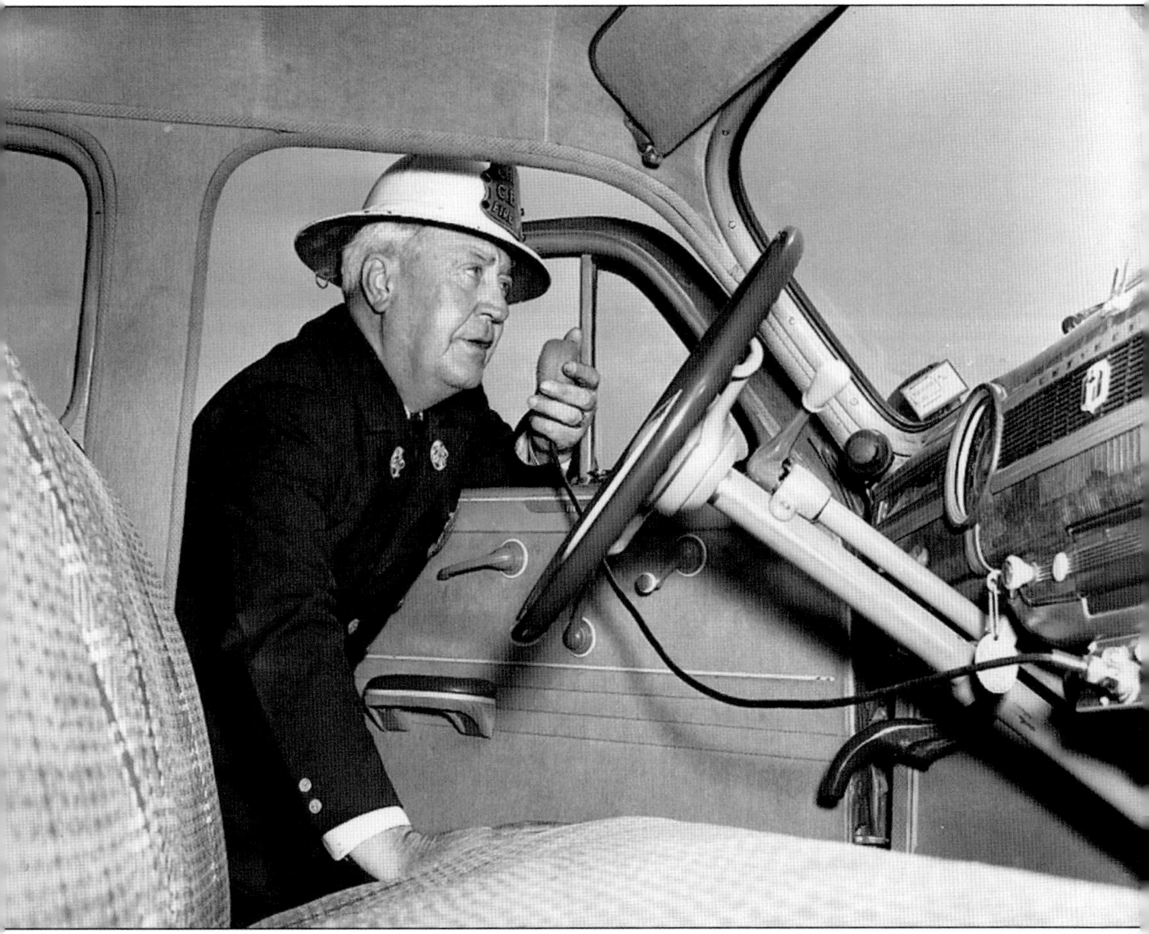

FIGHTING FIRES. Fire Chief Maples is seen communicating with his firemen through two-way radio. The fire department began with four men in early 1943 and grew to 201 men by 1946. Companies were stationed at eight fire halls strategically located in or around shopping centers or highly populated areas.

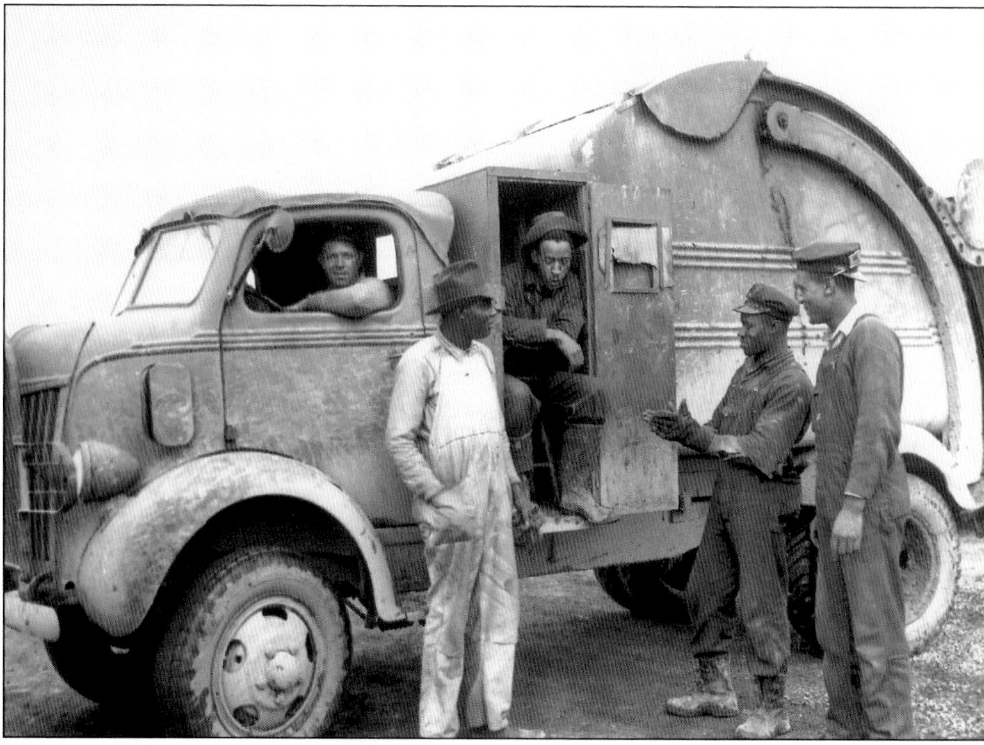

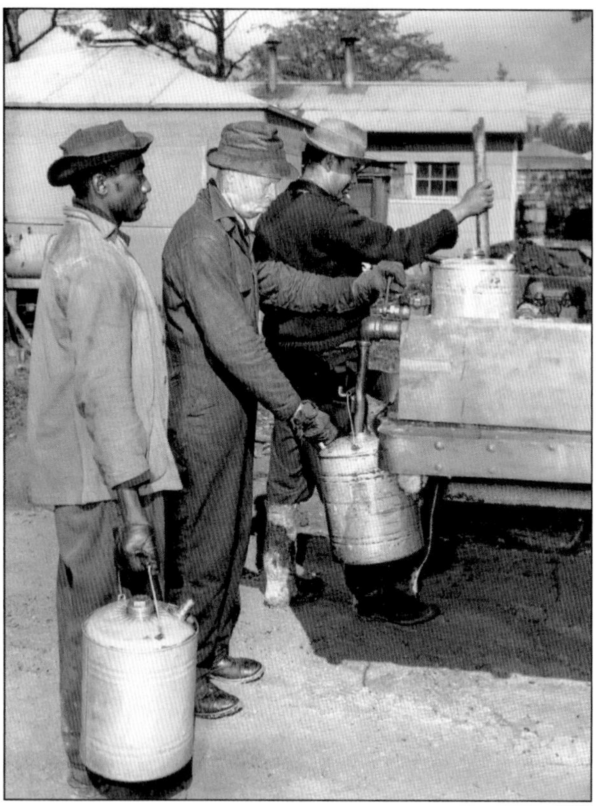

TRASH REMOVAL CREW. Roane-Anderson Company sanitation workers are taking a break from their busy schedule of daily trash pickup. The final destination of the rubbish was a large landfill located in the west end of Gamble Valley, across the street from what is now the South Hills golf course.

ANOTHER FORM OF HEATING. Hutments and Victory Cottages had their own source of heat. Fuel-oil heating was used due to the construction type of these living quarters and their limited floor space. During the summertime, heating stoves were removed from the hutments to allow more room to move about.

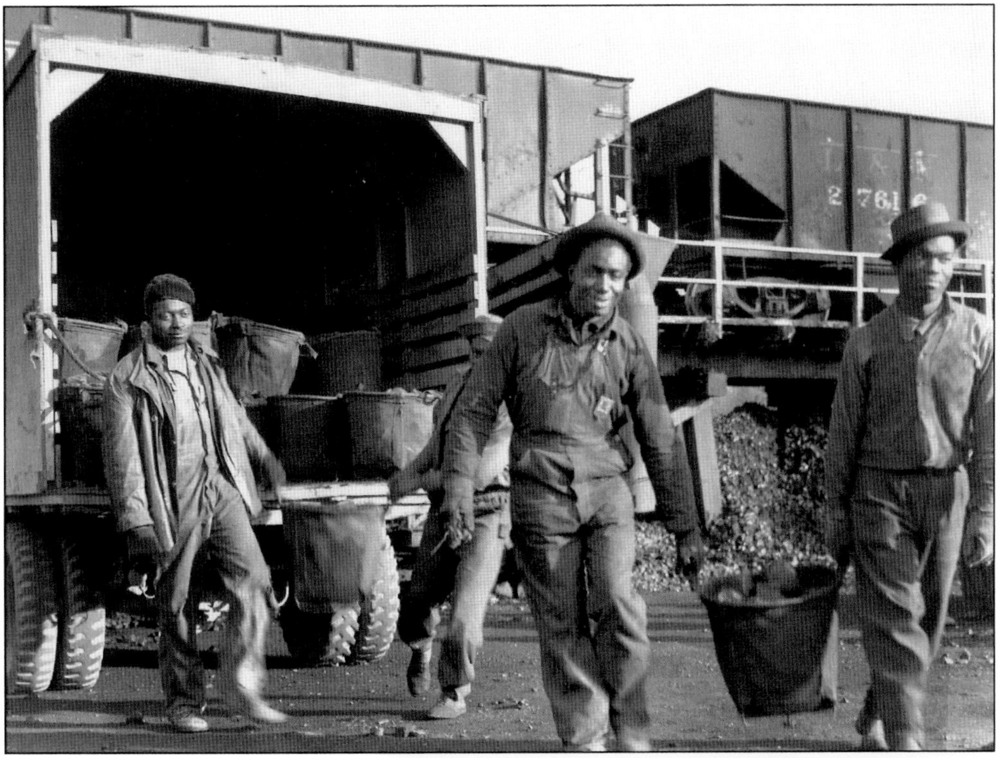

HEAVE-HO. Roane-Anderson Company coal delivery workers are unloading baskets of coal. The train in the background has deposited its load in the coal yard. Once the truck was loaded with baskets, it would make its way to the residential neighborhoods, where the coal was distributed to coal bins at each home.

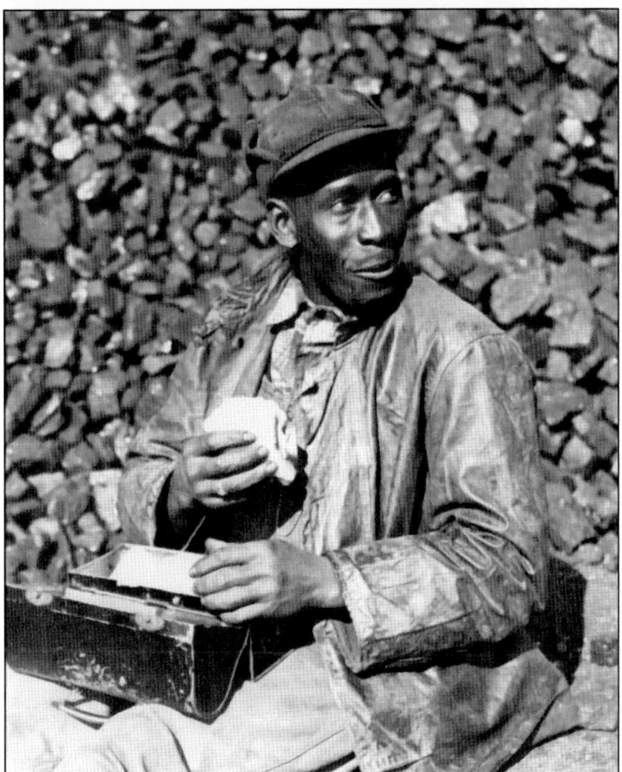

FRIENDLY FACE. A coal worker takes a break for lunch. Coal fuel was the most economical and readily available form of heating fuel for the homes and plants. The coal was mined from Windrock Mountain, located north of Oak Ridge.

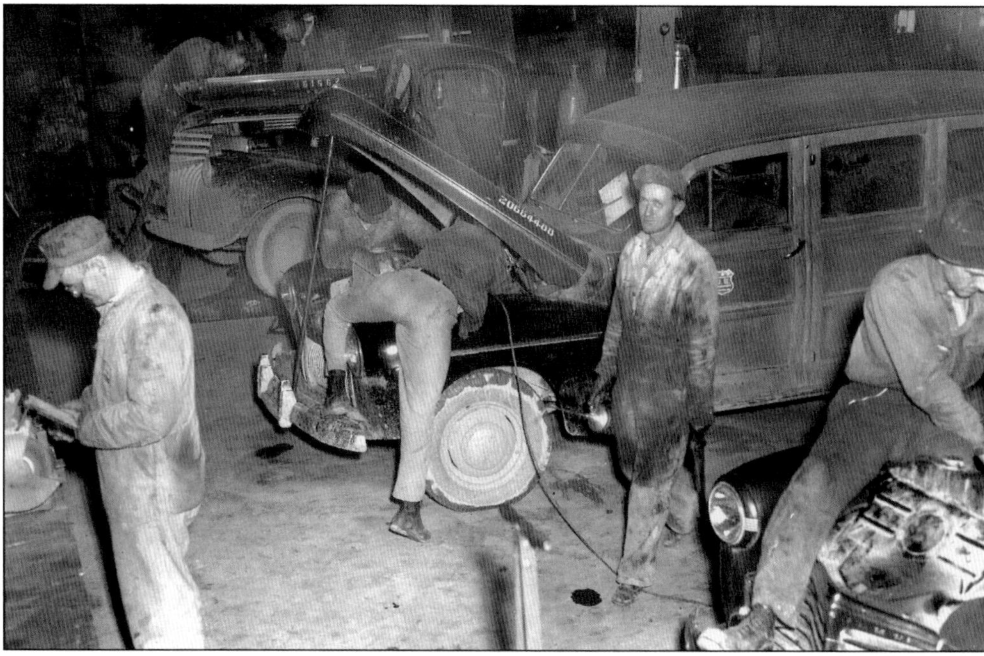

KEEPING AUTOS RUNNING. Unpaved road conditions on the reservation played havoc on trucks and automobiles. These mechanics worked 24-hour shifts performing maintenance on government vehicles used by officials. Manufacturing of automobiles was suspended due to the war effort, so upkeep was important on their assigned fleet.

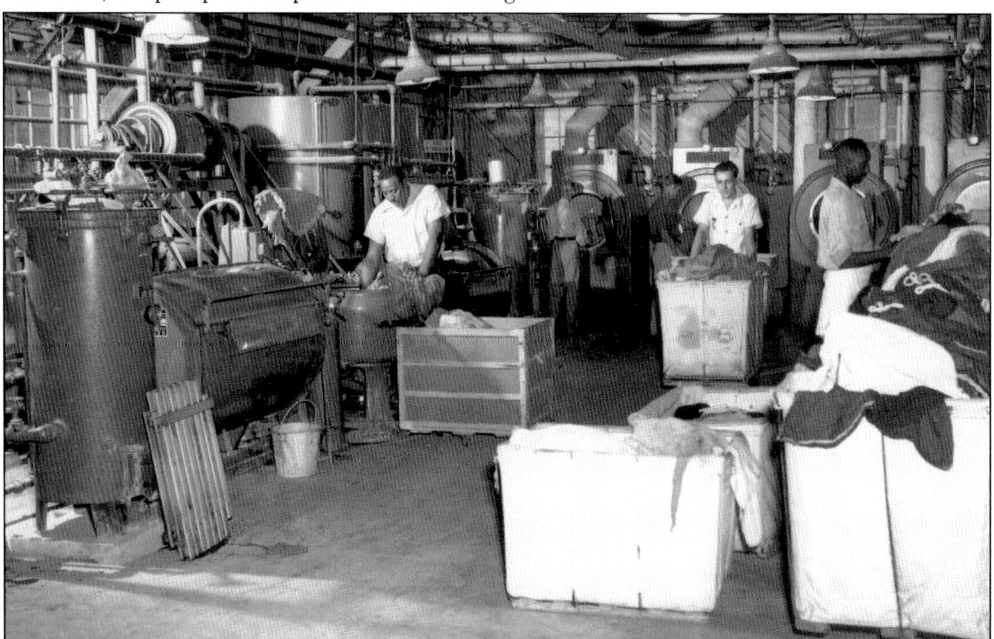

NO TICKIE, NO WASHIE. Being built simultaneously in the Townsite area were the first laundry, dormitory, and cafeteria. Pictured here are workers operating clothes-cleaning machines. Most dwellings (hutments and trailers) had limited space and could not store a washing machine. The cleaning charge was minimal, and fresh clean clothes were plentiful.

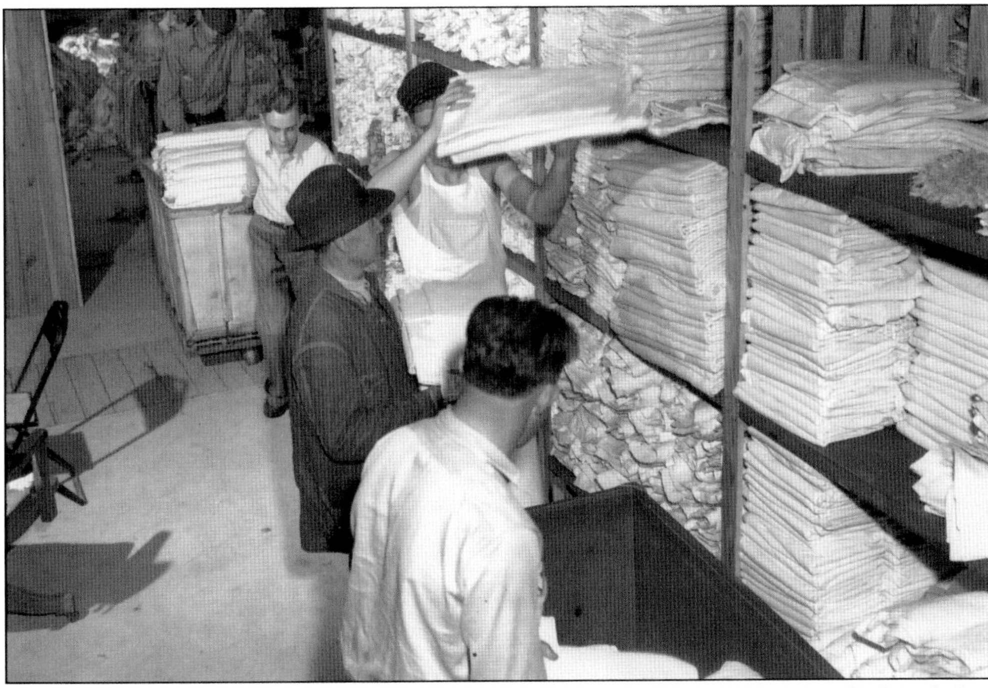

CLEAN SHEETS FOR THE DORMITORIES. Stacks of clean, fresh linen are being stocked on shelves for the beds at the men and women dormitories. These dwellings were occupied by military and plant workers and had hundreds of beds to be made daily.

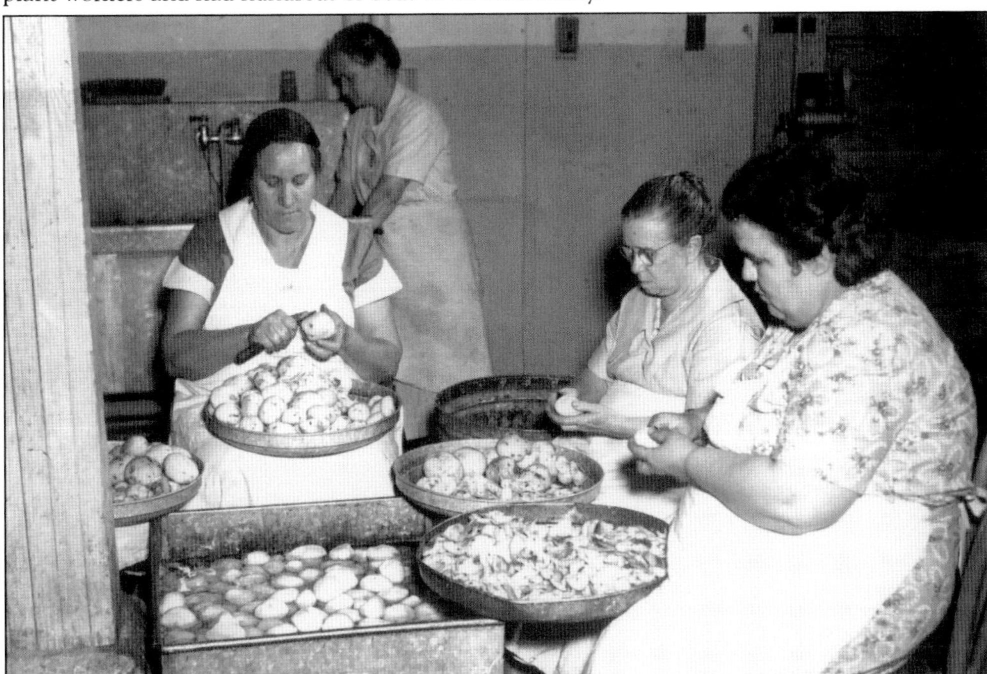

SPUDS FOR THE MASSES. Kitchen workers peeled and washed potatoes constantly for one of five cafeterias in the city of 75,000 people. The best potatoes from Idaho were railroaded in several times a week. Open 24 hours a day, the cafeterias served workers from all shifts.

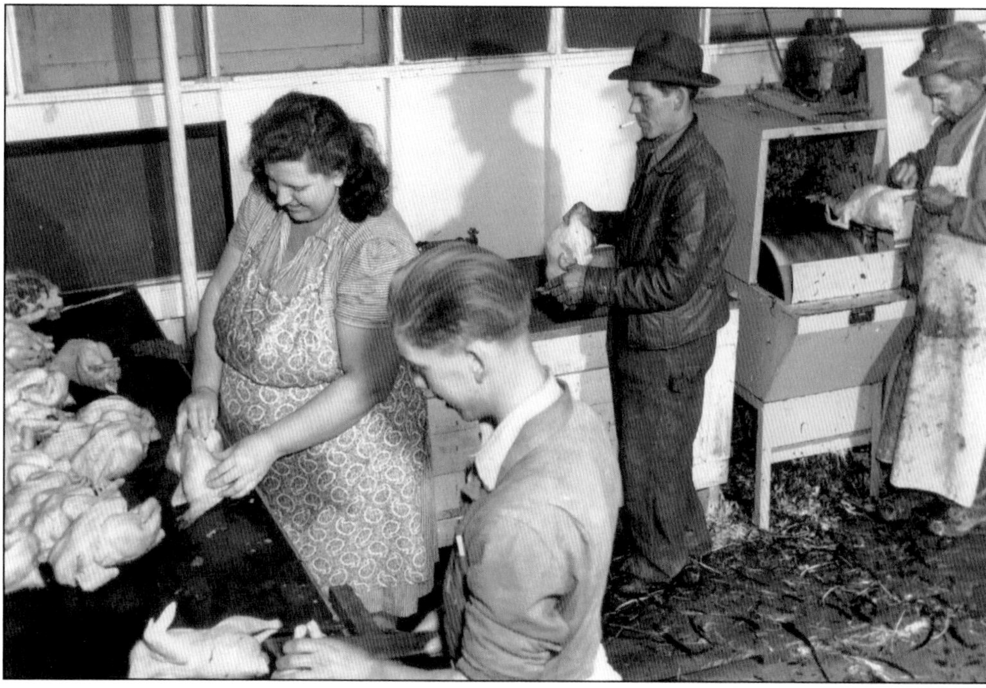

WHY THE CHICKEN CROSSED THE ROAD. To feed hungry plant workers, these poultry process workers are preparing chickens for meals at the Central Cafeteria. The man on far right is operating a defeathering machine, while others complete preparation for cooking.

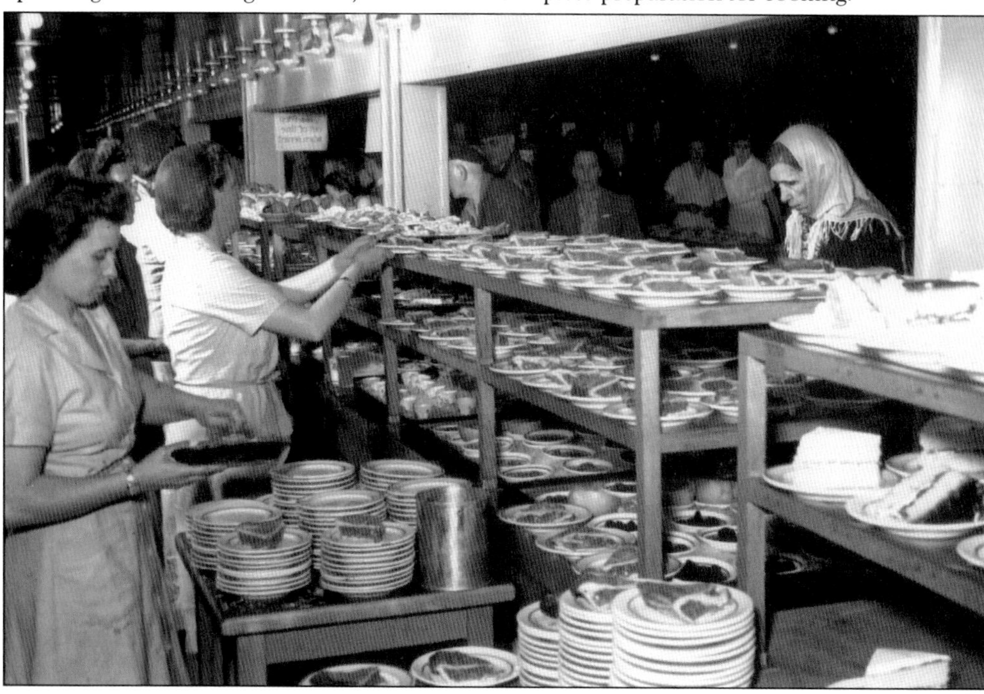

FULL SHELVES. Cakes and pies are being readied for the hungry workers. After a hardy meal, the workers will enjoy freshly baked desserts prepared in the kitchen of the cafeteria. The ovens never had a chance to cool down because of the enormous amount of meals being prepared.

Four

Elections, VIPs, Bond Drives, War Ends

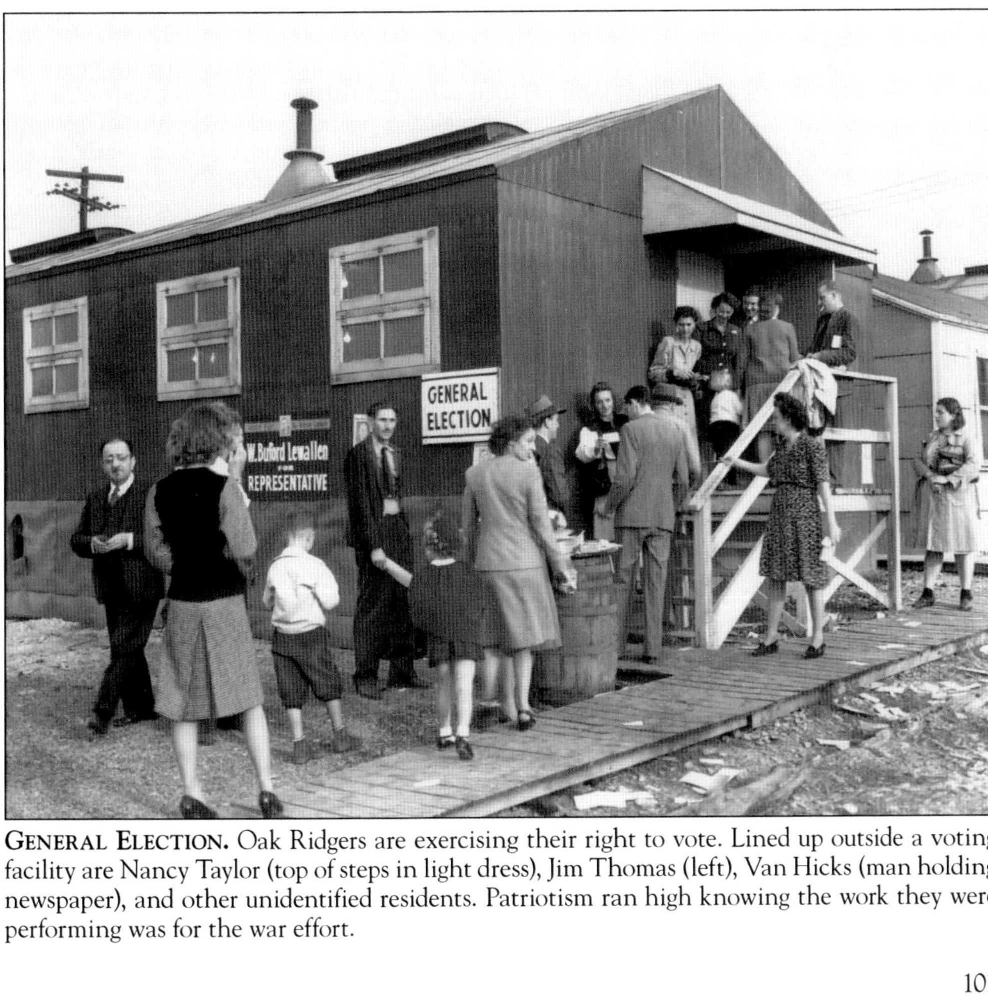

General Election. Oak Ridgers are exercising their right to vote. Lined up outside a voting facility are Nancy Taylor (top of steps in light dress), Jim Thomas (left), Van Hicks (man holding newspaper), and other unidentified residents. Patriotism ran high knowing the work they were performing was for the war effort.

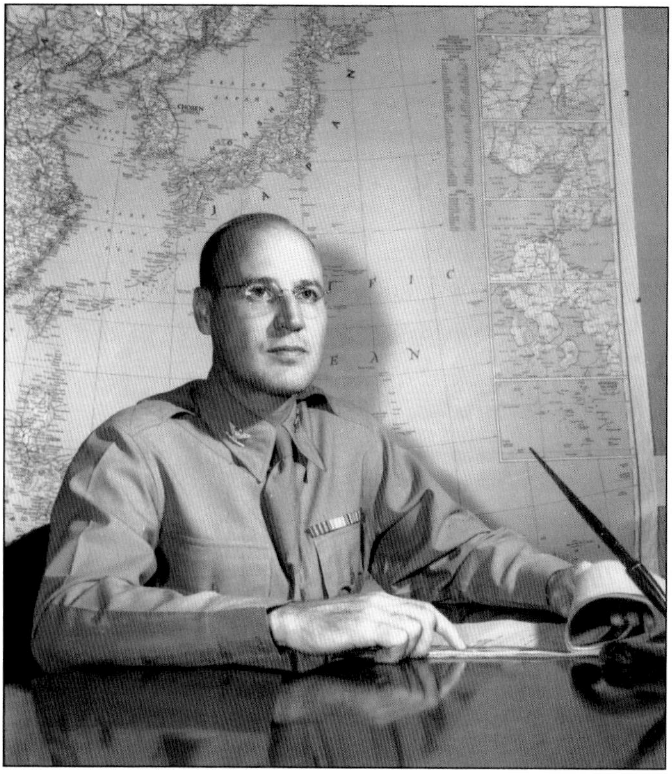

COL. KENNETH D. NICHOLS. In August 1942, the secretary of war, Henry L. Stimson, ordered the Army Corps of Engineers to create an engineering district to oversee the huge construction projects necessary to build an atomic bomb. Col. Kenneth D. Nichols, the deputy district engineer, was involved in the project even before General Groves was appointed chief engineer.

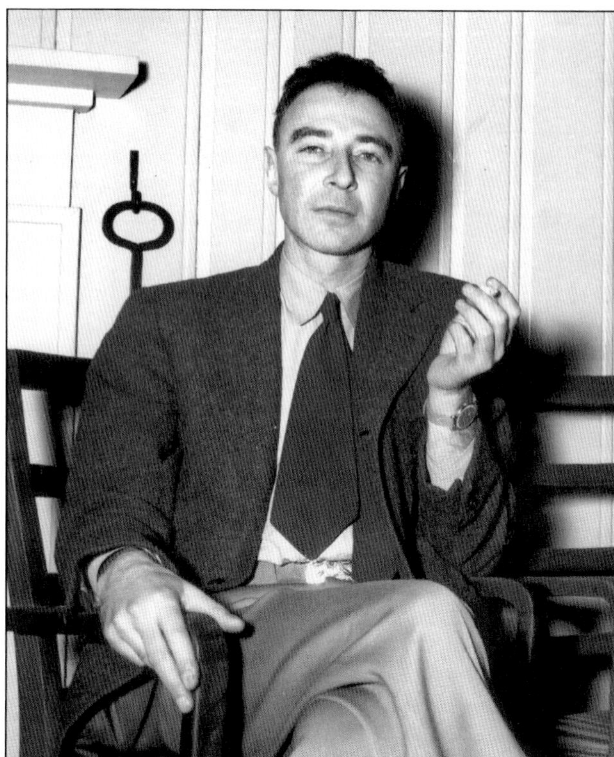

JULIUS ROBERT OPPENHEIMER. Born in New York City on April 22, 1904, Oppenheimer entered Harvard in 1922 intending to become a chemist, but he soon switched to physics. He graduated in 1925 and conducted research at Cambridge University's Cavendish Laboratory. After receiving his doctorate in 1927, he became a professor of physics at both the University of California at Berkeley and California Institute of Technology. In June 1942, Oppenheimer was appointed technical director of the Manhattan Project. On July 16, 1945, he and other scientists witnessed the first plutonium implosion bomb at Alamogordo, New Mexico.

GEN. LESLIE R. GROVES. On September 17, 1942, the army appointed 48-year-old Col. Leslie R. Groves (promoted to brigadier general six days later) to be director of the Manhattan Project, which created the atomic bomb. The decision to locate the nuclear project in East Tennessee was made personally by General Groves. Using the experience he gained while directing the construction of the Pentagon, he had impressive credentials and also had strong administrative abilities.

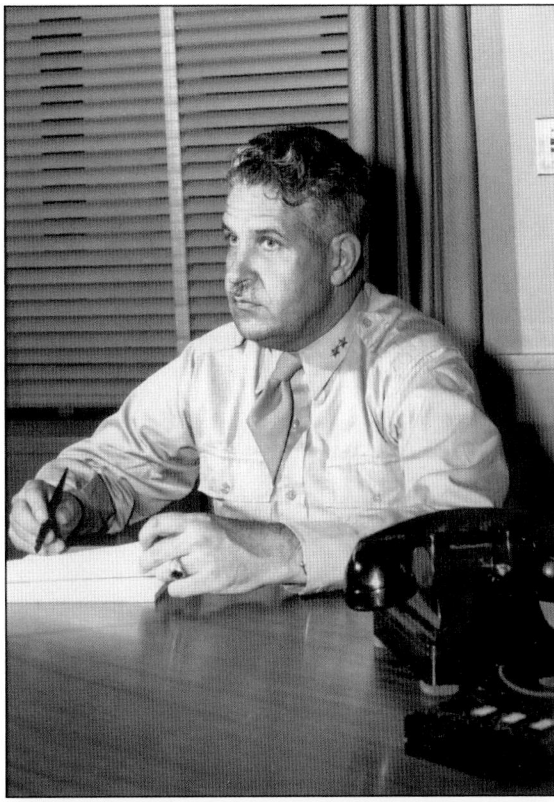

HANDING OVER CONTROL. The Oak Ridge community was transferred from military to civilian control in 1946. Maj. Gen. Leslie R. Groves (left) met with Tennessee Valley Authority chairman David E. Lilienthal in Oak Ridge on October 1, 1946. On October 29, 1946, Lilienthal was appointed by Pres. Harry S. Truman to be chairman of the newly formed Atomic Energy Commission.

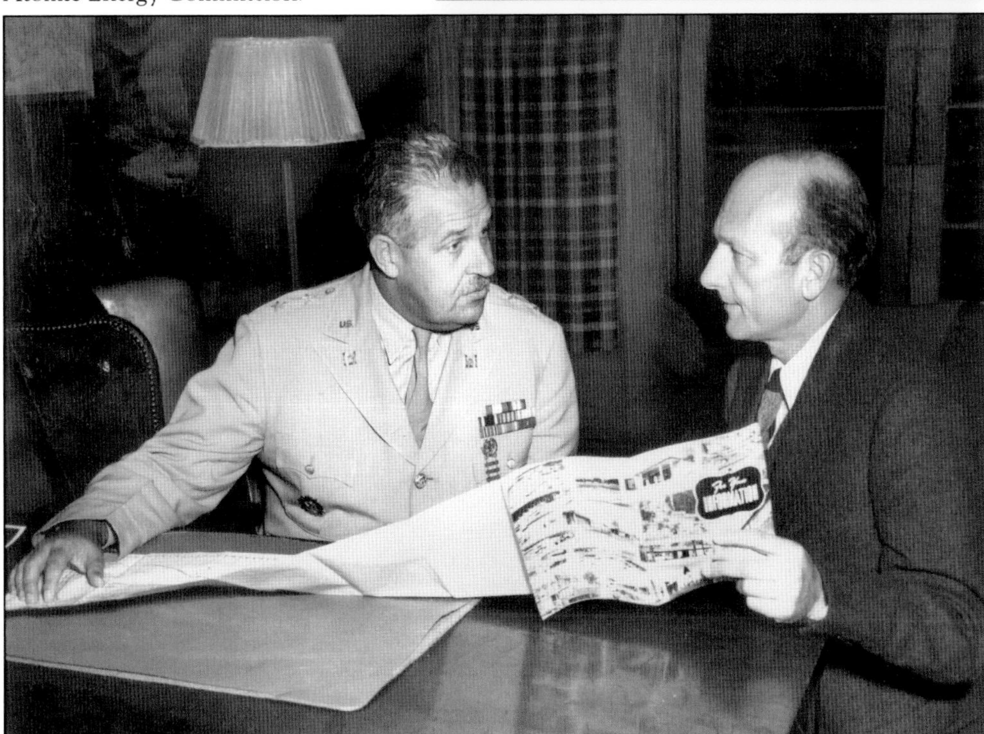

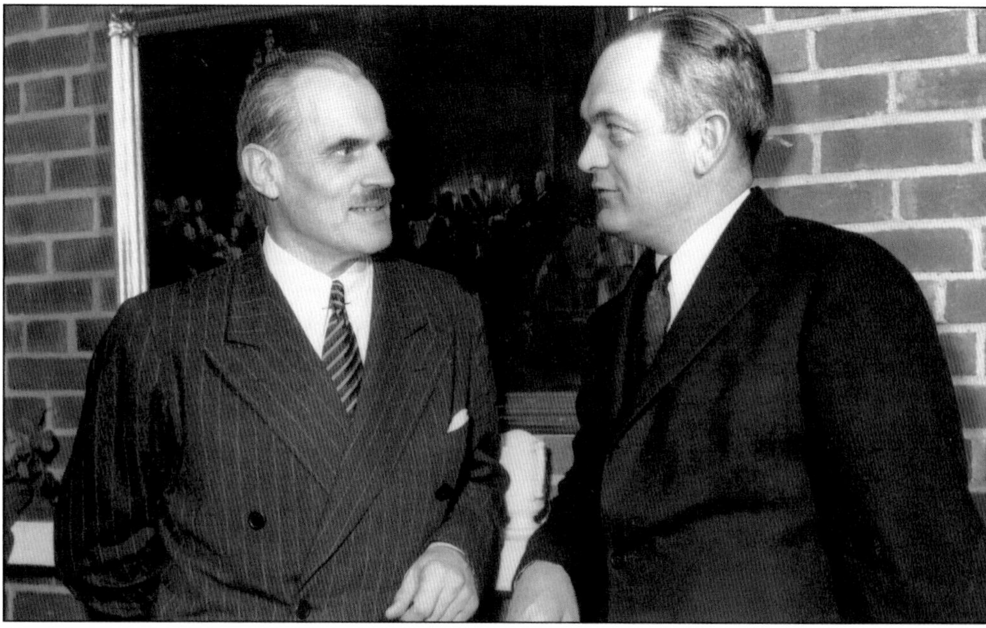

TWO LEADERS OF THE ATOMIC AGE. Arthur H. Compton (left) and Martin Whitaker are enjoying a friendly chat after a long day of intense work on the Manhattan Project. Compton was chairman of the National Academy of Sciences Committee to Evaluate Use of Atomic Energy in War. Whitaker was director of Clinton Laboratories, which would later be known as the X-10 Plant, and was instrumental in establishing mandatory health physics regulations for the working plant.

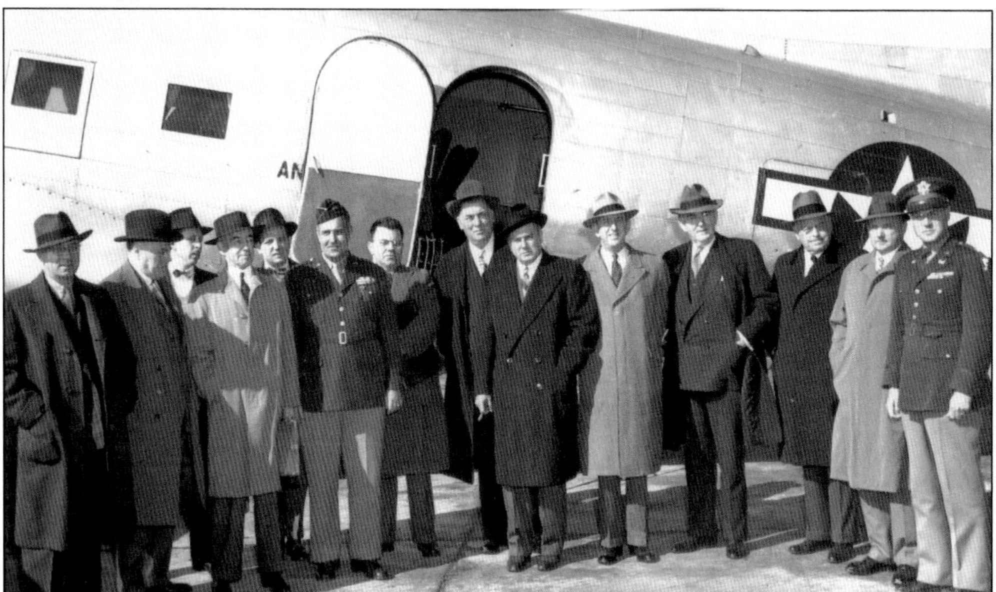

WATCHING OUT FOR OUR FUTURE. In 1945, the Joint Committee on Atomic Energy was created to become "the congressional watchdog over atomic energy." Landing at McGhee Tyson Airport in Knoxville, the committee pays a visit to Oak Ridge. Their main concerns were to safeguard the development of atomic energy and promote world peace.

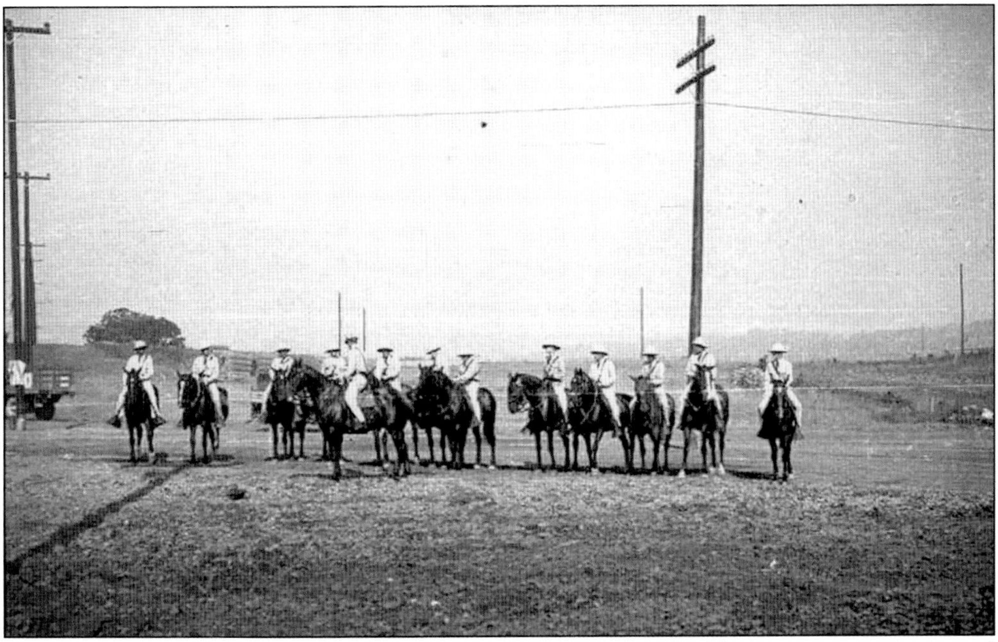

GUARDS ON HORSEBACK. In April 1943, an intensive security build-up got underway. Armed guards appeared at the seven defined entry points to the reservation, fencing was erected at strategic points on the exposed perimeter of the area, and mounted patrols guarded the area that boarded the Clinch River.

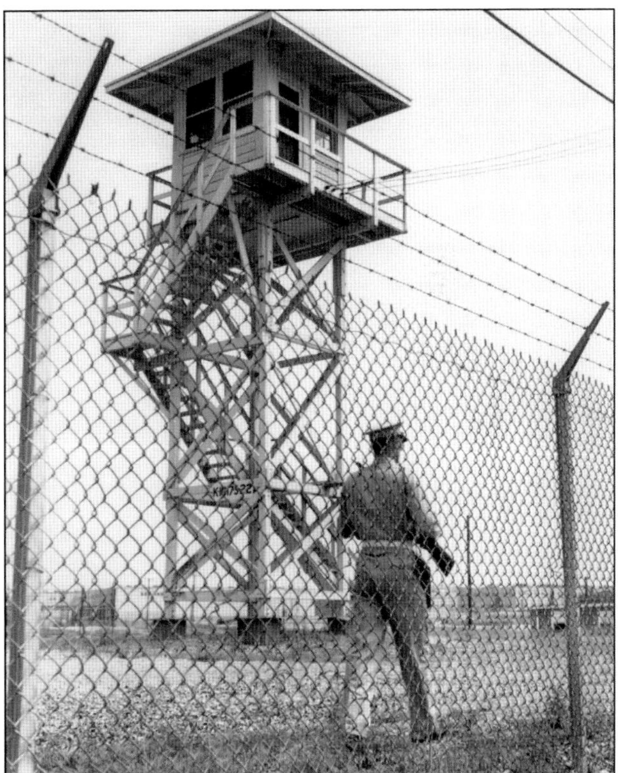

WALKING THE FENCE LINE. An armed security guard patrols the perimeter of a restricted area. By the end of the summer of 1943, the guard force, which had started as a group of un-uniformed, untrained, and inexperienced men, developed into a fairly smoothly operating force of approximately 1,000 men.

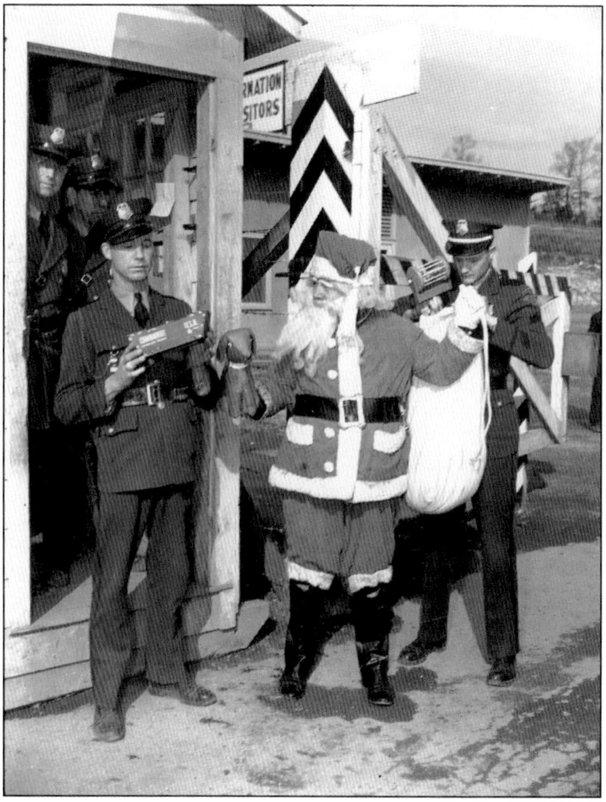

SHAKING DOWN SANTA CLAUS. Security was tight, even for St. Nick. Two security guards at Elza Gate checkpoint search Santa's goody sack while Santa holds up his hands. Everything coming and going through the checkpoints was investigated for the possibility of spying.

SECURITY FORCE. Standing in front of headquarters are city police ready for duty. By early 1945, security forces included 4,900 civilian guards, 740 military police, and more than 400 civilian policemen. The Intelligence and Security Division included approximately 500 agents.

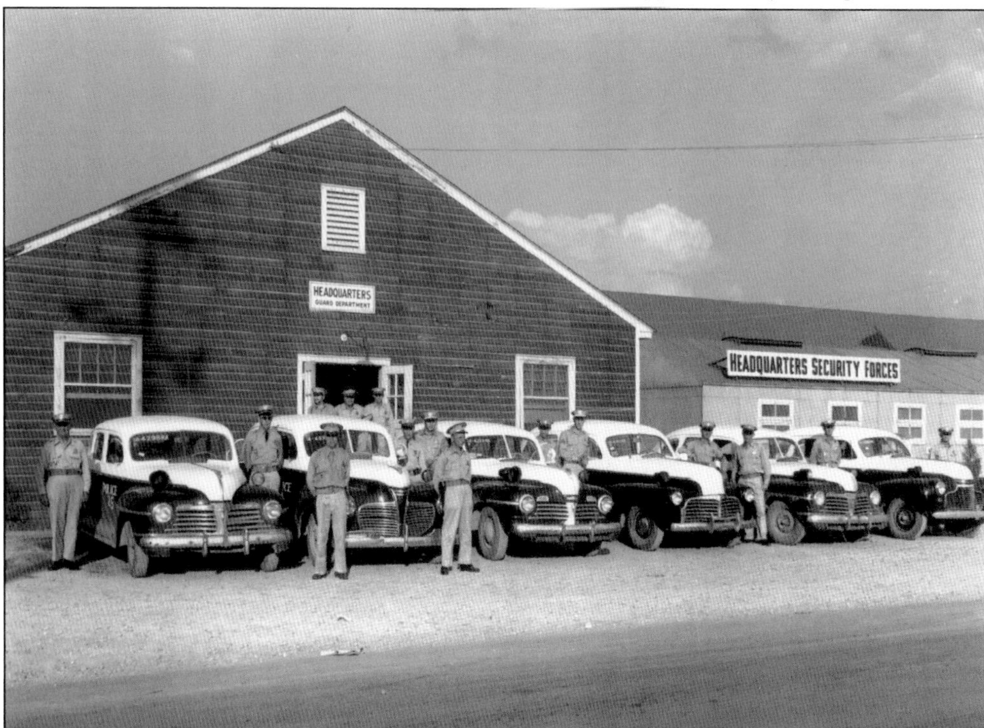

Directing Traffic Flow. In the early days of Oak Ridge, there were no traffic control signals. Pictured here is Elijah C. Terry, an auxiliary military policeman, standing on a platform directing traffic at the intersection of Kentucky Avenue and Tennessee Avenue, one of the busiest traffic spots in the Townsite area.

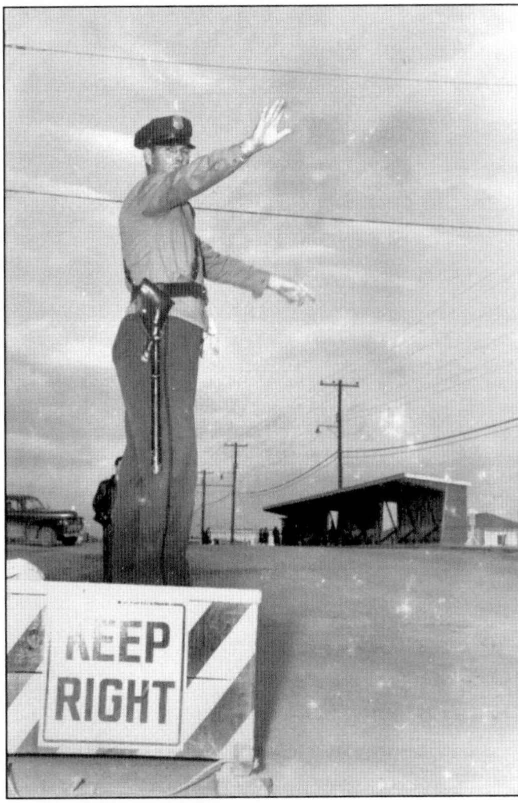

Attention to Detail. Military police Staff Sergeant Kennedy and Sergeant Bowling finalize details for an upcoming non-resident visit. All outside visitors to the area had to undergo scrutiny before they were able to enter the gates. Passes were issued to those who had a specific purpose to be on the reservation.

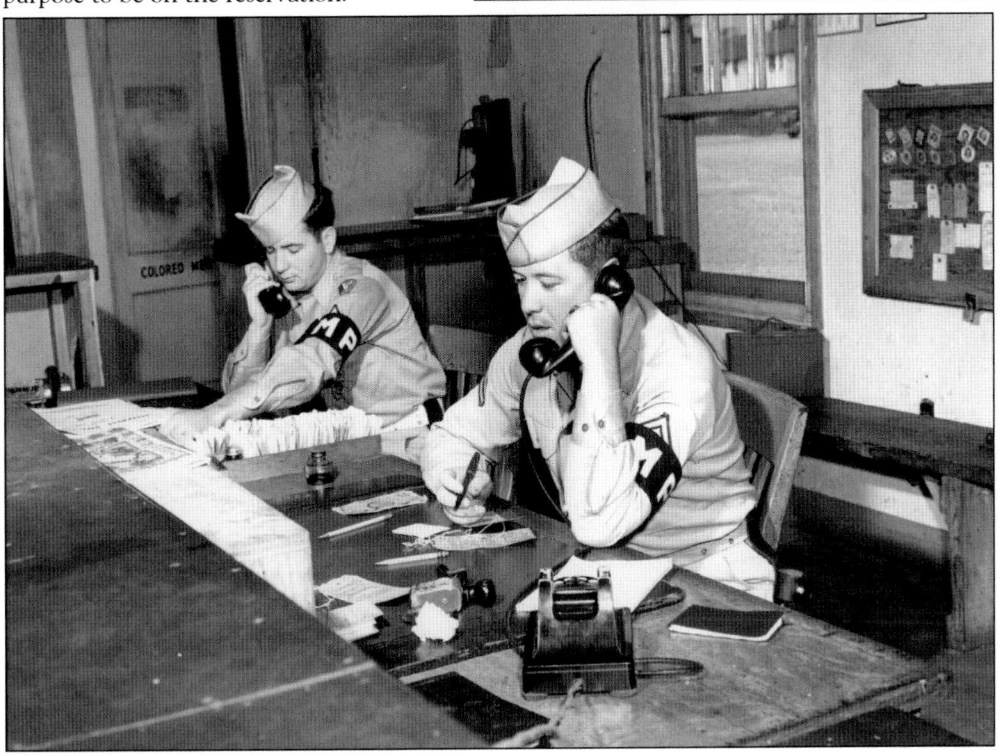

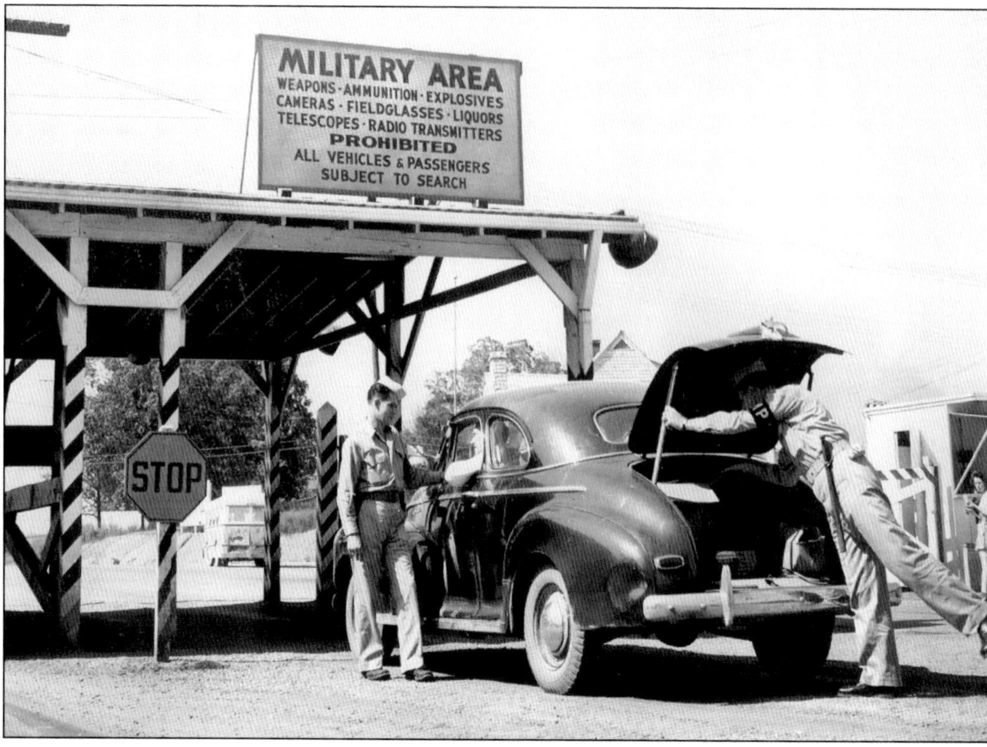

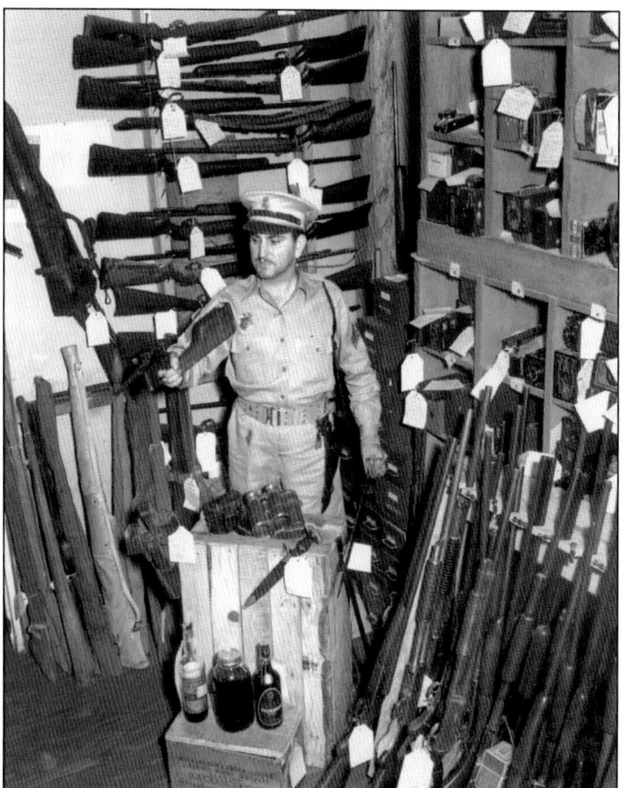

OPEN UP FOR INSPECTION. Elza Gate was by far the busiest of seven security checks. Rigid control over project entry was established April 1, 1943, when military police established gates at Elza, Edgemoor, Blair, Solway, Gallaher, Whitewing, and Oliver Springs entry points.

CONTRABAND. Police Sgt. C. M. Sillers exhibits various illegal items that were confiscated from individuals on the reservation. On any given day, 2,000 cars would enter and leave the area through the guard gates. Every car entering was searched, packs were opened, and bags were inspected.

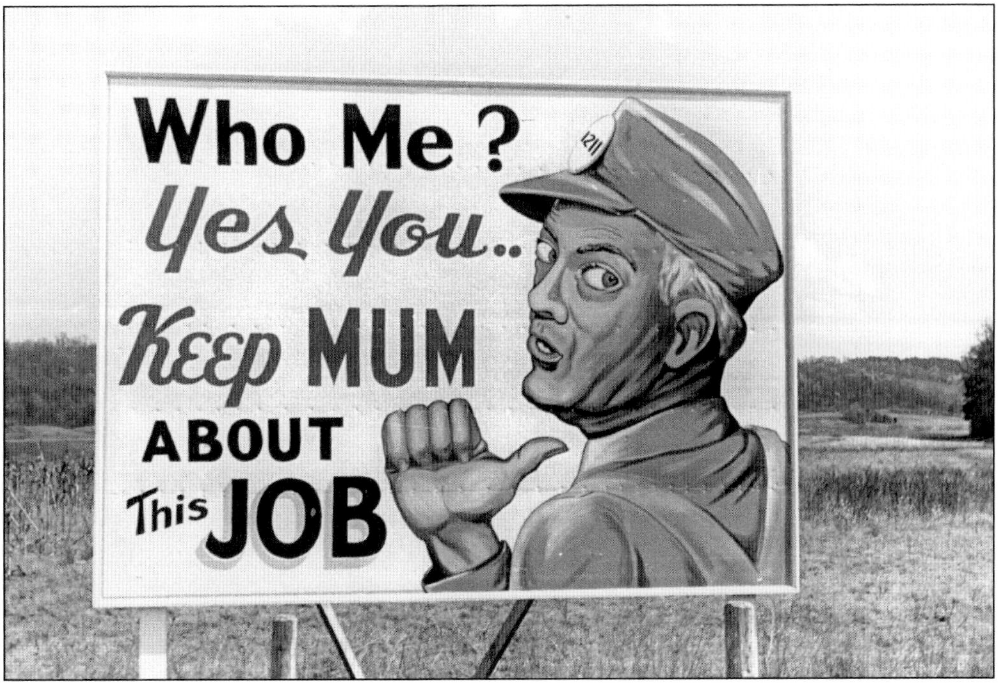

A Constant Reminder. In a special memorandum from the White House in the fall of 1942, President Roosevelt told Gen. Leslie R. Groves, the commanding general of the Manhattan Project, that "secrecy" and security were to be paramount. To carry this mandate out, there was set up in the Manhattan District an Intelligence and Security Division, which was later described as having successfully accomplished the outstanding security mission of the war.

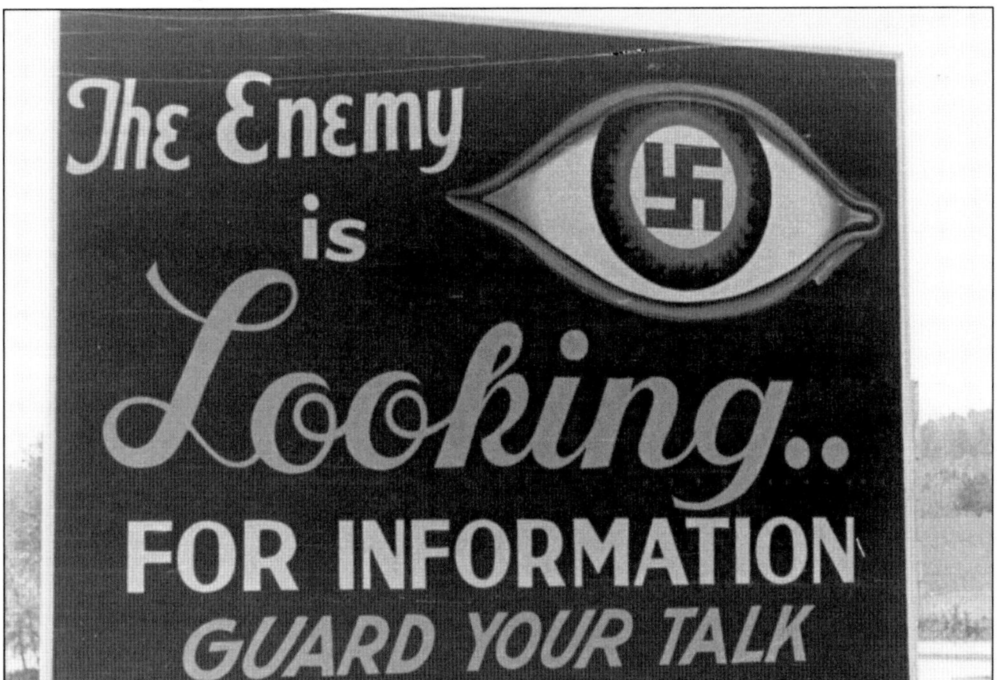

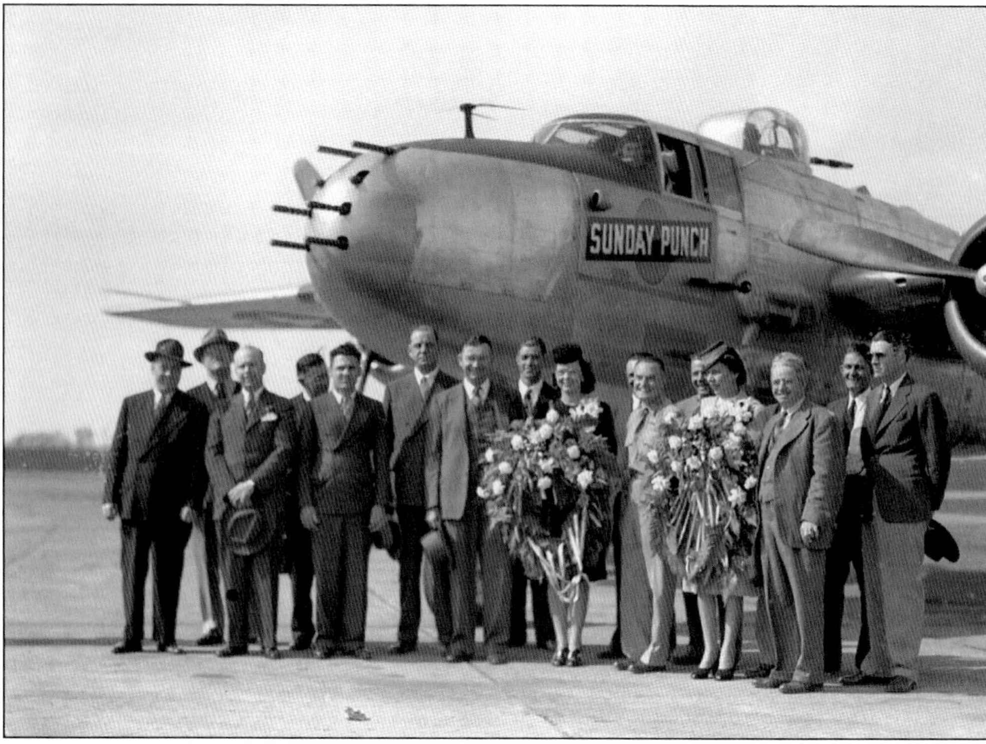

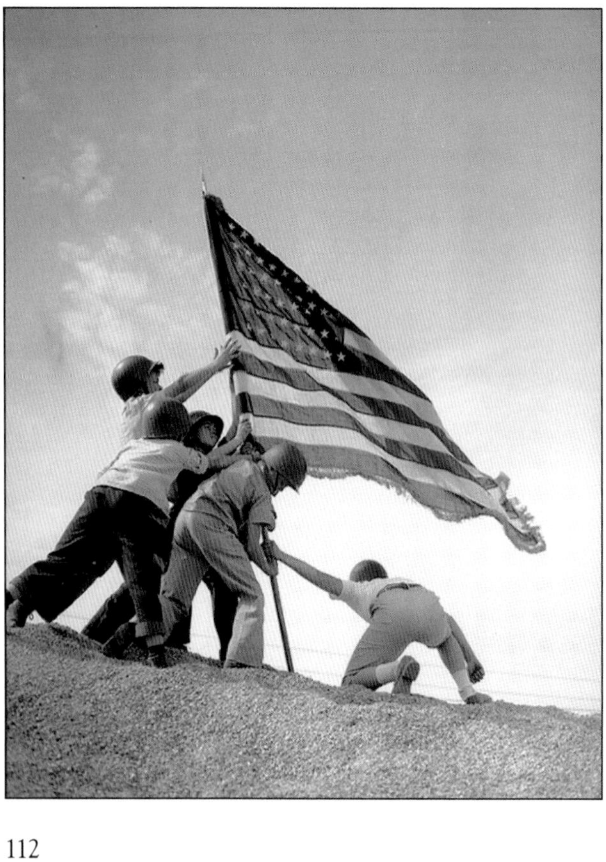

THE SUNDAY PUNCH. The K-25 Plant workers pooled their wages together for three Sundays to purchase a B-25 bomber as a gift to the U.S. Army Air Forces. This dedication took place at Knoxville Airport in April 1945. It was assigned to the 12th Bomber Group, 81st Squadron, and flown by Comdr. Tom Evans, a 1941 graduate of Knoxville High School in Knoxville, Tennessee.

UNCOMMON VALOR WAS A COMMON VIRTUE. The most-used photograph in American history, taken by Associated Press photographer Joe Rosenthal, was the flag-raising atop Mount Suribachi in Iwo Jima, Japan, signifying the defeat of the Japanese on that island on February 23, 1945. Back home, four Elm Grove School boys reenact that famous flag-raising on May 20, 1945. This photo was used in the seventh bond drive promotion.

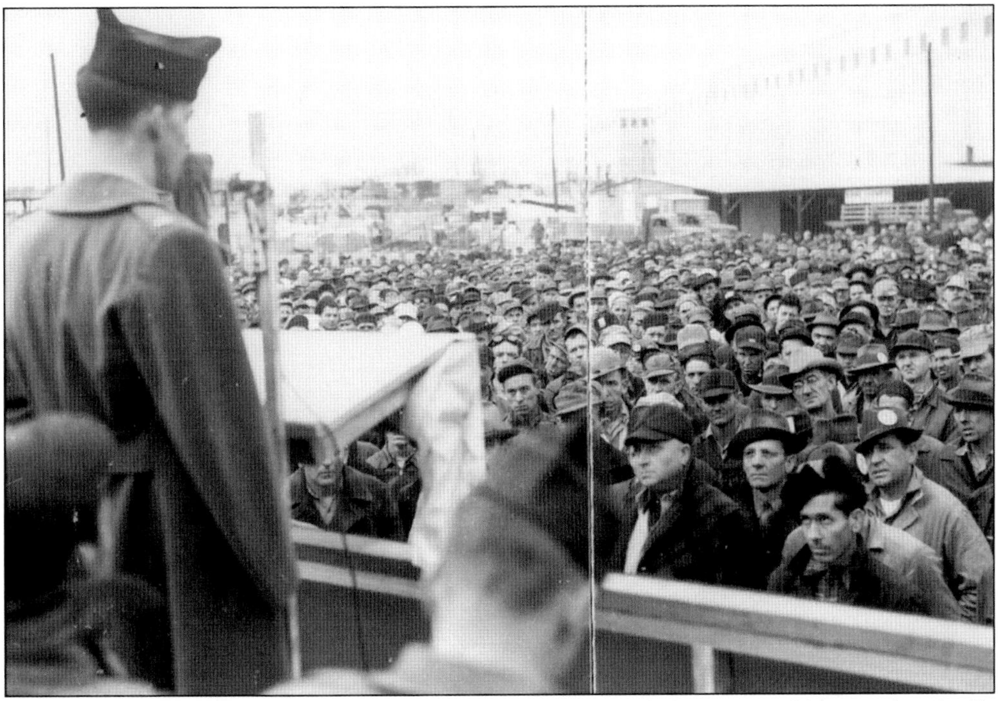

A VEIL OF SECRECY AT OAK RIDGE. Sgt. Mike Miller, a disabled veteran, addresses a bond rally at the K-25 Plant and urges workers to stay on the job. Army Intelligence cut the negative of this photograph, taken December 13, 1944. The left section was published, but the right side, showing the gaseous diffusion plant, remained classified until after the war. Below, a close-up of the workers shows some very intent facial expressions.

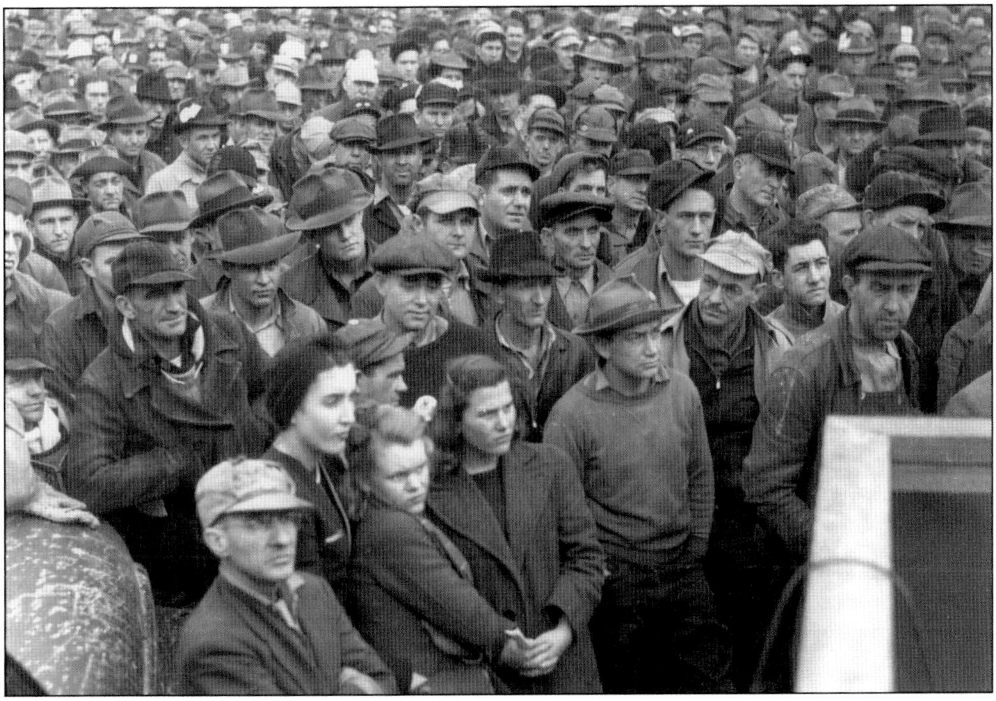

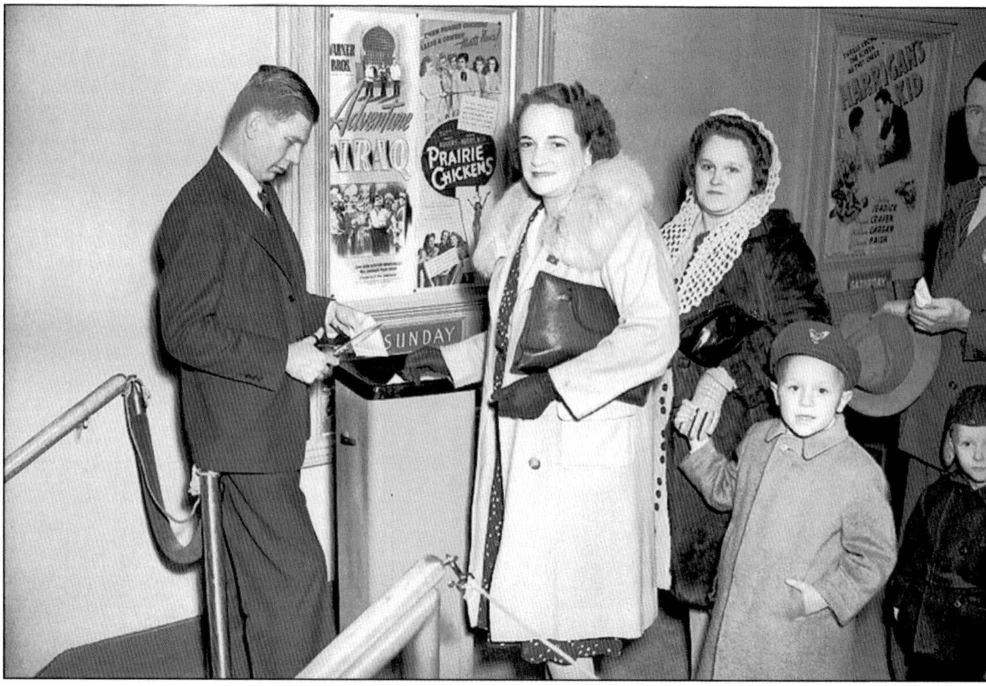

LEADER OF THE BOND DRIVE. Virginia S. Houston is pictured presenting her free movie pass to the showing of the *Guadalcanal Diary*. Miss Houston purchased $7,700 in bonds after she sold some real estate and became the largest bond-drive investor in Oak Ridge.

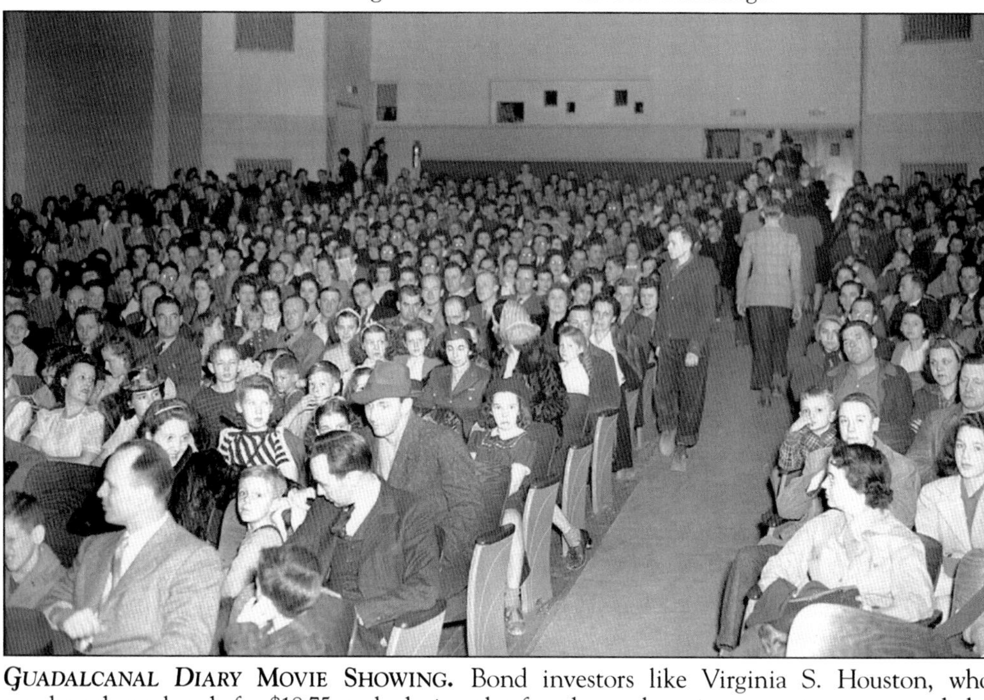

***GUADALCANAL DIARY* MOVIE SHOWING.** Bond investors like Virginia S. Houston, who purchased war bonds for $18.75 each during the fourth war loan investment, were awarded a free pass to a movie showing at Ridge Theater. As you can tell from the crowd, there was a lot of enthusiasm in the bond drive.

UNCLE SAM GETS TOUGH. This sign, located in Townsite, was a constant reminder to residents of the fifth bond drive campaign. Showing contributions of almost $2 million means employees and the families of the Clinton Engineer Works would have to dig deeper into their pockets to reach the $3 million goal.

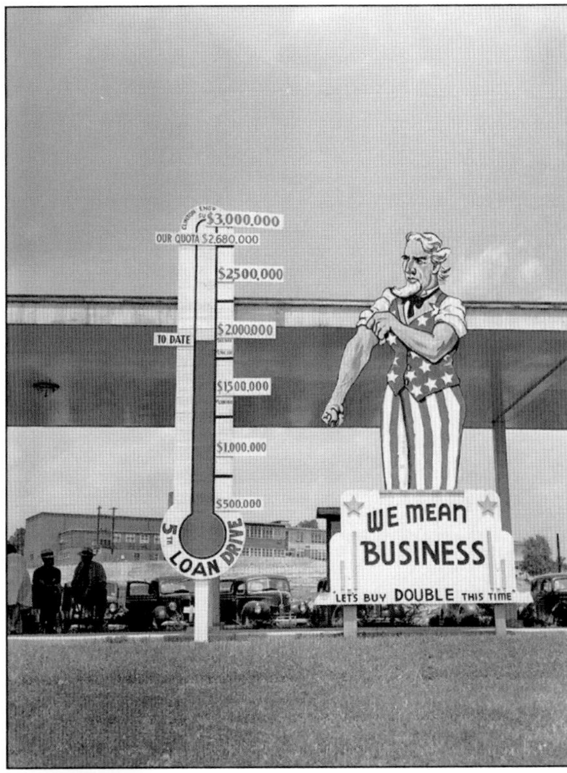

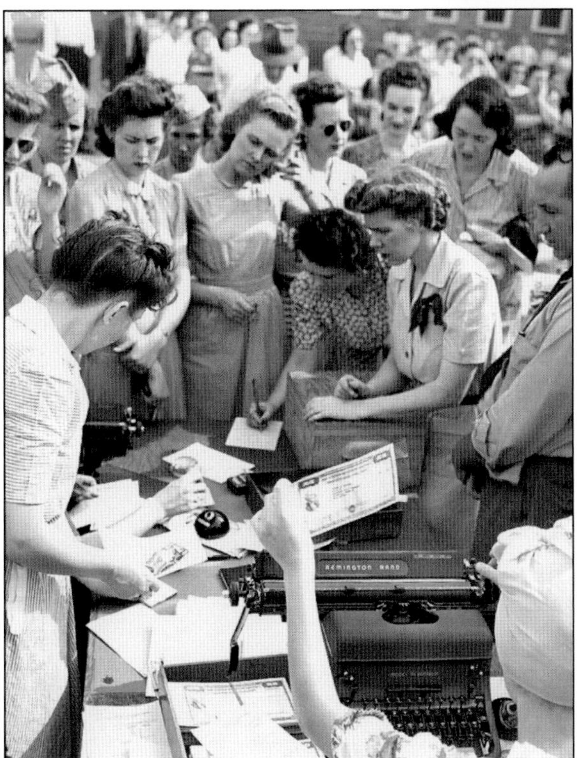

SUPPORTING THE WAR EFFORT. Ladies look on as others sign-up for the bond drive. In the foreground, a seller is showing a bond issued to a contributor. The sale of war bonds provided a way in which patriotic attitudes and the spirit of sacrifice could be expressed.

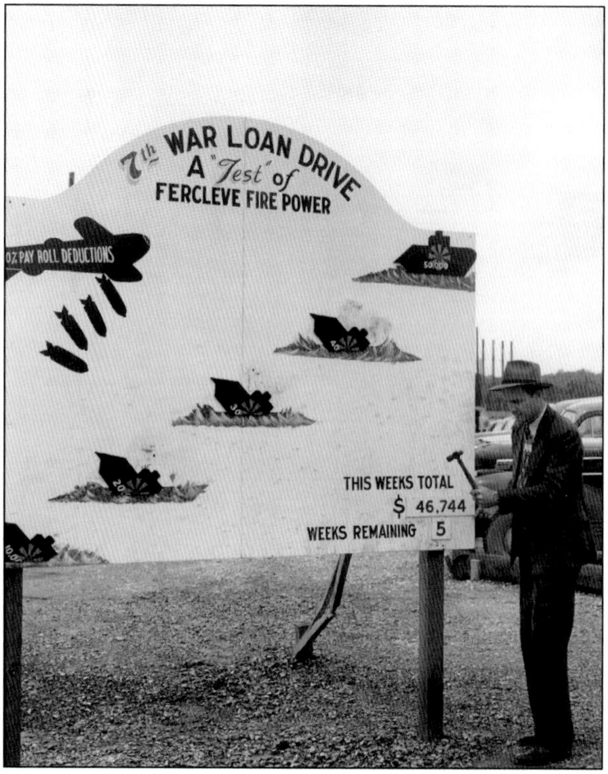

SEVENTH WAR LOAN DRIVE. Joe Torrance, a Roane-Anderson employee, updates the weekly total of payroll contributions with five weeks remaining in this drive. Nationally planned special promotional events far surpassed those planned for any other bond drive, and the Office of War Information pledged 50 percent of all available radio time to advertise the seventh loan drive. The final tally recorded was over $26 billion.

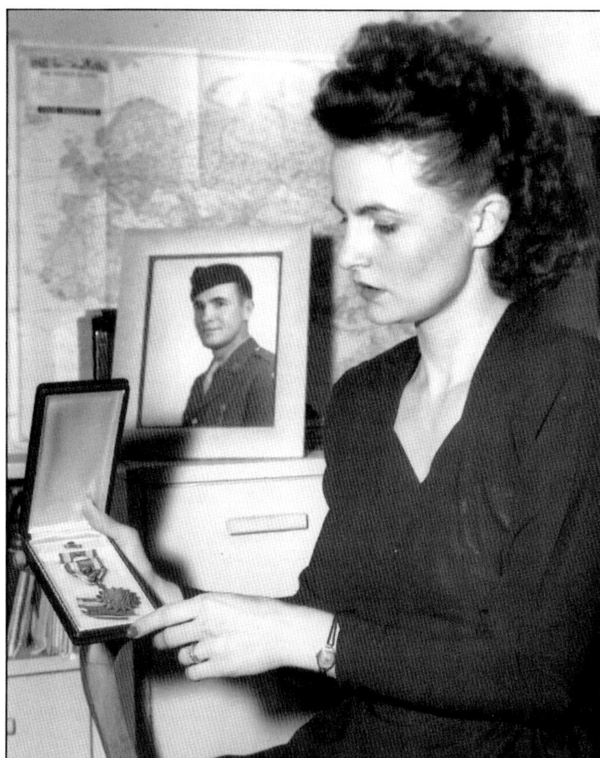

EXCEPTIONALLY MERITORIOUS CONDUCT. An oak-leaf cluster was awarded posthumously to Sgt. Jasper Richardson for his support to military operations during World War II. Mrs. Richardson received the award from Lt. James E. Thornton, U.S. Army Air Corps. A photo of her late husband and a map of Europe are in the background.

AN AWARD FOR COLONEL NICHOLS. Secretary of War Robert P. Patterson pins the Distinguished Service Metal on district engineer Col. Kenneth D. Nichols on October 4, 1945. Patterson expressed accolades to Nichols, described as a key man for the entire project by Gen. Leslie R. Groves, saying, "His dedicated team effort helped win the war."

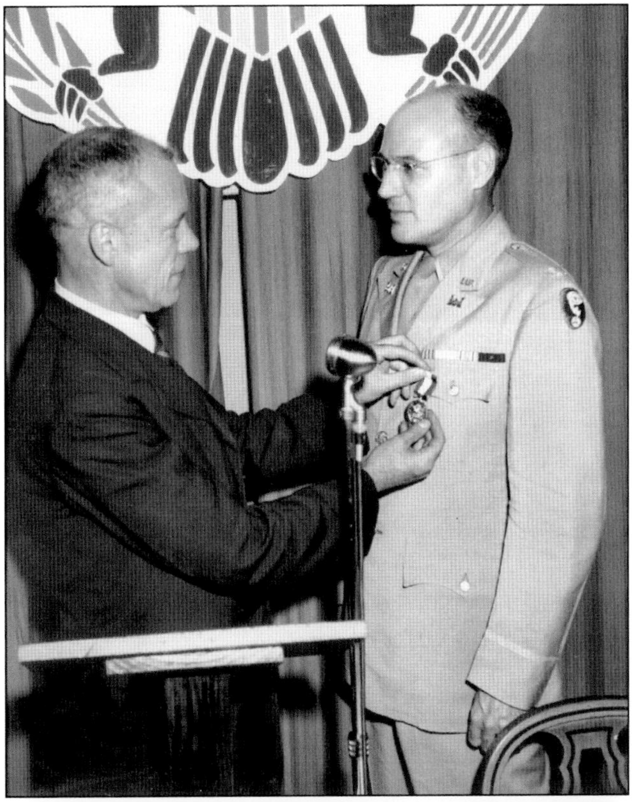

MARCHING TO A DRUM CADENCE. The members of the Special Engineer Company are in a rhythmic flow as the drum major uses his spontoon, a weapon carried by infantry officers during the 18th century, to command the drum corps. The full dress review was held at Blankenship Field, which was adjacent to the high school in Townsite.

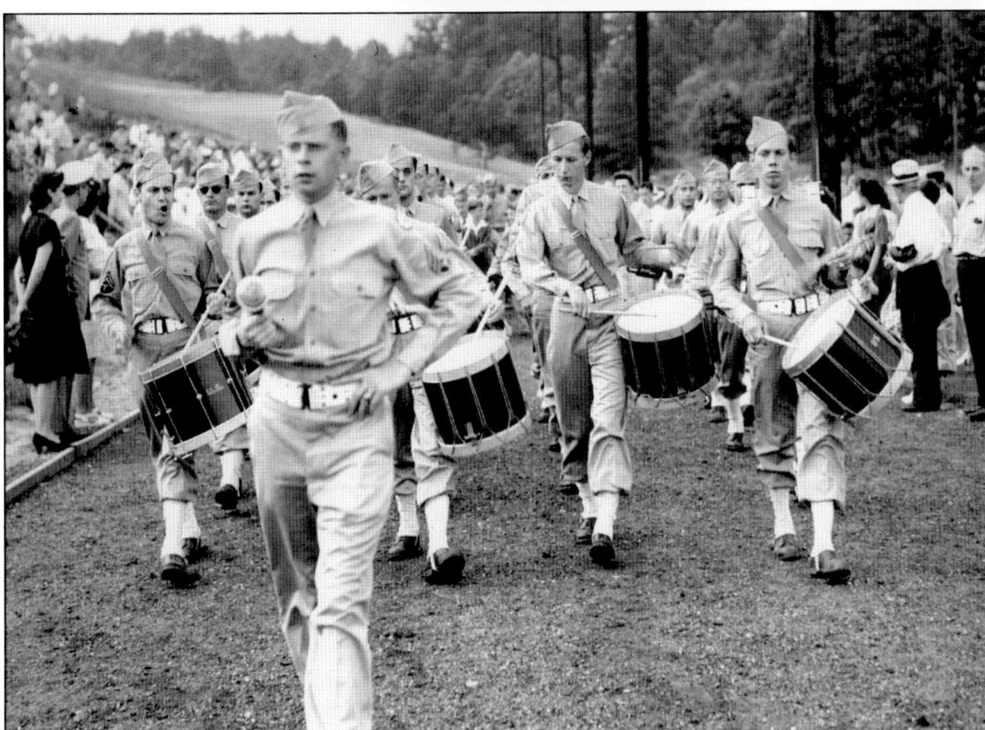

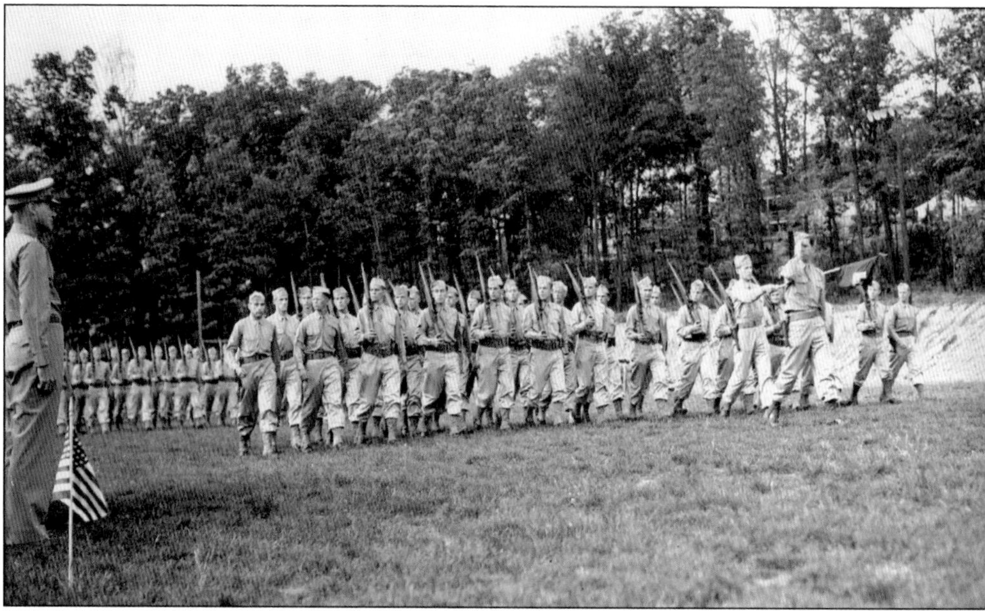

MILITARY REVIEW. Gen. Kenneth D. Nichols stands at attention to review members of the Special Engineer Company. So many rumors spread among the workers as to what was going on behind all the secrecy that the irritation threatened completion of certain operations. In 1944, the Manhattan District ordered a full-dress publicity campaign to arouse citizens to the danger of loose reference of operations at Clinton Engineer Works.

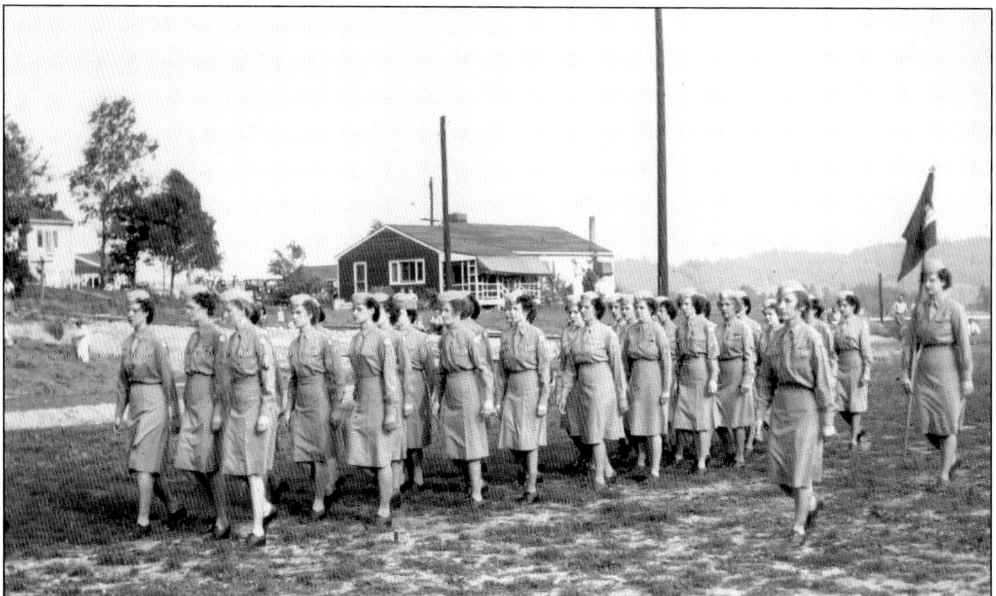

WOMEN'S AUXILIARY CORPS IN MILITARY REVIEW FLYING THE CORPS OF ENGINEERS FLAG. Early in 1943, preliminary construction work for the Manhattan Engineer District was progressing well. This progress also increased the volume of classified information regarding the project. On June 3, 1944, the adjutant general authorized establishment of a Manhattan District Women's Army Auxiliary Corps Detachment to utilize women in uniform who had skills, training, and experience in clerical fields.

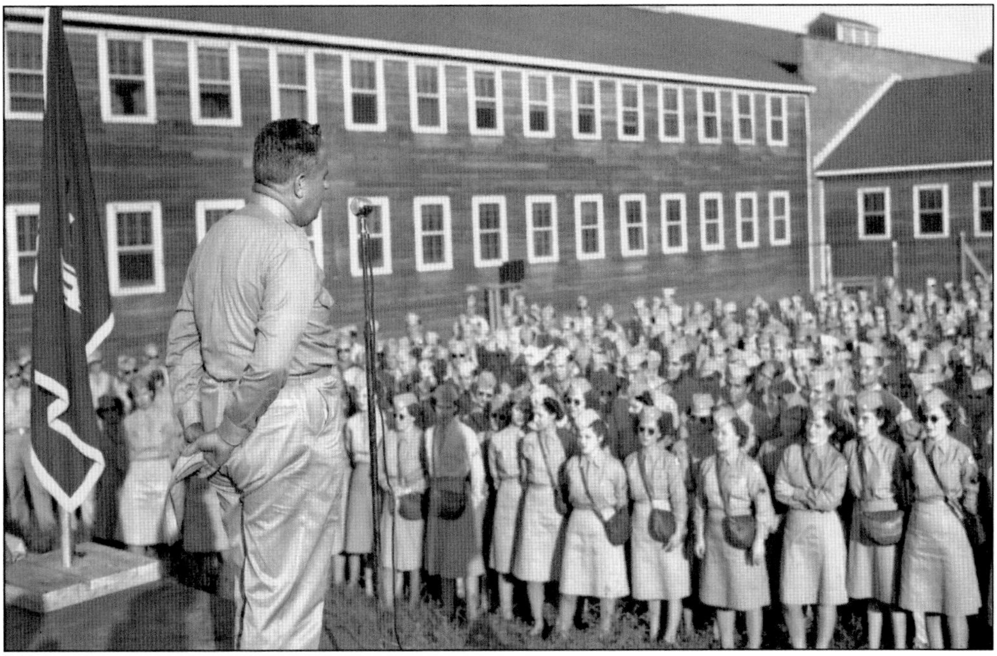

General Groves Addressing WAC Detachment. Outside their quarters, Women's Army Corps (WAC) are listening to information given by Gen. Leslie R. Groves. This detachment consisted of a specialized group of chief clerks, stenographers, telephone operators, scientific technicians, clerks general, and teletype and cryptographic technicians. In recognition of superior performance, the 9812th WAC detachment was awarded the Meritorious Service Unit Plaque and Star from the War Department for "outstanding devotion to duty."

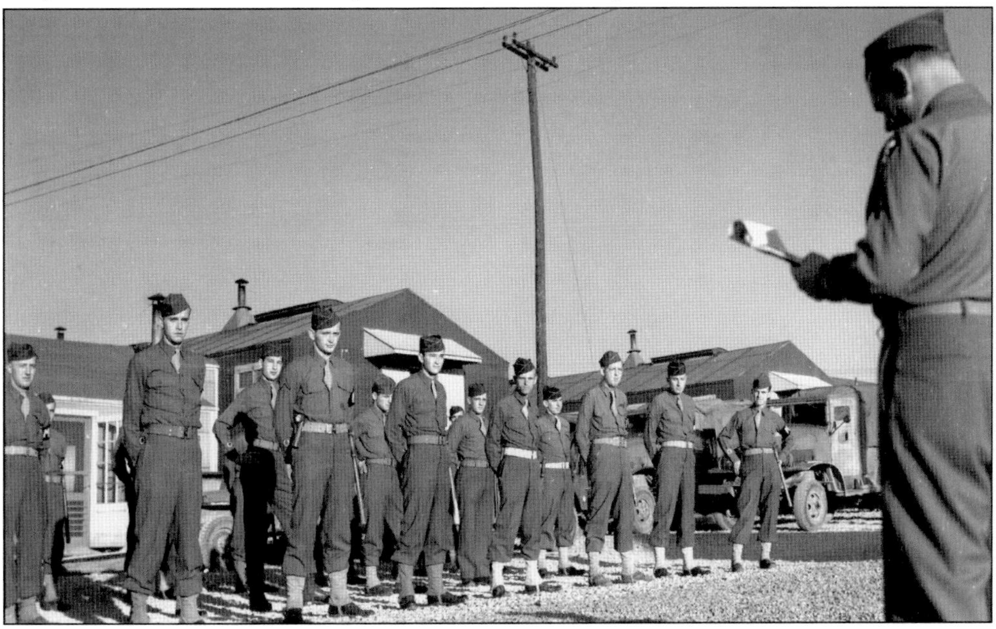

Military Police at Ease. M. P. Detachment No. 1 of the 4812th Service Unit stand at ease to receive their orders for the day's duty. These guards are responsible for gate and perimeter control of the reservation. By their side is a baton, which was also known as a "billy club."

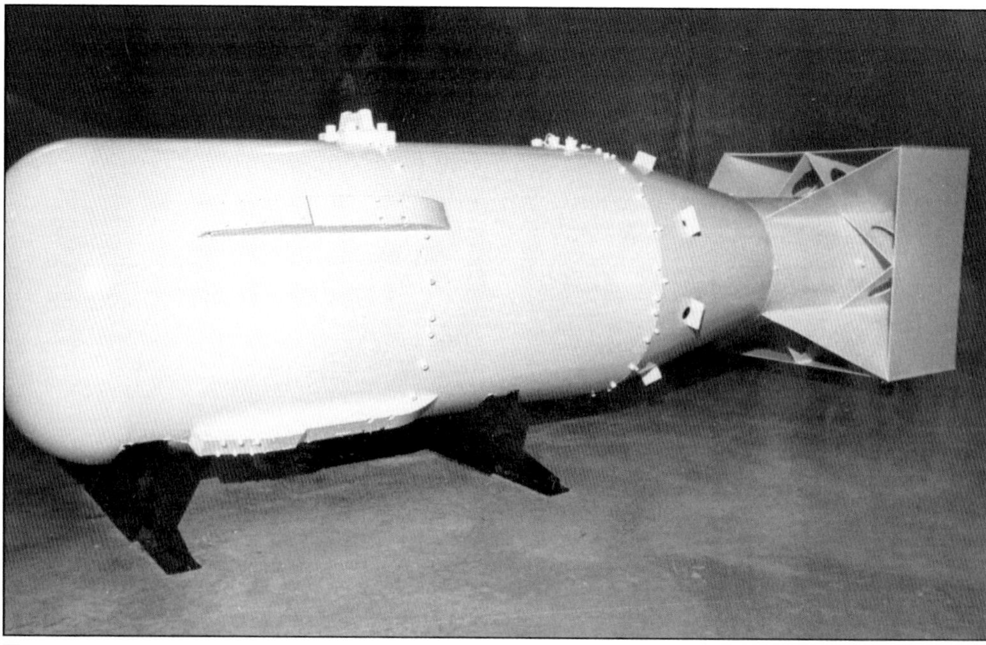

THE LITTLE BOY. On July 25, 1945, the first shipment of uranium-235 necessary for what would become the Hiroshima bomb left Oak Ridge, arriving at its destination on the Pacific island of Tinian on July 27. The bomb was 120 inches long and 28 inches in diameter. It weighed 9,000 pounds and had an explosive force equal to 20,000 tons of TNT. (Photo courtesy of the Manhattan Project.)

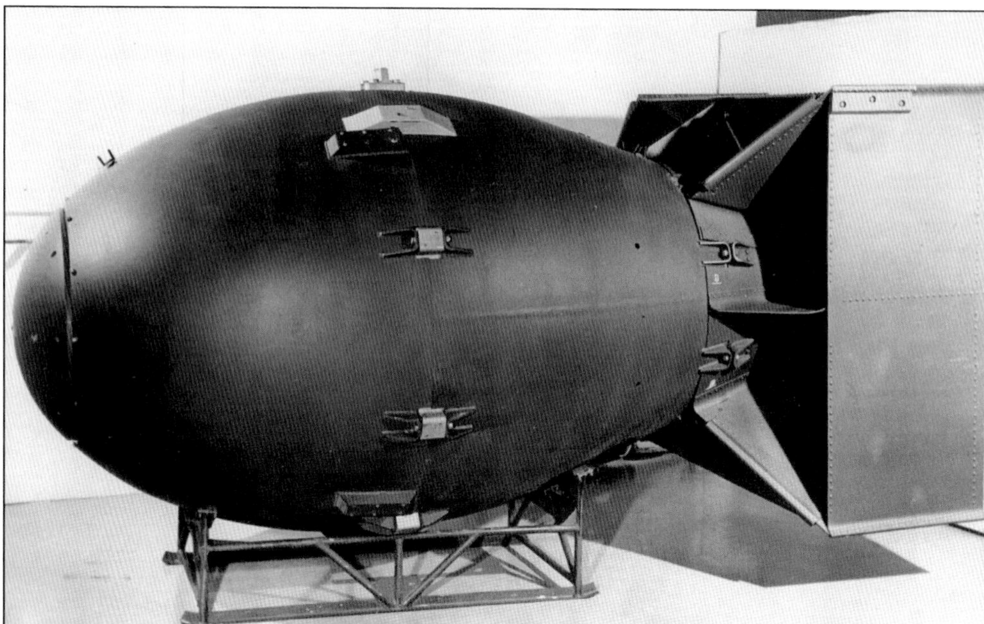

THE FAT MAN. This plutonium implosion bomb was detonated over Nagasaki, Japan, at 11:07 a.m. on August 9, 1945. The bomb was 60 inches in diameter, 10-feet-8-inches long, and weighed 10,800 pounds. Fat Man exploded 1,650 feet above the city with a yield of approximately 20,000 tons of TNT.

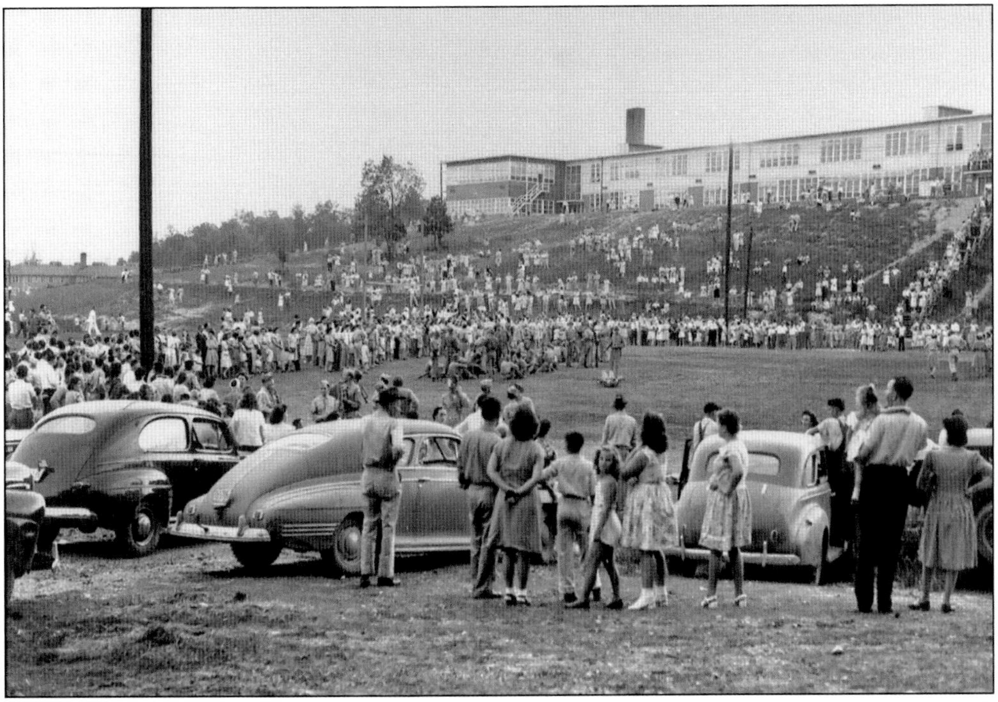

SOLDIERS SURROUNDED. Townspeople gather at Blankenship Field on August 6, 1945, and will soon learn the great news "War Ends." In the background is Oak Ridge High School on Kentucky Avenue. A group of off-duty soldiers and WACs (center) also await the announcement.

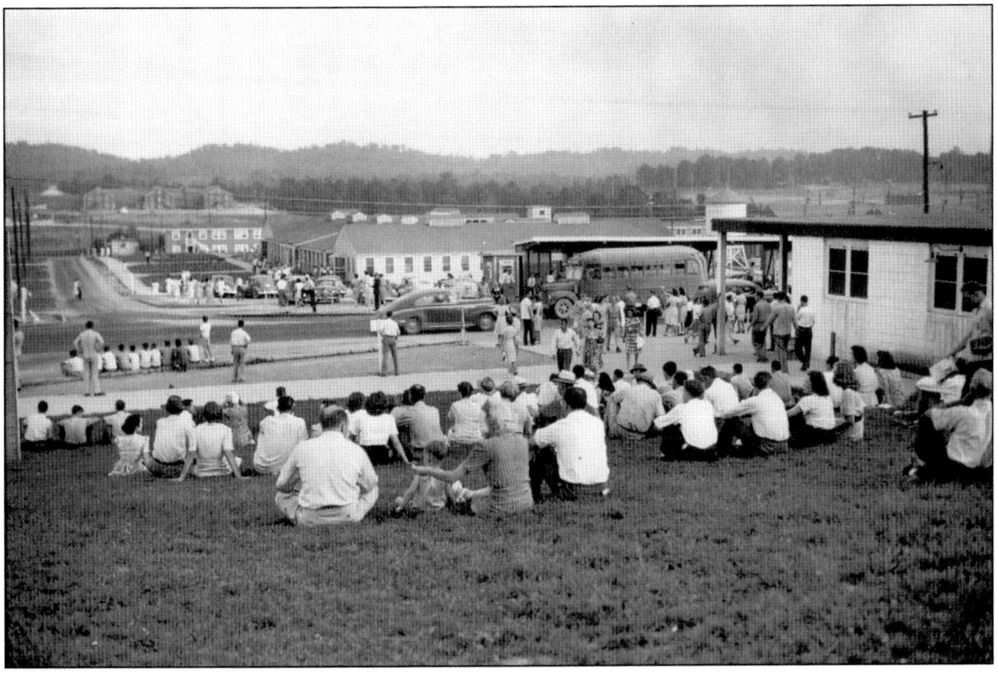

WAITING ANXIOUSLY. Hundreds of citizens, looking toward Corps of Engineering Headquarters, the "Castle on the Hill," are awaiting news of the end of the war. News came later that evening by newspaper delivery to Oak Ridge.

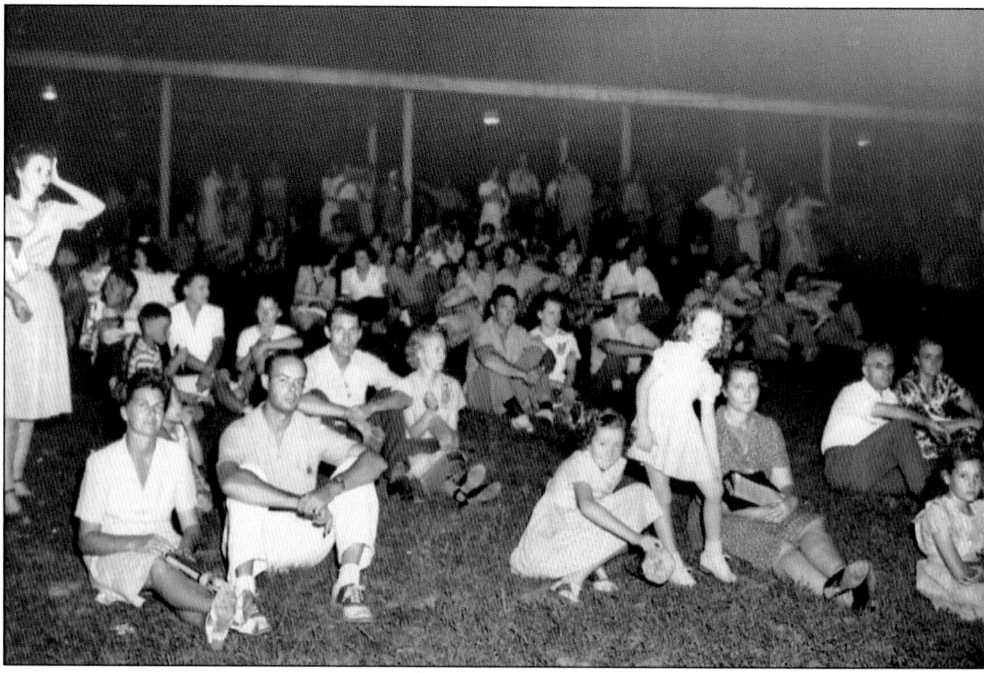

ABOUT 9:30 P.M. The people were still at the Townsite area expecting to hear the official announcement that had been rumored all day about the ending of the war. Patience paid off as the official word came by newspaper delivery.

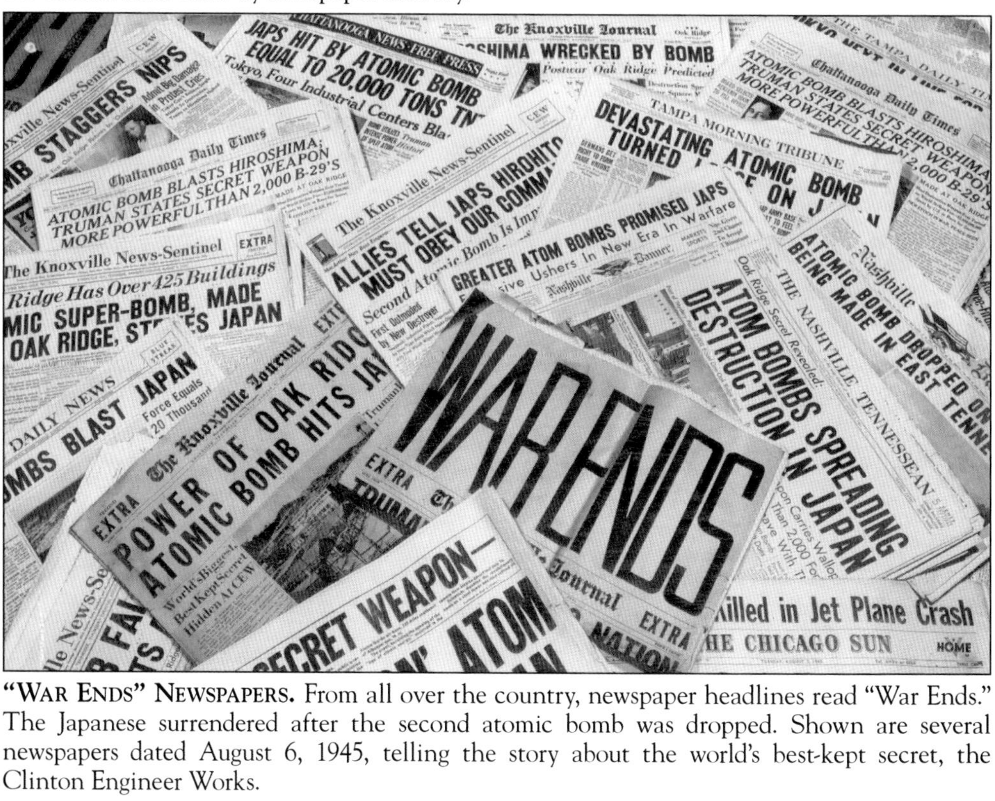

"WAR ENDS" NEWSPAPERS. From all over the country, newspaper headlines read "War Ends." The Japanese surrendered after the second atomic bomb was dropped. Shown are several newspapers dated August 6, 1945, telling the story about the world's best-kept secret, the Clinton Engineer Works.

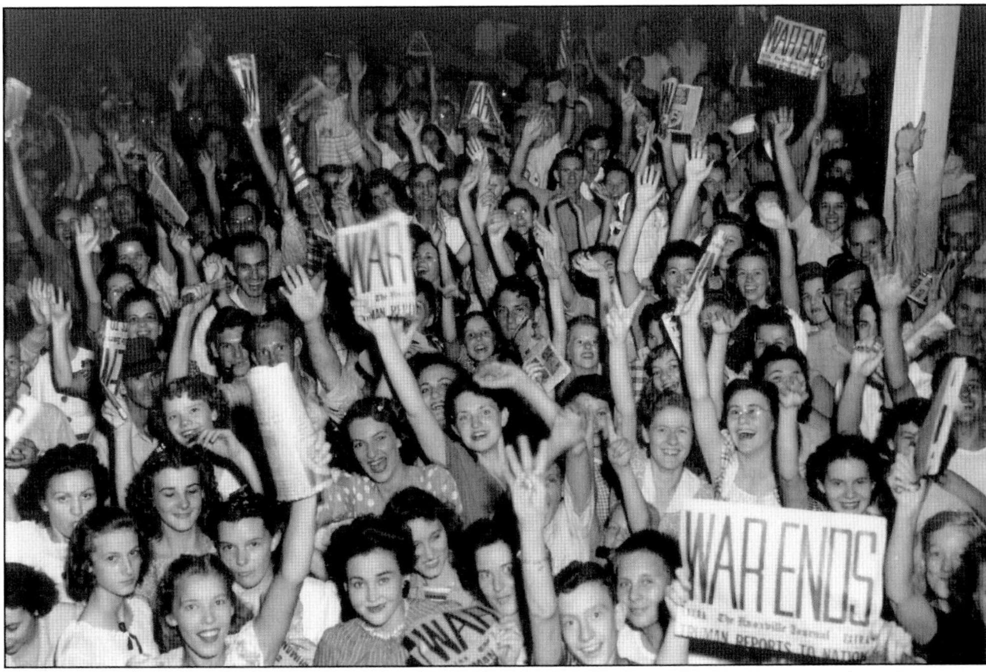

The Crowd Goes Wild! It was finally official. As soon as the newspapers hit the street, residents were waving them in jubilant celebration. Newspapers that once sold for 50¢ were sold this night for $1 and were soon sold out.

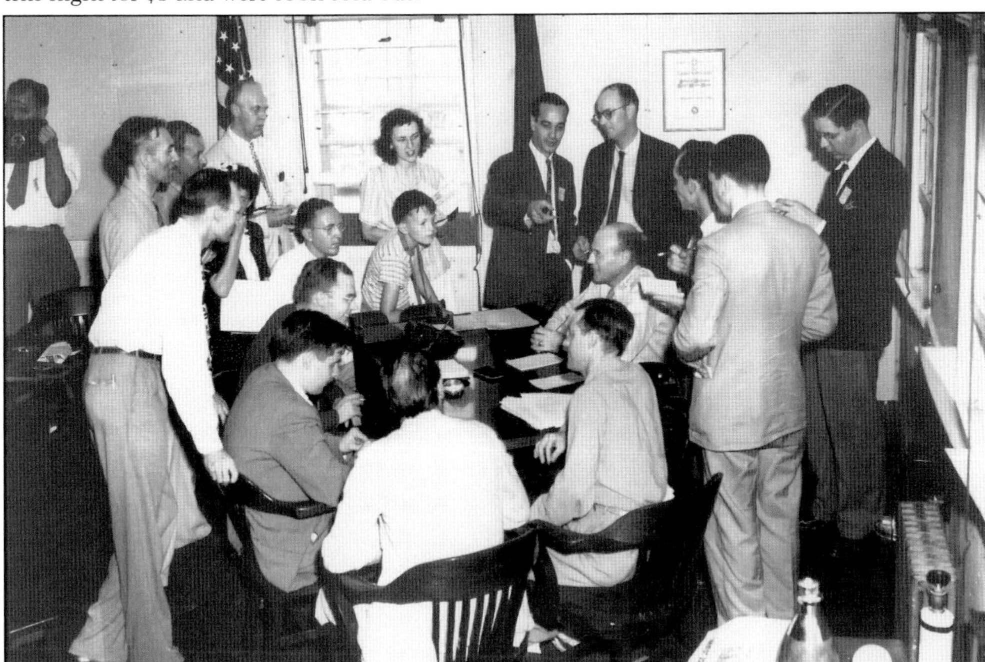

Press Conference. After the bomb was dropped on Hiroshima, the world was told of the fabulous work the Manhattan Engineer District had produced. Seated at the table, right center, Gen. Kenneth D. Nichols briefs the local press as to the role Oak Ridge and the secret operation played to help win the war.

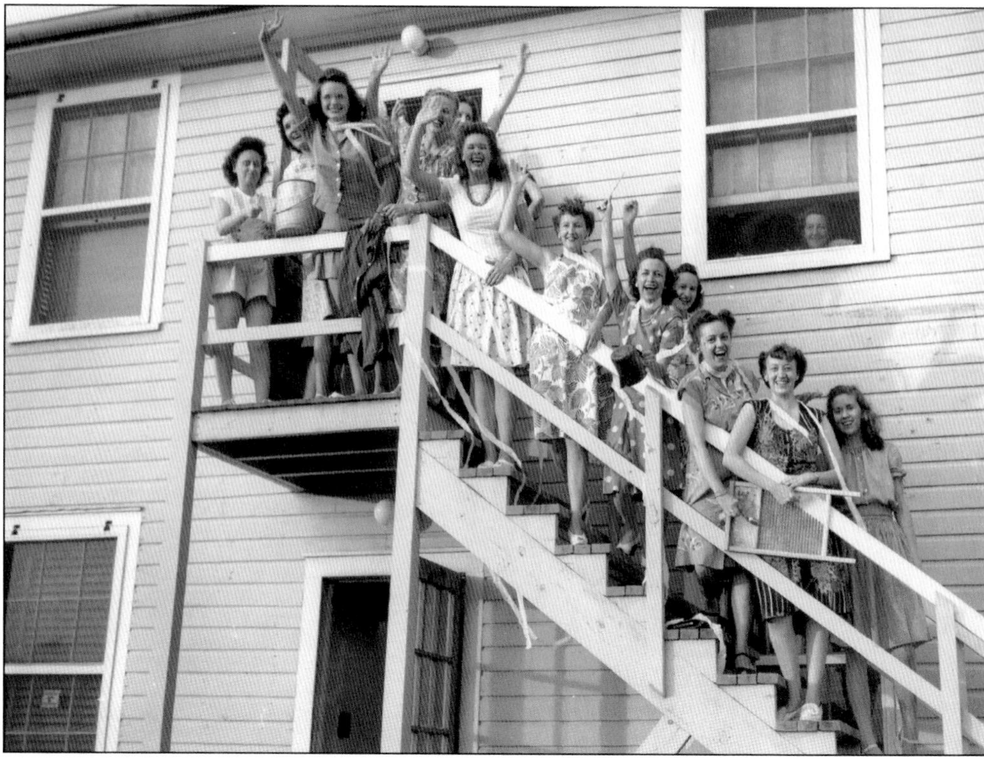

A HAPPY GROUP. Ladies from a dormitory prepare to hit the streets and make a joyful noise to help celebrate the end of the war. Knowing that their hard work and sacrifice benefited the war effort as it did, a street party was in order.

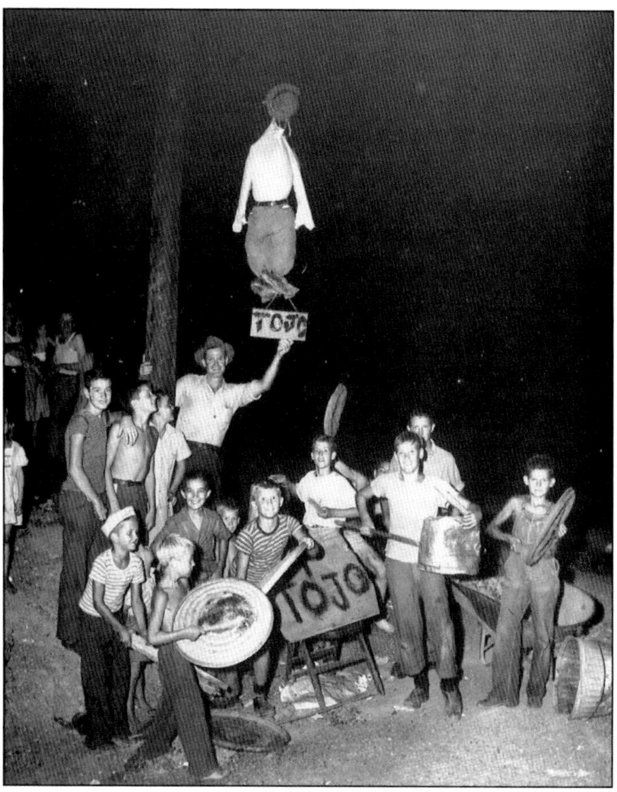

ALL OVER TOWN. The entire town of Oak Ridge was celebrating. This picture shows young revelers hanging an effigy of Tojo, which represented the toppling of Japan. Neighborhood street parties broke out all over town to commemorate the work they did to help end the war.

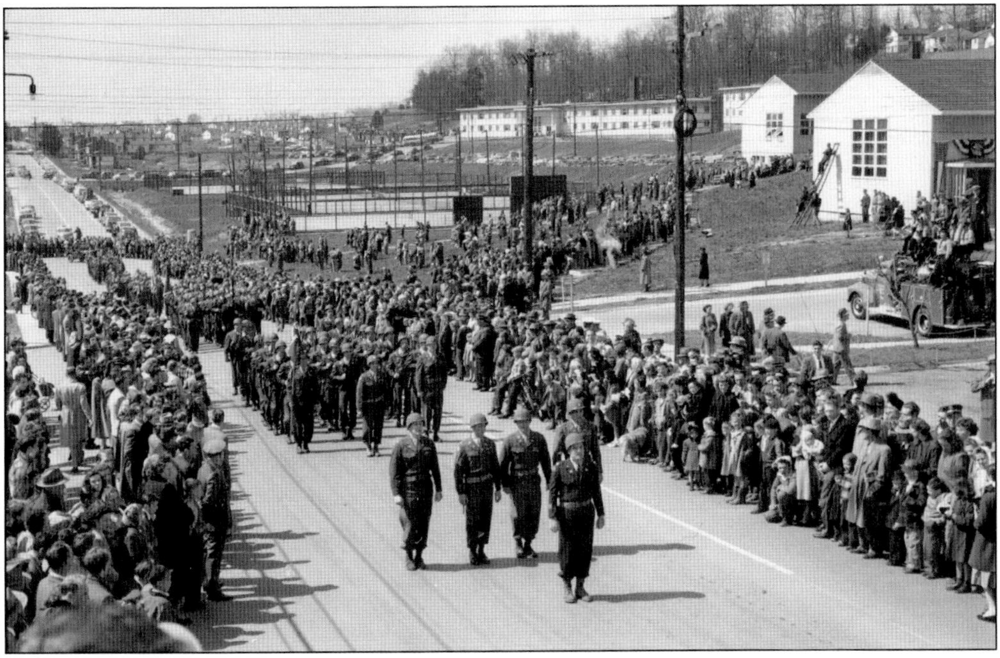

GATE-OPENING CELEBRATION. A parade marched down Tennessee Avenue at Townsite, commemorating the gate opening of Oak Ridge, which allowed people to pass through a "normal" city and not a guard gate. In the early afternoon of March 19, 1949, there were speeches and more speeches by visiting political leaders.

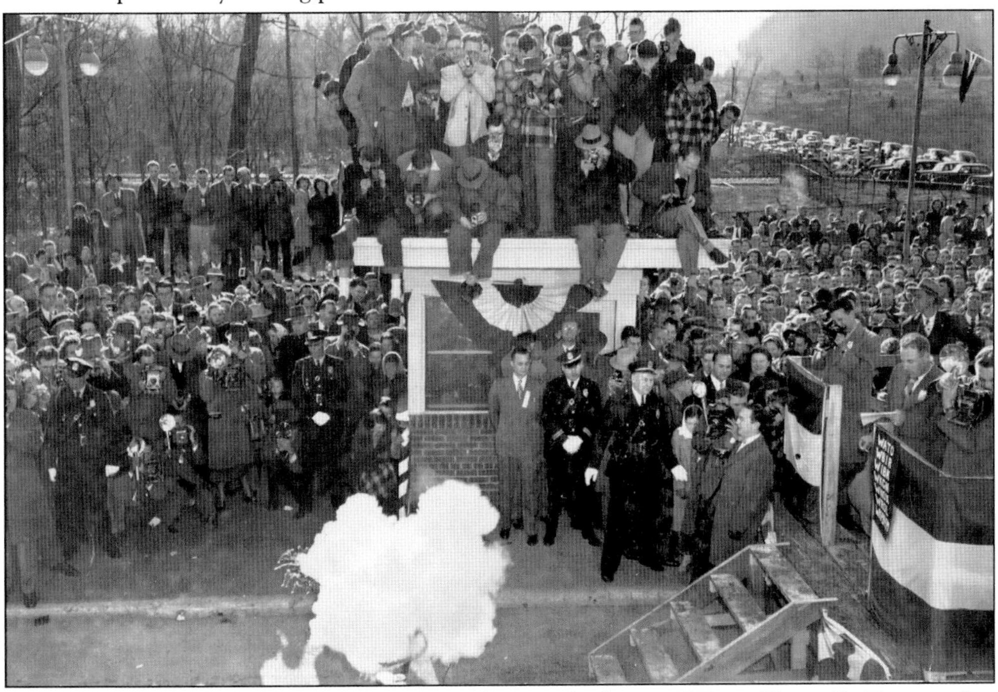

GATE-OPENING HOOPLA. The celebration planners had invited Pres. Harry S. Truman, but instead, Truman sent his vice president, Alben Barkley, who was from neighboring Kentucky. The ceremony at Elza Gate included a magnesium flare, showing a symbolic mushroom cloud.

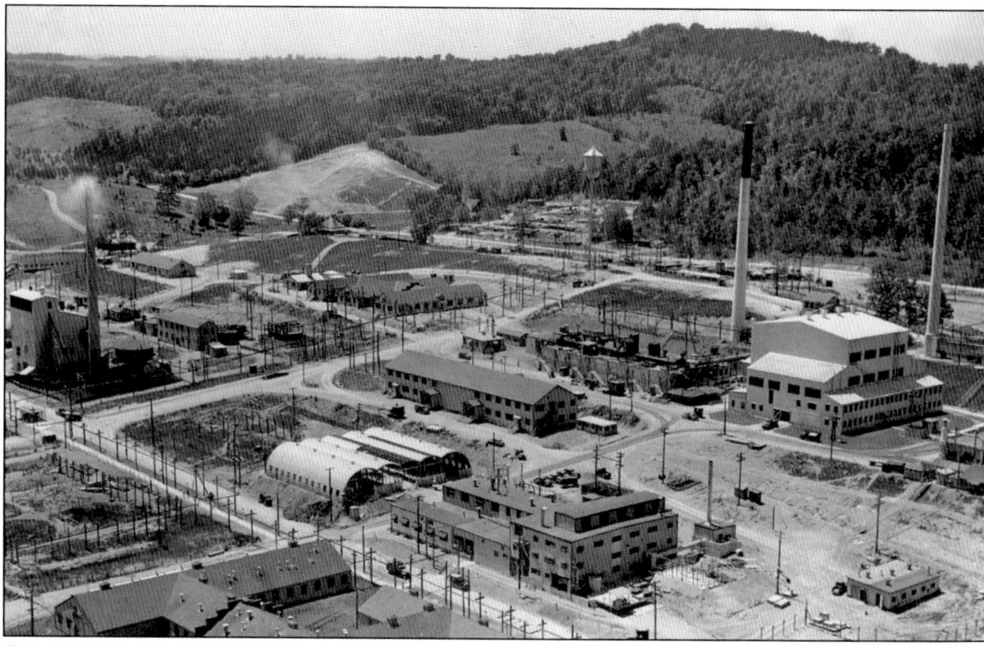

CLINTON LABORATORIES. This aerial view shows the Graphite Reactor (right center). X-10 was the code name given to this plant, which was built by E. I. du Pont de Nemours and Company. X-10 went critical at 5:00 a.m. on November 4, 1943. By the end of the year, the reactor had produced 1.54 milligrams of plutonium for the Los Alamos scientists.

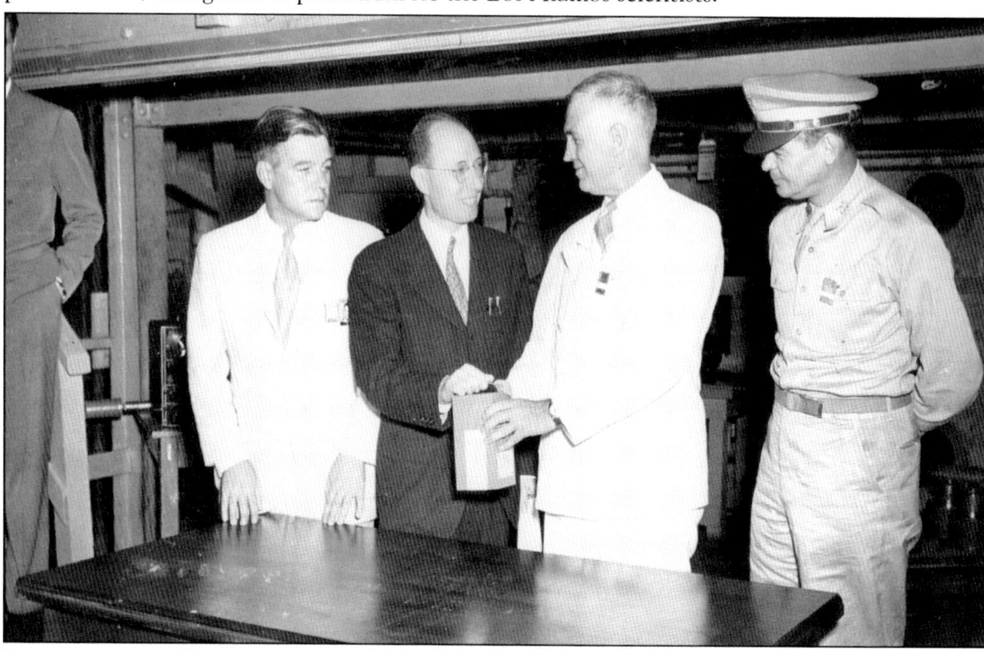

RADIOISOTOPES FOR HEALTH. The peacetime production of radioisotopes at the Graphite Reactor began in 1946. On August 2, 1946, the Clinton Laboratory's research director, Eugene Wigner, second from left, handed the first shipment of reactor-produced isotopes, carbon-14, to E. V. Cowdry, third from left, the director of the Barnard Free Skin and Cancer Hospital of St. Louis, Missouri.

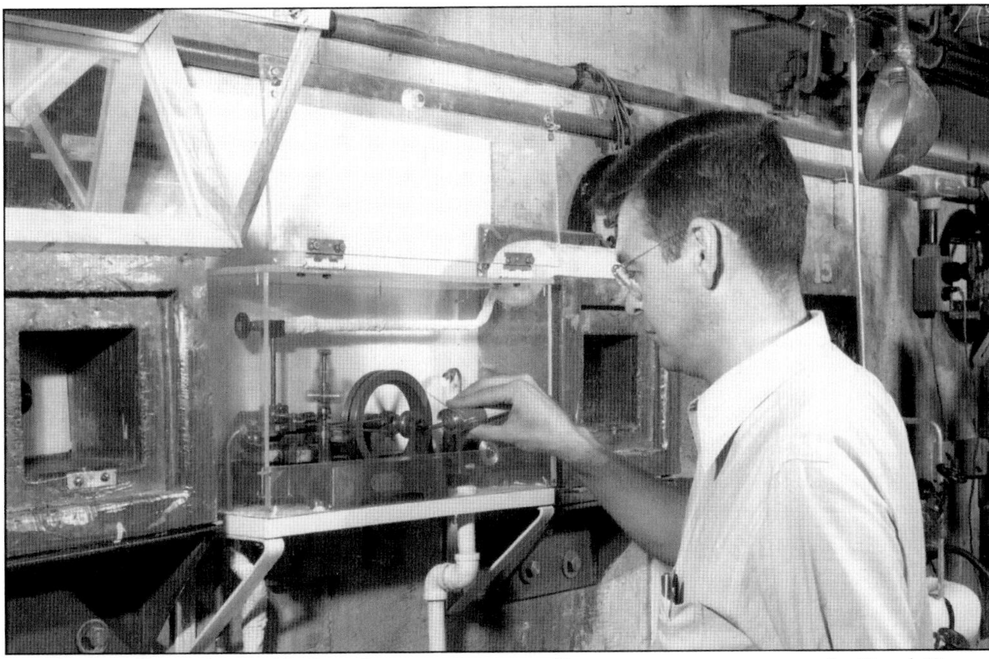

NOT JUST A TOY. The world's first electricity generated by atomic energy came at the South Face of the Graphite Reactor on September 3, 1958. Dr. Logan Emlett is shown with a 1/1000-horsepower toy steam engine driven by steam from the reactor, which lit a small light bulb.

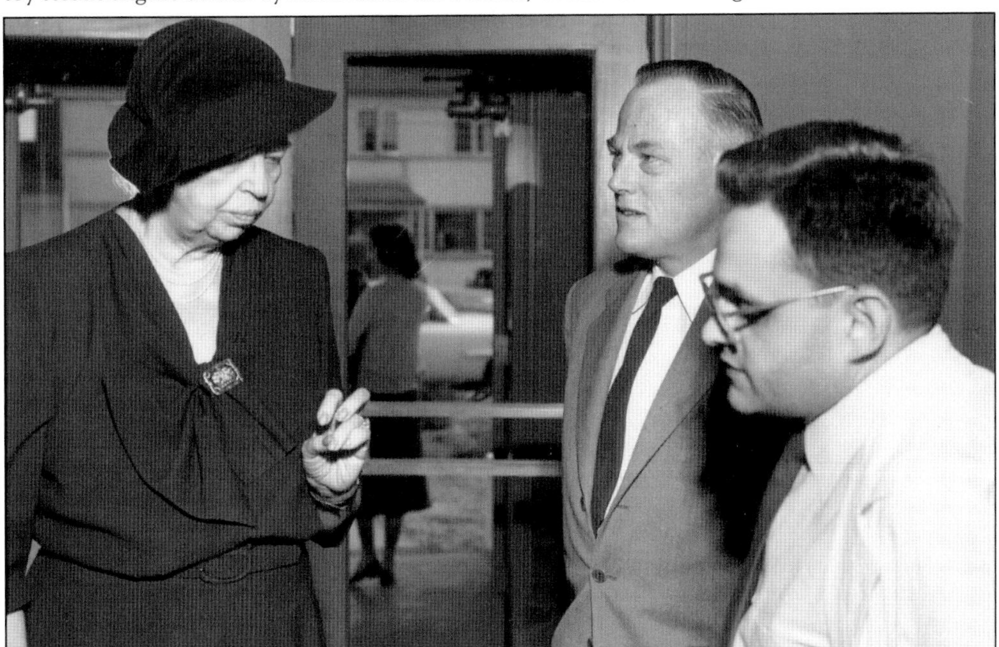

A DISTINGUISHED VISITOR. Welcoming Eleanor Roosevelt (left) to the Oak Ridge Institute of Nuclear Studies (ORINS) are William Pollard (center) and Gould Anderson (right). ORINS was created in 1945 to partner university students with Clinton Laboratories Biology Division. The nonprofit corporation later trained scientists in the use of radioisotopes, which were used for cancer treatment.

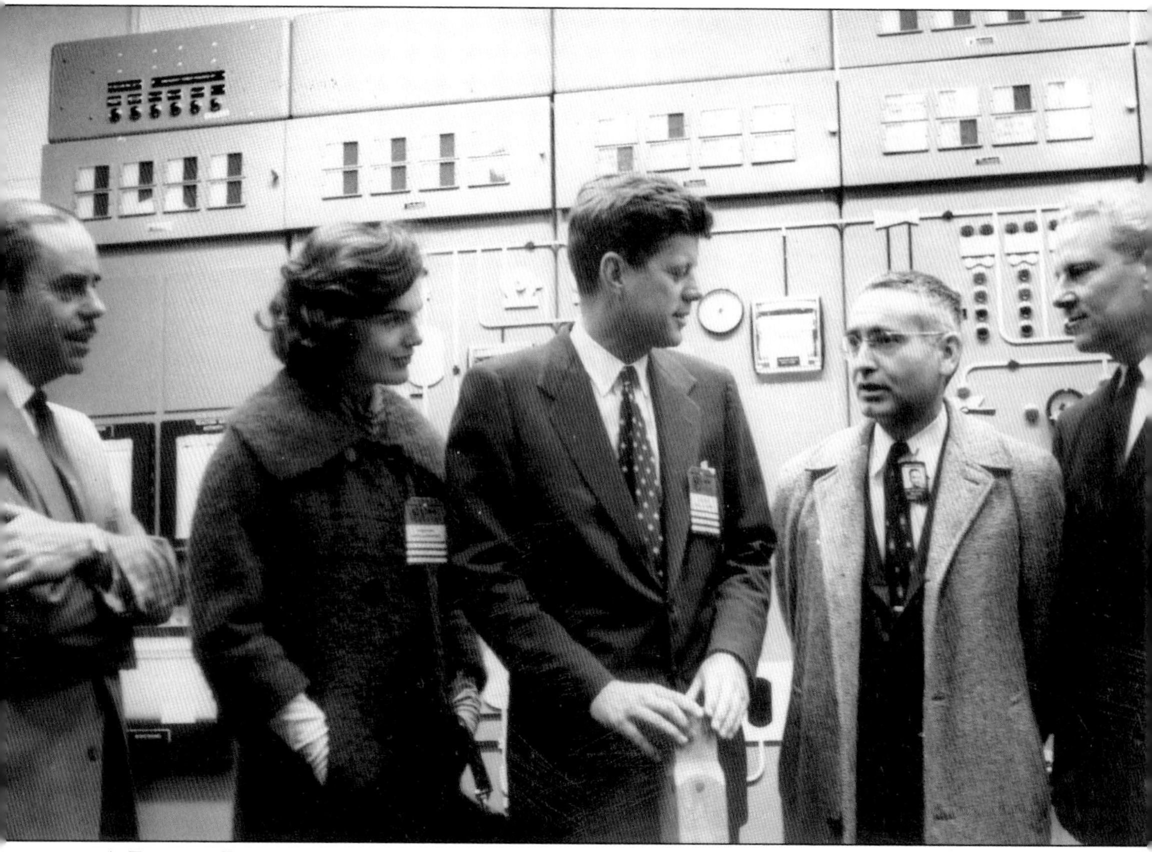

A FUTURE PRESIDENT VISITS. Sen. and Mrs. John F. Kennedy visited the Oak Ridge Research Reactor on February 24, 1959. Kennedy said in his talk to some 300 people at the Oak Terrace Restaurant, "Here in Oak Ridge this nation has demonstrated the vast power which results from the combination of many talents and resources—abundant power, scientific personnel, industrial capability, fuel supplies, and zealous government administration." Pictured from left to right are S. R. Sapirie, Atomic Energy Commission manager; Jacqueline Kennedy; Senator Kennedy; Alvin Weinburg, Oak Ridge National Laboratory director; and Sen. Albert Gore.